The Horror Sensorium

The Horror Sensorium
Media and the Senses

Angela Ndalianis

McFarland & Company, Inc., Publishers
Jefferson, North Carolina, and London

Chapter 1 is reprinted from *Popping Culture*, sixth edition, by Murray Pomerance and John Sakeris (2010), by permission of Pearson Learning Solutions, a Pearson Education Company.

Chapter 3 was published in an earlier form as "Dark Rides, Hybrid Machines and the Horror Experience" in *Horror Zone: The Cultural Experience of Contemporary Horror Cinema*, edited by Ian Conrich (London: I.B.Tauris, 2010). Used by permission.

Chapter 6 was published in an earlier form as "'Hail to the King!' The Return of Doom" in *Tijdschrift voor Mediageschiedenis* no. 2 (December 2004): 100–117. Used by permission.

LIBRARY OF CONGRESS CATALOGUING-IN-PUBLICATION DATA

Ndalianis, Angela.
    The horror sensorium : media and the senses / Angela Ndalianis.
    p.   cm.
    Includes bibliographical references and index.

ISBN 978-0-7864-6127-1
softcover : acid free paper ∞

    1. Horror films — History and criticism. 2. Horror television programs — History and criticism. 3. Motion picture audiences. I. Title.
PN1995.9.H6N35 2012
791.43'6164 — dc23   2012028777

BRITISH LIBRARY CATALOGUING DATA ARE AVAILABLE

© 2012 Angela Ndalianis. All rights reserved

No part of this book may be reproduced or transmitted in any form or by any means, electronic or mechanical, including photocopying or recording, or by any information storage and retrieval system, without permission in writing from the publisher.

Front cover: Amanda Walker in *28 Weeks Later*, directed by Juan Carlos Fresnadillo, 2007 (Fox Atomic/DNA Films/UK Film Council/The Kobal Collection/Susie Allnut)

Manufactured in the United States of America

McFarland & Company, Inc., Publishers
   Box 611, Jefferson, North Carolina 28640
   www.mcfarlandpub.com

To the four little monsters
who always make me smile:

Zoe, Amelie, Madeline and Dione.

Contents

Preface 1
Introduction 3

1. Horror Aesthetics and the Sensorium 15
2. Dancing with the Living Dead: Video Games, Avatars and Arms on the Brain 40
3. Dark Rides, Hybrid Machines and the Multisensory Experience 56
4. Paranormal Romance: Anita Blake, Sookie Stackhouse and the Monsters Who Love Them 73
5. Payback's a Bitch! *Death Proof*, *Planet Terror* and the Carnivalization of Grindhouse Cinema 107
6. Hail to the King! Techno-Intertexts, Video Game Horror and *Doom 3* 143
7. Transmedia and the Sensorium: From *Blair Witch* to *True Blood* 163

Chapter Notes 195
Bibliography 207
Index 217

Preface

In *The Horror Sensorium* I examine the ways in which current horror media connect with their audiences. Media examples as varied as films, television shows, video games and theme park attractions all immerse their audiences in their fictional worlds through combinations of storytelling practices, emotional and sensory experiences, cognitive responses and a physicality that fires the sensorium into action. Through an analysis of a variety of examples — ranging from the films *The Hills Have Eyes, 28 Days Later, Zombi 2, Planet Terror* and *Death Proof*; the video games *Resident Evil 4, Batman: Arkham Asylum,* and *Doom 3*; the theme park rides The Revenge of the Mummy, Haunted Mansion, and The Scary Adventures of Snow White; the television series *True Blood* and *Lost*; the paranormal romance novels featuring Anita Blake and Sookie Stackhouse; and the transmedia alternative reality viral experiences produced in conjunction with the film *The Dark Knight* and television show *True Blood*—this book examines how our sensorium is addressed and responds to horror media texts. The sensorium refers both to the sensory mechanics of the human body and to the intellectual and cognitive functions connected to it: it's integral to the process of perceiving, and to processing the gamut of sensory stimuli individuals may experience in order to make sense of the world around them. Moving away from traditional spectatorship approaches that focus primarily on narrative and thematic analysis, or visual analysis that centers on the psychic or ideological properties inherent to the reciprocal function of gaze on and from the screen, I turn instead to one that especially considers the centrality played by perception through the senses in our consumption of entertainment media. I'm also concerned with exploring the range of sensory and intellectual encounters horror texts can throw our way, both within the same medium but also across media. As will be argued, each medium addresses us corporeally, sensorially and intellectually in its own medium-specific way. Whether film, or video game, theme park ride or transmedia experience, each encounter is a double affair that involves an intimate relationship between the medium and the human body. In short, what this book is concerned with is how we and our horror games, films and television shows meet and affect each other.

There are, of course, many people I'd like to thank for their support. My family, as always, has been amazing: Athanasios, Panagiota, Cleopatra, Louisa, Paris, ZAM, and Dione have helped bring me back down to planet Earth when my brain insisted on traveling into unchartered territory. I also extend thanks to my dear friends who are always there, offering their guidance, humor, and friendship. I especially need to mention and acknowledge the following: Lisa Beaven, Leonie Cooper, Pamela Golden, Wendy Haslem, Alison Inglis, Christian McCrea, Simon McLean, Anne Marsh, Maureen Plavsic-Kerridge, and Sally Smart. You guys rock. I also need to mention the fur balls—Bats, Elektra, Loki and Zorro—who are nature's calming therapy.

Finally, I'd like to close by extending my deepest thanks to Alexandra Heller-Nicholas and Jim Collins for the indispensable and enlightened comments and advice they offered on this book in its various stages. Alex became my horror buddy extraordinaire and, in addition to her feedback, I greatly value her time, words of wisdom, and taste in all things horror. Jim's friendship and faith in me have helped drive me on; his intellectual capacity and knowledge of all things popular culture never cease to astound me, and he shared this ability generously, challenging me to clarify and complicate many of the ideas in this book. The generosity of both are greatly appreciated and helped bring clarity when, at times, I thought none was there.

Introduction

The Horror Sensorium is about the horror genre and how it interfaces with its audience. According to the Oxford English Dictionary, an interface is "the point where two subjects, systems, etc. meet and affect each other"; to interface, therefore, means "to be connected with something using an interface." Computing aside, in the realm of entertainment it's media technologies that provide the means to the interface. As the word implies, this is a space where the medium and the human body collide; where they meet and affect each other in very real ways that play themselves across and deep into the mind and body of the spectator. Media examples as varied as films, television shows, video games and theme park attractions all engage their audiences through combinations of storytelling practices, emotional and sensory experiences, cognitive responses and a physicality that fires the sensorium into action. Yet, as will be argued, each medium addresses us corporeally, sensorially and intellectually in its own medium-specific way. This book is concerned with how and why the sensorium is integral to perception: physiologically it comprises the sensory and intellectual capacities of the body; it processes sensory information and, in doing so, it facilitates our understanding of and reaction to the world around us. The spaces of horror media not only fictionalize — in vividly sensory ways — their own sensorium, but they also demand that we cognitively and physiologically respond to their fictions by translating their sensorial enactments across our bodies. Concentrating on the horror genre, I consider the centrality played by perception through the senses and how this operates across a range of media. I also focus on the interrelationship that exists between corporeal and sensory responses, and intellectual and evaluative processes.

Film theory has, until recently, highlighted the centrality that vision and the image plays in the ways audiences immerse themselves in the representational spaces created by narrative-based cinema. However, many cracks have appeared over the last decade or so, which have destabilized the ocular-centric model that dominated film theory in the 1970s and 80s (and which, in turn, supported psychoanalytic and ideological frameworks). Important studies dealing with the affective, phenomenological and sensorial power of the cinema have redirected film theory's previously myopic focus on the visual — some of the key theorists in the field being Giuliana Bruno, Vivian Sobchack, Laura Marks and Jennifer Barker. Over the last decade, the cinema has vied with many media competitors for attention and the more overt physical and sensory responses required of theme park attractions and video games, in particular, have served to throw into sharp relief the major gap that had been present in film scholarship: the lack of acknowledgment of the significance of the sensorium and the network of relations it triggers in the body's experience and interpretation of entertainment media, ranging from the perceptual and cognitive to the corporeal and sensory. Any attempt to come to terms with how the film or television "viewer," game player or theme park attraction participant interface with their chosen media example needs to recognize the diverse nature of that experience from the sensory reactions and impulses to perceptions that activate cognitive processes of understanding and interpretation.

One of the concerns of this book is to offer alternative approaches to exploring the types of interconnections we make with entertainment media, approaches that don't necessarily privilege homogeneous models that speak for all spectators or which offer singular interpretations that prioritize vision over the other senses. Focusing on examples of contemporary horror media, each chapter focuses on a series of horror case studies that evaluate different kinds of horror media experiences. Why horror? As a genre, it's capable of intensifying the range of reactions and experiences in which we can become enmeshed when connecting with media texts and, over the last decade in particular, the proliferation of horror texts across media have amplified their focus on sensory encounters. As will be discussed throughout this book, there's a greater emphasis on corporeality both within the fictional worlds that viciously decimate and cause suffering to the human body in glorious, gory detail, but also beyond the fictions. The diverse media that are the study of this book all generate specific corporeal and sensory responses from their spectators, players, readers and participants.

In her book *Atlas of Emotion*, Giuliana Bruno describes the film experience as "geopsychic architexture"[1]; not only are films considered to be psychogeographic journeys that trigger affective responses from their audiences but they're also modes of travel that take the spectator to fictional places and embroil them in the lives of characters who travel their own life journeys onscreen. Watching a film is an emotional journey that relies on cognition and perception; our understanding of the characters, their stories, the way they interact with each other and the spaces around them affects us in immediate ways in that beyond the level of narrative comprehension (and often because of it), we're also drawn into emotional journeys. The spaces "in there" impact on our space "out here." But Bruno goes beyond this to argue that the cinematic experience is also a sensory journey that extends beyond cognition (and the emotional affects this can bring about) and which can affect the audience physically. Questioning the ocularcentrism that's dominated interpretations of audio-visual media, Bruno focuses on haptics. The haptic, however, isn't limited to the sense of touch; instead it's connected to vision and, as such, a film experience becomes a "haptic way of site-seeing"[2] that "constitutes the reciprocal con*tact* between us and the environment, both housing and extending communicative interface."[3] Contact as a point of visual, perceptual or emotional bond is extended to also encompass the tactile. Sight is intertwined with touch and to see is to also become immersed in the site of the film space: its textures, the atmosphere it creates, and the spatial relationships it establishes — what Bruno calls "a touching experience of feeling through the eye."[4] Our perception of onscreen kinetics has the potential to give way to a "type of kinesthetics"[5] that activates the senses and creates for the "viewer" an offscreen response to the onscreen space.

As early as the 1910s, in his book *The Photoplay: A Psychological Study* (1916), Hugo Munsterberg discussed "the kinesthetic properties of our cinematic machine," which produce the perception of travel.[6] Of course, the cinema has always relied on this perception; however, the current structure of the entertainment industry, the competition for diverse media experiences, the advances in digital effects that deceptively conjure astonishing illusions that promise more immersive experiences all amplify the "haptic way of site-seeing" in their own media-specific ways, with games and theme park rides delivering the kinetic and kinesthetic thrills more literally and in ways that leave their direct physical imprint on the body and the senses.

The first part of this book focuses primarily on the body and the senses and explores the crucial role both play in our comprehension of and immersion in media texts. Chapter 1, "Horror Aesthetics and the Sensorium," looks at how New Horror Cinema deliberately addresses its spectator through an intense and unforgiving corporeality that demands the attention of the senses. Onscreen, characters suffer graphic violence at the hands of the monsters, and this violence continues to be played out offscreen and across the body of the spectator. Taking my cue from Vivian Sobchack, in her book *Carnal Thoughts: Embodiment and Moving Image Culture*, my interest is in what she calls the "cinesthetic subject," which is "a neologism that derives not only from *cinema* but also from two scientific terms that designate particular structures and conditions of the human sensorium: *synaesthesia* and *coenaesthesia*." She explains that both "point to ways in which the cinema uses our dominant senses of vision and hearing to speak comprehensibly to our other senses."[7] Whereas synaesthesia refers to the ability sense modalities have to translate themselves into other senses, coenaesthesia "names the potential and perception of one's whole sensorial being."[8] In many of the horror films since 2000, the new focus has been on assaulting the spectator with extreme violence, gore and a merciless social critique that understands the social fabric as coming apart at the seams. Films like *The Hills Have Eyes* (Alexandre Aja, 2006), *Halloween* (Rob Zombie, 2007) and *28 Weeks Later* (Juan Carlos Fresnadillo, 2007) plunge the spectator into spaces of extreme violence that translates itself across the body of the spectator through the senses. Focusing on Sobchack's cinesthetic subject, my interest is in exploring how, in addition to immersing ourselves in the narratives and character actions, we also extract meaning through our bodies. But, as will be explored later, while film is an audio-visual medium, sight and sound often migrate their sensory effect onto other sense modalities, therefore making the horror experience all the more potent.

At the core of New Horror Cinema is an aesthetic of disgust. The bite that ravages fragile skin, the hands that tear open an abdomen to reveal slippery internal organs, the same hands that rip limbs from pulsating bodies: how do we begin to articulate the aesthetics of disgust that washes over our senses when confronted by these images? As Brigitte Peucker explains in her book *The Material Image: Art and the Real in Film*, a certain reciprocity exists between the film spectator and image.[9] Her interest is with "the physiological perceptual" and she argues a case for "the spectator's somatic responsiveness" to the projected image. In this somatic responsiveness, Peucker argues that the image itself is granted the semblance of materiality. In gore-intensive horror films and, in particular, New Horror, while not literal, the disgusting subject matter imbricates itself into our bodies and across our skin by inciting our senses directly, and synaesthetically, in very real ways. A similar point is made by Bruno who, referring to the writing of Michael Taussig, states that the "mimetic version of tactile optics ... [is] sensitive to physiognomic manifestations of visual worlds." This form of haptics "can push mimesis to the edge of mimicry, taking us into the image as the image, in turn, is ingested."[10] In a sense, the extremity and textural surface of violence in New Horror plunges us into such a state of discomfort until, ironically, like the zombies that often navigate its fictional universes, we ingest the disgusting material presence that's onscreen into ourselves so that our bodies are forced to respond physically.

Chapter 2, "Dancing with the Living Dead: Video Games, Avatars and

Arms on the Brain," continues examining the role of the sensorium in our engagement with horror media but turns instead to our corporeal relationship to video games. Focusing on *Resident Evil 4: The Wii edition* (Capcom, 2007), which is an evolution of the popular survival horror genre, I return to the figure of the zombie (who features prominently in Chapter 1 and who is a character that also dominates many examples of New Horror Cinema), in which I articulate the relationship between the player and their onscreen avatar. Using the creation myth as a critical tool, I explore how the myth replays itself through the technological mediation that occurs in the human-machine interface. I argue that, as players, like the living dead who populate the landscapes of *Resident Evil 4*, we struggle to gain control of our avatar body as it plods (and eventually masterfully maneuvers) its way through the game space. In games, we don't just "interact," we actually undergo a state that's akin to entering someone else's skin and, in the process, we *animate* previously inanimate matter. Whereas the power of horror films is visible in its capacity to disempower the spectator who remains incapable of affecting the linear unraveling of story events, video games demand the player's interaction with the story world and this interaction brings with it a sensory experience that's absent in film. Discussing the haptic nature of film spectatorship, Giuliana Bruno argues that the "site-seeing" central to film spectatorship requires "a shift away from the long-standing focus of film theory on sight and toward the construction of a moving theory of site."[11] As will be argued in this chapter, this understanding of haptics and a moving theory of site becomes all the more powerful in the world of video games where, via their avatars and through the intensely haptic relationship to game controllers and, more recently, systems like Xbox Kinect, Wii, and iMove, the physiological motion and sensory interaction of the player becomes integral to the unraveling of fictional worlds onscreen. Using the metaphor of the arm on the brain, this chapter discusses how intellect and the senses, cognition and the body work in unison to give shape to the action in the game world.

The third chapter, "Dark Rides, Hybrid Machines and the Multisensory Experience," focuses on the formal parallels and differences between horror rides of the theme and amusement park industries and horror cinema through a close analysis of Revenge of the Mummy — the Ride (Universal, 2004). Against the backdrop of media conglomeration and the focus on diversification of media experiences, this chapter focuses on the ways in which Revenge of the Mummy — the Ride cross-pollinate elements from past amusement rides into a new theme park hybrid (that the Universal marketing department dubbed a "psychological thrill ride"). In particular, attention is drawn to the "dark ride," which has been common to the amusement park since its beginnings at the turn of the 20th century. In dark rides, participants board a buggy, train or boat and enter a dark, enclosed space; any storytelling that's present plays itself out across the body of the attraction participant. Relying on an intertextuality that appropriates and enhances past technologies, Revenge of the Mummy takes its cue from the hybrid dark rides like Jurassic Park (Universal), The Amazing Adventures of Spiderman (Universal) and the Indiana Jones Adventure (Disneyland). In doing so, Revenge of the Mummy relies on an excessive remediation of media old and new: dark ride, roller coaster, film, television, theater, architecture, music—all vie for the attention of the participant and seek to make the experience an intensely kinetic and sensorial one. In horror rides we, the ride participants, become the main character as we enter "real" spaces that we can see, smell, touch, hear and even taste; the sensory experience is intense and immediate and relies less on the process of synaesthetic transfer. Likewise, as is the case with video games, such horror theme park attractions bring to the fore the expansion of the number of senses to include proprioception or the kinesthetic sense; equilibrioception, the sense of balance and acceleration; and nociception, the sense of pain. In the dark ride attraction, the horror is aimed more directly at the participant's body; the senses have no choice but to react to being thrown about in various directions and to being propelled forwards and backwards at hair-raising speeds that literally make the flesh and muscles on our bodies shudder against their will. Of all entertainment media, it's only the theme park ride that can deliver such intense somatic and visceral effects on the body.

Chapter 4, "Paranormal Romance: Anita Blake, Sookie Stackhouse and the Monsters Who Love Them" turns initially to the novel, specifically, horror-paranormal romance fiction. Focusing on the Anita Blake series by Laurell K. Hamilton and examples from the Dark series by Christine Feehan, this chapter traces some of the origins of paranormal romance back to the 18th-century romance genre and Gothic fiction. In particular, in this chapter I explore how sensations of passion, sensuality and seduction, which are associated with romance, are affected when placed within the context of the horror genre. By overlaying the romantic with stories and sensory experiences that are more aligned with horror, many of these texts seek to complicate and challenge the nature of desire and sexuality. Frequently, pleasure, danger and horror merge, often taking the reader into a place that takes illicit delight in the darkness and chaos that can lie at the core of eroticism. Horror-paranormal romances focus on the coupling of a usually human heroine, and a supernatural love interest—most popularly a vampire or werewolf. Connecting these novels to the beast-man motif common to fairy tales, I explore Marina Warner's argument that such stories complicate the erotic desires they represent, often celebrating "polymorphous perversity" and "the potential eroticism of aggressive appetites."[12] I argue that the dangerous seductive vampire is heavily coded both in the horror genre and in horror-paranormal romance and his presence targets the sensorium in distinctive ways. Like the beast of fairy tale romances, the figure of the vampire makes possible the probing of boundaries relating to sex, passion and desire. They allow both the heroine and the reader to explore what Davies calls "the darker side of eros."[13]

Exploring the sensory pleasures of horror-paranormal romance, the chapter turns finally to the recent screen expression of these stories in television shows like *True Blood*. I argue that, like the cinema, television is an aesthetic form that encourages mimetic identification in ways that differ radically to text or static image. The cinesthetic subject that was the focus of Chapter 1 returns here. As Linda Williams asserts, when sex is screened, the attraction isn't just directed to the eyes but to the flesh. Quoting Sobchack she continues: "Our entire sensorium is activated synesthetically, all the more so ... when the moving image shows two (or more) beings touching, tasting, smelling, and rubbing up against one another ... in watching them [bodies engaged in sex] I am solicited sexually too."[14] Sensory contact is made between "the very body of the perceiver and the perceived"[15] so that through our eyes and ears, our other senses join in. As I will argue in this chapter, Williams's words take on powerful meaning when considered in relation to the merging of horror, violence and sex that's often at the core of *True Blood*.

The final three chapters of this book focus on the senses but shifts attention towards the cognitive and intellectual games that are intimately connected to our sensory encounters with horror. But before launching into the content of the last three chapters, it's important to provide a little aside about the entertainment industry's underlying structure. Increasingly since the 1960s, media corporations have expanded their businesses by investing in multiple company interests that include film and television companies along with other unrelated businesses (including soft drink and cereal companies), thus minimizing financial loss or maximizing financial gain by dispersing their financial investments. It wasn't until the 1980s, however, that conglomeration began to focus more effectively on building a network of subsidiary companies that had shared media-related investments that complemented one another, but which were diverse enough to disperse financial loss/gain. While it's common for companies to collaborate outside their conglomerate (for example, the collaboration between Sony Pictures and Marvel Entertainment on the *Spiderman* film/comic book cross-over), the primary aim is to try to disperse and diversify a franchise within the same conglomerate structure. As one example, the Walt Disney Company — the largest of the media conglomerates — focuses its business around four interrelated divisions that include: Walt Disney Studios, which handle film, music and theatrical productions and include Walt Disney

Motion Pictures Group, Marvel Entertainment, Pixar Animation and Walt Disney Theatrical; the Disney theme parks and resorts, with Disney theme parks now operating in the U.S.A., France, Japan and China; the toys, clothing and merchandise generated by Disney Consumer Products; and the television, cable and internet operations including Disney-ABC, the Disney Channel and the Disney Interactive Media Group (which includes computer game production), which come under the domain of the Media Networks division.

Obviously, there's great cost effectiveness in exploiting the fluid transition of a product across a conglomerate's film, computer game, television, theme park or comic book companies. Economics aside, the formal significance of these convergences is that not only do they encourage extended, cross- and transmedia storytelling practices, and alternative modes of sensory interaction with the diverse media technologies, but they also require greater intellectual activity on the part of the audience. In order to make sense of the fictional spaces that often extend across sequels or series within the one medium as well as across multiple media, a more committed and active engagement with these texts is encouraged. In addition, there's an increased expectation of media literacy both on the part of media creators and consumers. In the case of cult media — which many horror examples often become — this activity on the part of the media consumer is amplified further still, especially when fan activity enters the picture. The horror genre, whether expressed through film, comic book or television, is notorious for amassing followers who possess an obsessive understanding of the genre, its rules and its history.

An impulse that's important to contemporary media, and especially to horror, is the pervasive intertextuality that's expressed through seriality, allusionism and a level of media literacy that requires the active engagement of the participant beyond the simple interaction with a story or character level. When Barthes announced the "death of the author" he also acknowledged the "birth of the reader." For Barthes,[16] no work is an original; the author is transformed into the scriptor who combines pre-existing texts (through allusionism, refashioning, direct quotation, etc.) into new variations. According to this logic, the text becomes "writerly" rather than "readerly" in that it's not simply passively consumed by the reader, but rather the text waits to be actively deciphered so that it can come into being. Applying this reading it's possible to argue, therefore, that processes of intertextuality and active audience engagement have been an important mode of interface since the birth of popular media, and even earlier. Yet, Barthes's concept of the writerly text has reached a new level of intensity. The extent of media literacy required of the audience in the post-modern (and post–post-modern?) era has now become a deliberate media strategy that's intent on making the most out of the cross-media synergies that sustain the industry — an industry that's also aware of the mainstreaming of fan culture and the cult text, which has always relied on the notion of the replayability of the text. So much so that often deeper "meaning" is reliant upon an audience that's capable of crossing multiple "texts" and, often, multiple media, in order to give coherence to a specific work that's brimming over with intertextual references and allusions. Of course, the rise in audio-visual technologies such as DVDs, cable, and the Internet (and the ability to access online — and not so legal — download facilities) has created an easily accessible archive of film, television and game history, therefore amplifying the ability of audiences to familiarize themselves with a multitude of examples of entertainment culture. The final three chapters focus on intertextual journeys and shift the focus on the sensorium away from the more immediate sensory and synaesthetic experiences that horror media can inflict on their participants and towards more cognitive and intellectual processes, which bring with them their own sensory delights.

In his book *Sensuous Geographies* Paul Rodaway makes a crucial point, explaining that the tendency to create a binary between sensory and cognitive processes creates a false understanding of perception: perception involves both sensation and cognition, and the two are always in play simultaneously. Chapter 5, "Payback's a Bitch! *Death Proof, Planet Terror* and the Carnivalization of Grindhouse Cinema," speaks to the interplay between sensation and cognition. In this chapter I extend William Paul's analysis of the bodily expressiveness of the gross-out horror tradition of the 1970s and explore how it's self-consciously explored in the films *Planet Terror*, directed by Robert Rodriguez, and *Death Proof*, directed by Quentin Tarantino. I analyze both these films as modern expressions of the carnivalesque tradition as theorized by Mikhail Bakhtin in the 1930s and '40s. This chapter is concerned with the meta-genericity of *Planet Terror* and *Death Proof* and with the dialogic discourse that's generated within the films about generic process and the pleasures of horror. Both films carry their generic history and evaluate it reflexively. These films address the audience directly, demanding their critical participation in a game that's about the construction of the films' meaning. *Planet Terror* is clearly aware of the debt it owes to gross-out films like *Dawn of the Dead* (George Romero, 1979), *Evil Dead* and *Evil Dead II* (Sam Raimi, 1981 & 1987). Grossing-out the spectator films not only embrace bad taste but disgust and, as the title implies, gross-out is their aim. In *Planet Terror*, Rodriguez relies on a dual interplay between the delights of the intertextual recognition of '70s gross-out horror and the physiological and sensory reactions central to this tradition. In *Death Proof,* Tarantino has a similar agenda to that of Rodriguez: his primary concern is to expose the ever-changing, dialogic process of genre. Tarantino is especially interested in exploring and deconstructing the narrative logic of the slasher/stalker subgenre of horror.

The film examines and teases the audiences with its conventions and then injects new elements taken from other exploitation genres, especially rape-revenge, carsploitation and girl-gang films. The result is that *Death Proof* becomes a performance that's a rewriting of the slasher convention that places the "final girl" heroine as passive victim of the psycho-killer monster. Both films perform a ludic function in that they don't require the spectator to merely observe, but to also actively and critically engage with their form, their history and their revisions. The corporeal and sensory encounters we have with horror media texts still present to maximum effect, but these are amplified by the more cerebral pleasures we can also extract through intertextual encounters with media texts: an active role that fuels the spectator's horror-philia.

Chapter 6, "Hail to the King! Techno-Intertexts, Video Game Horror and *Doom 3*," continue with the subject of intertextual pleasure but turn instead to the popular *Doom* video game franchise (id Software). Focusing primarily on the *Doom* games and, in particular *Doom 3* (id Software, 2004), this chapter explores the ways in which players are absorbed in playful and inventive perceptual puzzles that are about the process of meaning construction in horror video games—meaning that's about both the stimulation of the senses and the intellect. In addition to drawing attention to the intertextual web of sources that the game draws upon to construct its game world, which includes reference to its own predecessors, *Doom3* also immerses the player in a game that's about how its creator, id Software, pushed the technological boundaries of game technology. Not only did the game set new standards for the look of 3D games but it also altered the gamer's perception and sensory reactions to the game world action. The game is obsessed by its technological intertexts, asking the player to recognize the technological advances its made, and to revel—while in game play—in what is a virtuoso performance and celebration of digital effects that heighten the gamer's sensory pleasures.

The final chapter, "Transmedia and the Sensorium: From *Blair Witch* to *True Blood*," takes the senses to the streets. This chapter explores the interplay between reality and horror fiction but it does so by focusing on a more recent phenomenon that's been embraced by the entertainment industry: viral marketing as a form of extended storytelling. These fictions rely on social networks such as Twitter, Facebook and YouTube, mobile technologies, and websites, as well as real world events that include the placement of posters and advertisements on billboards, and the pervasive use of the urban landscape as a theatrical space that requires our performance as actors and puzzle solvers. Focusing on the film and television examples *True Blood* (HBO 2008–), *The Blair Witch Project* (Myrick and Sánchez, 1999), *Cloverfield* (Matt Reeves, 2008) and the hybrid-genre examples *Lost* (ABC, 2004–10) and *The Dark*

Knight (Christopher Nolan, 2008), this chapter examines how game aesthetics have become an integral way of immersing the audience into the story action. But here, fiction escapes the screen and moves into the cityscape, in the process requiring a different role of the sensorium when compared to film, television, or video games, because here the participant is often required to physically navigate city spaces so that the fiction can be told. Adapting fan-culture strategies to create more active narrative structures, viral campaigns have become a key element in interweaving the audience more intensively into the narrative universe of the primary franchise. My interest in this chapter is in exploring how the transmediality that's at the center of viral experiences relies on stories spilling invasively into the social sphere; a networked environment is created that weaves through a variety of media and into the public realm and, in doing so, creates spaces that both perform for the audience and which are for performing within. Players participate in an emerging narrative that operates like a puzzle to be solved. They actively recompose an ensemble of networked bits of information that are distributed across media and across the urban landscape, which combine cumulatively to give the participant a more cerebral and participatory experience of the primary franchise. The transmedia alternative reality games shift the focus towards sensory experiences that rely on multiple media and spatial encounters that are associated with a "lived experience" that takes place in the participants' everyday environment. The transmedia performances and their demanding theatricality become intimately intertwined with our bodies, which are integral to the articulation of their media fictions. We, as participants, become part of the work of art.

And so begins the horror media sensorium...

1

Horror Aesthetics and the Sensorium

New Horror Aesthetics

> Bobby, leave Doug alone. He's a Democrat. He doesn't believe in guns.—*The Hills Have Eyes* (2006)

Since the release of Alfred Hitchcock's *Psycho* in 1960, the direction of the contemporary horror film increasingly led to a disturbing confrontation between the spectator and his or her worst fears about the collapse of identity, system and order. The entry of the monster—whether Nosferatu, King Kong, Count Dracula or Michael Myers—serves a crucial function in the horror film: by embodying society's dark side, it tests the rules, morals and ideological structures that operate in our culture, holding these structures up for analysis, contesting their worth, and exposing the instability of the system that inform the social order. The horror film is about crossing boundaries. One side of the border constitutes order; the other chaos: the horrific manifests itself where meaning, which is established by civilization, collapses. The horror genre has been one of the longest surviving and most consistently popular genres in the cinema and, over the last decade it has made its presence felt intensively through the influx of what has come to be known as New Horror, which is the subject of this chapter. Unlike the playful, self-reflexive and parodic trend in horror that dominated in the 1990s and which is typified by *Scream* (Wes Craven, 1996) and its sequels, in the horror films of the first decade of the 2000s there's a different agenda: in films such as *Cabin Fever* (Eli Roth, 2002), *Saw* (James Wan, 2004), *Hostel* (Eli Roth, 2005) and *Wolf Creek* (Greg McLean, 2005), the audience is ruthlessly confronted with violence, intense gore and, often, a social critique that refuses to hold back the punches.

In New Horror Cinema, the label often given to this recent phase of the genre, the horror spectator enters a space that operates as a ritualistic violation of taboos and, in the process, fears and desires are unleashed that often threaten "normal" society and its onscreen ideologies: murder and displays of sadomasochistic violence, perverted sexual acts, incest and interbreeding, the return of the dead, cannibalism—these themes are at the core of New Horror. Yet these themes rely heavily on the spectator's senses in order to achieve their full impact. New Horror, like all horror, relies on the sensorium, an integrated unit that combines cognition and the senses, the mind and the body. Horror media offer us a gamut of experiences—horror, laughter, fear, terror, the cerebral pleasures of intertextual play—and, depending on the sensory, emotional and intellectual encounters each example throws our way, we perceive, sense and interpret the fictional spaces of horror in diverse and distinctive ways. The sensorium, therefore, refers both to the sensory mechanics of the human body, but also to the intellectual and cognitive functions connected to it: it's integral to the process of perceiving, and to processing the gamut of sensory stimuli the individual may experience in order to make sense of their understanding and impression of the world around them. This chapter explores how we perceive horror and how and why New Horror, in particular, delivers its message by placing greater emphasis on the sensory impact of graphic depictions of horror, violence and bodily destruction. Using the example of New Horror and some of its influences, this chapter explores how we, the audience, engage with, make sense of, and encounter these horrific spaces.

New Horror tests the limits of the filmic social order to such a degree that often the suggestion is that there can be no turning back. Whereas in the past horror narratives clearly coded the flawed characters who were marked for destruction at the hands of the monster (by being sexually promiscuous, lacking morality, being a mega-nerd, etc.), New Horror is unforgiving; in films like *Hostel* and *Hostel II* (Eli Roth, 2007), *Wolf Creek*, *30 Days of Night* (David Slade, 2007) and the remakes of *Texas Chainsaw Massacre* (Marcus Nispel, 2003) and *The Hills Have Eyes* (Alexandre Aja, 2006) there is little rhyme or reason as to why the films' multiple victims become the target of monstrous acts of bloody destruction. The world appears to be in a transition state, teetering at a point that threatens to collapse into absolute chaos. While the story premise, main characters and nature of the destruction may differ markedly in these films, one thing that does dominate across the board is the depiction of human beings (and, by extension, society) who reach their limits as the world around them collapses. For example, Rob Zombie's remake of *Halloween* (2007), the horror classic originally directed by John Carpenter, rewrites the 1978 events by providing greater detail of the factors that pushed the child Michael Myers into becoming "the Bogeyman." Unlike Carpenter, who played on the powerful ambiguity of Michael Myers's nature—is he sociopath or Bogeyman?—Zombie releases Myers's identity from the realm of the unknown and supernatural, blaming his monstrous nature on the social environment that nurtured him: repeated bullying at school, the backdrop of a horrific home life, an abusive stepfather, a self-obsessed and sexually zealous older sister, and a mother who spent more time at the strip joint where she worked than at home providing support to her ten-year-old son. In case we miss the blame being placed on society (and the real, as opposed to the supernatural), Zombie further drives home the trigger to Michael Myers's (fig. 1) violent nature by exposing his predilection for the torture of animals—a clear sign of someone who, at the age of ten, was already coming apart at the seams. Whereas horror cinema pre–*Psycho* unleashed horror in order to test the borders that demarcate society, order and normality from the anti-social, chaotic and abnormal, the social status quo was reinstated in the end. Horror cinema post–*Psycho* has demanded intellectual engagement of its audience, whether on the level of social critique presented by the film narratives or in the intertextual games that demand to be deciphered by the spectator (a topic I'll deal with in Chapter 5). Yet paralleling or, more correctly, in conjunction with this cognitive and intellectual involvement is an insistent focus on the body on- and offscreen. Horror films, especially since the 1960s, have performed their textual journeys on the bodies of the characters that populate their fictional worlds. In turn, the bodily destruction depicted onscreen unrelentingly weaves its way offscreen and onto the body of the spectator. New Horror ups the ante on this focus on the body and gives voice to the theme of society in decay through intense sensorial and carnal engagement. New Horror speaks to a sensorium that invests in the sensory intelligence of its spectator.

In an article about Walter Benjamin and aesthetics, Susan Buck-Morss states the following:

> *Aisthitikos* is the ancient Greek word for that which is "perceptive by feeling." *Aisthisis* is the sensory experience of perception. The original field of aesthetics is not art but reality—corporeal, material nature. As Terry Eagleton writes: "Aesthetics is born as a discourse of the body." It is a form of cognition, achieved through taste, touch, hearing, seeing, smell—the whole corporeal sensorium.... The senses maintain an uncivilized and uncivilizable trace, a core of resistance to cultural domestication. This is because their immediate purpose is to serve instinctual needs—for warmth, nourishment, safety, sociability—in short, they remain a part of the biological apparatus, indispensable to the self-preservation of both the individual and the social group.[1]

Aesthetics and its capacity to incite the whole sensorium—the senses, the body, cognition and intelligence—is the primary focus of this chapter. New Horror takes us on an intense journey on two fronts: our cognitive and intellectual

Figure 1: Michael Myers (Tyler Mane) meditates over one of his violent acts in *Halloween* (Dimension Films, Spectacle Entertainment, 2007) (Kobal Collection).

abilities are called into full action, but so are our senses, and both (sometimes independently and sometimes in unison) drive home messages that can be powerfully brutal and uncomfortable about the human condition. In doing so, New Horror amplifies something that's always been inherent to "film spectatorship." The reality of film spectatorship is that it's never truly engaged vision alone, even during the silent era.[2] In the cinema, vision and sound (one of the greatly neglected yet directly active senses in the film experience) have always acted as mediator-senses that facilitate states of perception, which, in turn, can activate additional sensory responses from the "spectator." Despite the recent research focus on the senses and the body by Vivian Sobchack, Laura Marks, Jennifer Barker and Brigette Peucker, film theory has persistently prioritized the role played by vision in the cinematic experience. Perhaps horror genre theorists have been even more guilty of the prioritization of sight, especially because horror films like *Psycho*, *Peeping Tom* (Michael Powell, 1960), *Suspiria* (Dario Argento, 1977), *Halloween* (John Carpenter, 1978) and *Demons* (Lamberto Bava, 1985) have (through the iconic image of the eye) deliberately asked their audience to ponder the pleasures inherent in viewing horror *while in the act of viewing horror*. But even when reflectively deconstructing the relationship between vision and the pleasures of horror, the contemporary horror film has insistently demanded of its spectator a multisensory response to the world it conjures onscreen.

In this chapter, examples of New Horror Cinema will be explored and compared to examples of 1970s horror, which set the scene in terms of its unapologetic attack on "normality," its depiction of violence and its intense viscerality. In particular, I'll return to the "apocalyptic" horror films of the 1970s as typified by the films of George Romero, Wes Craven and Tobe Hooper; and the vividly graphic, intensely somatic and often controversial Italian horror films of Dario Argento, Lucio Fulci and Ruggero Deodata — all of which later impacted on the aesthetics of New Horror in varying degrees of intensity. New Horror's themes deal primarily with the "uncivilized and uncivilizable"; the conformity of the civilized is stripped away and, for horror film protagonists, the primal and the sensory become crucial weapons when struggling against the abject and chaotic worlds that horror unleashes. The most successful horror films mercilessly propel this heightened emphasis on the senses into the realm of the spectator and, as I'll argue below, consequently amplify the tendencies of most horror cinema. New Horror is "a discourse of the body."

For the sake of convenience — and for want of a more all-inclusive word that embraces the sensorium — I'll be sticking with the word "spectator" here and in the rest of this book; however, my use of the term is aligned more with Giuliana Bruno's definition of the haptic spectator. In *Atlas of Emotion: Jour-*

neys in Art, Architecture and Film, Bruno considers spectatorship as a state not dominated by vision but by touch; the eyes may see but they are, in turn, touched emotionally in ways that ignite the entire body into a state of "kinesthetic perception." "The haptic," she explains, "allows us to come into contact with people and the surface of things. Thus, while the basis of touch is a reaching out — for an object, a place, or a person (including oneself) — it also implies the reverse: that is, being touched in return."[3] The cinema presents cartographic journeys that both move us and which we move in. Vision and, I'd add, sound become the way into spaces that take us on "psychogeographic" journeys whereby a form of "geopsychic site-seeing" occurs.[4] While immersed in film worlds we follow and experience the paths of the protagonists and the spaces they navigate; we also allow those spaces to write themselves across our own bodies in that our site-seeing may trigger memories of our own encounters with the world, or open up new ones.

Whereas Bruno is concerned more with the affective nature of the haptic, my interest extends beyond this to consider ways in which our cognitive engagement with the ideological issues raised by horror films (the social and family dramas they evoke, their exploration of the borders that define the human, their reflexive dialogue with the generic tradition of which they are part) rely on our sensory responses to the horror. In discussing the senses, while I'm interested in the haptic in the sense that Bruno uses the term, I'll also be looking at the synaesthetic properties inherent to the cinematic experience; in other words, the ability of sense modalities such as sight and hearing to trigger other senses. In exploring some of the paths that the sensorium may follow while absorbed in an encounter with New Horror Cinema, I'll begin with some of the films' intellectual interests before moving on to the sensory (dis)pleasures of New Horror film aesthetics.

The Apocalypse Is Coming

> I always thought of the zombies as being about revolution, one generation consuming the next. — George A. Romero

Much has been made of the social and political undercurrent that runs through the new 21st-century wave of horror films, and many of these films have been read against their socio-political backdrop. Axelle Carolyn (2008), for example, is typical of many writers on New Horror in establishing a correlation between the rise of hardcore, apocalyptic horror and the aftermath of the events that took place on September 11, 2001. As a result, with the release of *28 Days Later* (Danny Boyle), the year 2002 is seen as a turning point that ushers in a horror film renaissance that aims to terrify its viewers as much as its film victims by reminding them of the grand-scale horrors that also lie "out there." For Carolyn, for example, there are "obvious parallels between *Hostel* and real-life atrocities that the Western world was only too familiar with, from Kana's (Jennifer Lim) burnt face recalling the blowtorch torture Saddam Hussein's troops used against Iraqi dissidents, to the image of Josh (Derek Richardson) hooded, stripped to his underwear and tied to a chair directly mirroring photographs from Abu Ghraib published by the U.S. media a couple of years earlier."[5] A high percentage of the New Horror boom comprises of the living dead/zombie films and cannibalism films that follow in the tradition of George Romero's Living Dead trilogy and Tobe Hooper's *Texas Chainsaw Massacre* (1977). According to Kyle Bishop, there's a parallel between the success of the living dead sub-genre of horror and current political events. Just as *Night of the Living Dead* (George Romero 1968) was placed by critics against the backdrop of the assassinations of Martin Luther King and Robert Kennedy, student riots, racial unrest, and the involvement of the United States in the Vietnam War, so too is the zombie comeback — as witnessed in *28 Days Later*, *Dawn of the Dead* (Zack Snyder, 2004), *Land of the Dead* (George Romero, 2005), *28 Weeks Later* (Juan Carlos Fresnadillo, 2007), *Day of the Dead* (Steve Miner, 2008), *Zombieland* (Ruben Fleischer, 2009), and so many others — placed in the current socio-political context of the September 11 events and their aftermath. Discussing the resurgence of the living dead in horror cinema, Bishop states, "This renaissance of the subgenre reveals a connection between zombie cinema and post–9/11 cultural consciousness."[6]

> In fact, some films move beyond the zombie-as-allegory for social issues to directly address the post–9/11 crisis. The post-apocalyptic backdrop present in the New Horror living dead films stresses "the collapse of societal infrastructures, the indulgence of survivalist fantasies, and the fear of other surviving humans. All of these plot elements and motifs are present in pre–9/11 zombie films, but they have become more relevant to a modern, contemporary audience.[7]

In the opening title sequence of the *Dawn of the Dead* reboot, Kyle Cooper (who directed the title sequence) makes this relevance very clear as he intercuts the titles of the film with scenes of mayhem and destruction. The social context is directly brought to the fore through a sensorial confrontation with the spectators. The result is a highly emotive and sensorially evocative sequence whose harsh and violent beauty delivers messages of horror and mass destruction. "Real" and fictional news footage bombard the viewer with scenes of riots, abandoned buildings, police beatings, burning bodies, explosions, zombie attacks, crowds in states of mass hysteria, and micro images of blood flowing through veins, while news readers report the events that have befallen the world with utter disbelief. To the accompaniment of Johnny Cash singing "When the Man Comes Around," snippets of audio interrupt to tell the story of viral infections that are spreading and bringing the dead back to life — an infection that even contaminates the film's titles as the red text leaks blood and disperses the titles across the screen. And the titles come to a close with the gravelly voice of Johnny Cash signaling the apocalypse: "And I heard a voice in the midst of the four beasts. And I looked, and behold a pale horse, and his name that sat on him was Death, and hell followed with him." The zombie invasion and scenes of global apocalyptic destruction are, through this title sequence, placed firmly within the context of real world events; and to drive home the connection between the zombie invasion and the 9/11 events further still, the titles begin with one seemingly anomalous act that stands apart from the destruction that dominates in this scene: the opening sequence depicts thousands of Muslims bowing their heads repeatedly to the ground in mass prayer, the suggestion being that religious zeal initiates the events that follow in the rest of the film.

In *Homecoming* (2005) — a film produced for Showtime's "Masters of Horror" anthology series — the director Joe Dante more explicitly develops this connection between the socio-political and the emergence of the horror. No plot summary can do justice to what Dante delivers with his typically satirical wit and flair, but this is what Brian Lowry has to say about the film:

> "Homecoming" is a full-frontal assault on the Bush administration, and as subtle as a punch to the jaw. Adapted by Sam Hamm from Dale Bailey's short story "Death and Suffrage"— but also vaguely reminiscent of Irwin Shaw's 1936 antiwar play "Bury the Dead"— Dante's hour darkly satirizes zombie movies, as dead soldiers arise to vote against the politicians who shipped them off to war.[8]

And in his *Village Voice* review, Dennis Lim explains that "as if in defiance of the Pentagon's policy to ban photographs of dead soldiers' coffins, Dante's film shows not just the flag-draped caskets at Dover Air Force Base but their irate occupants bursting out of them ... as *Homecoming* suggests, there are ways in which the current administration is essentially beyond satire."[9] According to Bishop, "Horror films function as barometers of society's anxieties, and zombie movies represent the inescapable realities of unnatural death while presenting a grim view of the modern apocalypse through scenes of deserted streets, piles of corpses, and gangs of vigilantes — images that have become increasingly common and can shock and terrify a population."[10] From "the torture, rape and possible homicide of Iraqi prisoners in Abu Ghraib by American soldiers" to "accounts of cruel and inhumane methods of interrogation and treatment of prisoners at the Guantánamo Bay detention camp in Cuba, which were reported to the media by soldiers, FBI agents and non-governmental organisations," to the hurricanes Ivan, Jeanne and Katrina, to the SARS epidemic and mad cow disease,[11] New Horror is understood as reflecting on and interpreting these events — manmade and natural — in self-consciously apocalyptic terms.

Aside from the many examples of New Horror that have been produced in the United States, Australasia, Europe and Latin America, it comes as no surprise that many of the films (and some of the most successful) have been the remakes of a wave of independent, low-budget horror films that hit the screens in the 1970s. Along with the invasion of the living dead, which began in the late 1960s with *Night of the Living Dead* (George Romero, 1968), a number of these low-budget classics — *Last House on the Left* (Wes Craven, 1972), *Texas Chainsaw Massacre* (Tobe Hooper, 1974) and *The Hills Have Eyes* (Wes Craven, 1977) — led the way to the New Horror aesthetic, in particular, its focus on a dark, apocalyptic horror from which there appears to be no return. Rebooting the classics, the New Horror versions revisit the spaces of horror, but this time, from within the mainstream, with bigger budgets and a greater attention to the graphic punishment and destruction of bodies. The result is that the mental, psychological and sensory impact on the bodies of the characters who suffer at the hands of the monsters are not only depicted explicitly but this trauma also thrusts itself onto the body of the spectator.

Laura Marks writes that the kind of haptic visuality the cinema engages in not only relies on the eye of the viewer touching and being touched by the content of the screen: its atmospheric lighting, its editing, its characters in motion and states of emotion, its diegetic and non-diegetic sound, and so on. Haptic images, she explains, don't invite "identification with a figure but encourage a bodily relationship between viewer and image."[12] In New Horror Cinema, this bodily relationship is all the more marked in that the cinematic body — the audio-visual fictional world presented to us — reflects and amplifies the experience of the horrified, suffering and volatile bodies within the narrative space. Consider *The Hills Have Eyes* (2006), directed by Alexandre Aja, which was based on the 1977 classic directed by Wes Craven. Both films place the family as institution at the center of the horror: traveling across the desert, the Carter family (which includes Bob and Ethel Carter — who are celebrating their 50th wedding anniversary — the two teenagers, Brenda and Bobby, their other daughter, Lynn, her husband, Doug, and baby daughter, Catherine, and the German Shepherd couple, Beauty and Beast. Soon after the film's opening, a parallel is established between the "normal" Carter family and a mysterious mutant family that appears to be living in the desert mountain caves. Of course, any horror fan worth anything knows that, ever since the days of *Psycho*, leaving the safety of the freeway (which symbolizes the link to civilization) means trouble, and the Carters find trouble by the bucket load! Stuck in the desert (their caravan is damaged by the mutants) the Carters endure a series of attacks that rob them of Bob the father, Lynn the daughter, Ethel the mother, and Beauty the dog — all are brutally murdered. After the initial attacks, the Carters take more of a defensive stance against the mutants and, while Doug treks into the mountains to find his baby daughter who's been kidnapped, Brenda and Bobby stay behind and think of ways to protect themselves from further attacks. In the end Bobby, Brenda, Doug and Beast all survive, revealing a resilience and capacity for violence that had seemed barely possible in the first part of the film.

Despite having the same narrative focus, it's worth considering the differences between original and remake. Both films are vicious in terms of their depiction of violence, but *Hills* 2006 is far more graphic and grisly (for example, the scene in which the mutant Lizard suckles milk from Lynn's breast before shooting her in the head and kidnapping her baby; or, grotesque detail of Brenda's rape at the hands of two mutants). As I'll come back to below, the unforgiving representation of affective brutal acts of violence owes much to the Italian horror tradition, which relied heavily on masterful gore special effects. Like the earlier version of *Texas*, *Hills* 1977 relies on film style, in particular cinema verité techniques, which are heavily influenced by the low-budget production, to amplify the sensation of horror rather than locating

Figure 2: Doug (Aaron Stanford), patriarch-in-the-making with the canine patriarch Beast from *The Hills Have Eyes* (Fox Searchlight 2006) (Kobal Collection, Lacey Terrell).

and playing out the horror more explicitly and relentlessly across the fictional bodies. Yet, despite not excessively representing the acts of cruelty, there's something harsh about *Hills* 1977 that makes these acts appear to be less about represented violence and more about "real" violence, which becomes for the spectator an uncomfortable experience.[13] The multimillion-dollar budget that backed the production of *Hills* 2006 resulted in a much slicker and mannered look that differs dramatically from the documentary style of filmmaking of its predecessor. Despite being based on the same fictional premise, both films apply different storytelling and stylistic devices to create their horror fictions; the result is that each brings with it alternative ways with which to engage the sensorium.

Both *The Hills Have Eyes* films are gutsy, in your face, and have no qualms about sticking it to the American government and the military. Yet, whereas the 1977 version implies that the desert had been used for bomb testing, *Hills* 2006 makes this a core part of the film, the opening title sequence explicitly mentioning military tests in the desert between 1945–'62, which resulted in nuclear fallout and genetic mutations. Aja explains,

> We wanted to keep its savage, realistic aspect but at the same time add a story that involved the tests that the U.S. army conducted in the forties and fifties in the New Mexico desert — the armed forces conducted about 350 atmospheric tests, each time asking the people to leave the area, but not always making sure that they'd all gone.... That is how we wanted to explain why the region was deserted and where the mutant family comes from. It allowed us to tell a larger, more epic story elaborating on the original material.[14]

In his search for the kidnapped Catherine, Doug (fig. 2) discovers an abandoned Test Village that had been used as a site for nuclear testing. Rather than being cave dwellers, as is the mutant family in Craven's film,[15] Aja's mutants live in this town (the happy "nuclear" family?) and even have the convenience of television viewing (we see Big Mama, for example, in a blissful state, watching *Divorce Court* on an old television set). Meeting Big Mama and Ruby (the young mutant who decides to help Doug), Doug is also granted an audience with Big Brain (yes, he has a really big head, which presumably houses his really big brain and which drops like a huge watermelon over the back of his wheelchair), who tells Doug the story of the mutants, who were inhabitants of the area and were exposed to the fallout from the nuclear tests. ("You made us what we became. Boom. Boom. Boom.")

In his influential article "Return of the Repressed," Robin Wood provides a basic formula for the function of the horror film: normality is threatened by the monster.[16] Normality is defined as an order that conforms to dominant social norms — heterosexuality, monogamous couples, the family and social institutions, such as the police, the Church and the military which defends them. Wood's argument depends on the Marcusian thesis that, in a society based on monogamy and the nuclear family, there will be an enormous surplus of sexual energy that must be repressed. As a result, that which is repressed must inevitably return. New Horror is positively brimming over with sexual surplus, and its unleashing is played out violently, bloodily and without forgiveness. While the sexual surplus definitely rears its ugly head in both *Hills* films, the methods for depicting the threat to the social are where the two films differ. Both films place blame on the government and military as institutions that were clearly responsible for the horror families that are the films' monsters. Aja, however, chooses to be more specific about the backstory of the mutant family: they are the government and military's repressed, and they are the result of the cover-up and failure to remove all residents from their homes before turning the desert town into a nuclear test village. The mutant community comes back with a vengeance and attacks all who pass through the land with an extreme ferocity that, like the nuclear tests, has no respect for morality, civilized values or humanity.

Unlike Aja, Craven establishes a far more direct parallel between the "normal" Carters (who he sees as representative of "whitebread" middle America[17]) and the mutant family of Jupiter, his aim being to invite comparison between the two; the growing discovery, as the film progresses and as members of both families take out members of the opposition, is that it is the "normal" family that has the greater capacity for violence (the teenagers even use their dead mother's body as bait to draw Jupiter into a trap). We also get to know more about Jupiter's cannibalistic clan, which is smaller than the community of mutants that live in the nuclear town in the 2006 version. The result is that in the 1977 version the attack is far more explicitly on one of the foundations of civilization: the family, whose drive to continue is represented in three generations. On the side of normality we find Bob and Ethyl, the children Lynn, Doug, Bobby and Brenda, and the baby Catherine; and the monstrous family mirrors this in old Fred, whose absent wife is ripped apart giving birth to Jupiter, who, with Mama Jupiter, give birth to Mars, Pluto and Ruby (whose father may also be Mars or Pluto).[18] The struggle in *Hills* 1977 is the symbolic struggle for the survival of patriarchy and white-American civilization. When Bob dies, the mantle of patriarch is taken over by Doug and the men of the Jupiter tribe are murdered one by one. At the end of *Hills* 2006 we're invited to cheer on the transformed cell-phone-salesman-cum-hero as he wreaks havoc on the mutants (he even manages to stab a mini–American flag (fig. 3) into the head of one of them along the way!) and escapes with the baby Catherine in one hand and Beast on a leash in the other. In the final moments of the film, he returns to the other two survivors — his teen brother-in-law and previously lusted-after young sister-in-law — as they unite in a

Figure 3: Doug (Aaron Stanford) attacks a mutant and plants a U.S. flag in his head, from *The Hills Have Eyes* (Dune Entertainment & Major Studio Partners, 2006).

group hug that screams "reconfigured nuclear family." *Hills* 1977, however, leaves the spectator with little to cheer about as the camera freezes mid-action on surviving patriarch Doug's bloody form as he pounds down on one of the mutant victims, the close-up of his face finally morphing into a bloody red hue.

Discussing the Tobe Hooper version of *Texas Chainsaw Massacre*, Christopher Sharrett makes the observation that "Hooper's apocalyptic landscape is ... a deserted wasteland of dissolution where the once vibrant myth [of the frontier] is desiccated."[19] In *Texas*, we see the end product of the frontier myth in the form of the decaying mansions and families who can no longer make a living off the land because of the new concerns that drive the nation: "Thus, the long-term shifts in American culture, society and the U.S. economy have together conspired to spawn many monsters."[20] Merging horror with the Western, *Hills* 1977 also evokes the ghost of frontier history, not only in the presence of the Carters who travel west across the desert — in what is seen as an act of invasion by the mutant inhabitants — but Papa Jupiter's family (who we develop more and more empathy for as the film progresses) is clearly coded through their clothing to echo the American Indian. When Papa Jupiter addresses his speech to the decapitated head of Big Bob (while staring directly at the camera and, by extension, the viewer) the curse he wishes upon the seed of Bob and his progeny — "I'm gonna suck the brains of your children's children!" — is a curse on Western civilization and the European "civilizers" who invaded America. Both films test the limits of human nature by uncovering a darkness in the human spirit that questions the very nature of humanity. However, intellectually, on the level of story both films have a different agenda. *Hills* 2006 is more concerned with depicting the devastating outcomes of nuclear testing in recent American history; unlike the cannibal family in the 1977 film, which appears to look "normal" (with possible signs of interbreeding), the 2006 film focuses on the horrendous mutations caused by exposure to nuclear radiation. The journey of the Republican family and Democrat son-in-law can and has also been read as an allegory of the invasion of the Middle East by U.S. Forces (a connection driven home more forcefully in the sequel).

The film's other dissimilarity to the 1977 film lies in its interest in amplifying the spectator's corporeal reaction to the onscreen horror. The film body, in other words, offers a different performance for its spectator. In *Hills* 2006, scene after scene presents the viewer with a multitude of episodes that make our skin crawl and our bodies cringe, and the cinematic properties of cinematography, editing, acting, sound and special effects heighten the horror of body desecration: the terrified gas station owner whose brains and skull we see erupt after he shoots himself in the head; the burning of Bob's living body as close-ups expose us to the burnt and melting flesh, and as the sound amplifies his agonizing screams before they're finally silenced by his death; the mutant Lizard who rips off and eats the head of a love bird then squeezes its body so that the blood can flow more freely into his mouth; the squeals of pleasure we hear coming out of the deformed mouth of the mutant Pluto as he rapes the catatonic Brenda; the screwdriver that Lynn plunges and forcefully twists into Lizard's leg before he shoots her through the head, her blood and brains erupting through the air and across the interior of the caravan; Doug regaining consciousness in a freezer, his body and clothes dripping with blood and becoming hysterical as he realizes he's surrounded by a mass of bloody human limbs that have been kept in storage for later consumption; the perturbing sound of Big Brain's labored breathing and the revolting sight of his limp and wasted body as it languishes in a wheelchair that's barely capable of supporting the bulging, grotesque mass of bone and flesh that is his head; the violent force with which Doug plunges the pick axe repeatedly into the deformed mutant bodies, their flesh and bones collapsing under its weight. *Hills* 2006 takes the unforgiving display of horror that was present in its predecessor and amplifies the corporeal damage dramatically. How do we make sense of these actions?

The psychogeographic journeys of New Horror are dark and foreboding but their impact would be minimal without the sensory and emotional experiences that are at the core of these films. A structuralist like Lévi-Strauss may insist that to get to the core of myths it's necessary to strip away the surface; but horror and, in particular, New Horror, is as much about the surface as it is about the underlying structure. In his book *Cinematic Emotion in Horror Films and Thrillers*, Julian Hanich takes issue with Noel Carroll who, in *The Philosophy of Horror, or Paradox of the Heart*, argues that the spectator's main pleasure in horror comes from satisfying a cognitive interest concerned with proving that monsters exist.[21] Hanich argues that Carroll's definition of the emotion of "art-horror" (which relies on a combination of threat and disgust),[22] fails to consider the sensory and sensual aspects of film spectatorship.[23] For Carroll the threat of the monster involves a cognitive and evaluative response on the part of the viewer.

> Some nonordinary physical state of agitation is caused by the thought of the monster.... The audience thinking of a monster is prompted in this response by the responses of fictional human characters whose actions they are attending to, and that audience, like said characters, may also wish to avoid physical contact with such types of things as monsters.[24]
>
> The audience's psychological state, therefore, diverges from the psychological state of characters with respect to belief, but converges on that of characters with respect to the way in which the properties of said monsters are emotively assessed.[25]

According to Carroll, the characters become our mediator into the horror fiction, and also — through cognitive processes that decipher narrative and character development and action signal our emotional responses to what appears onscreen. And yet, as Hanich explains, Carroll "overemphasizes cognitive pleasure and overintellectualizes somatic experience."[26] I agree with Hanich that the spectator's cognitive response to a film is important, and to dismiss this response in favor of an analysis that only favors the emotion, the body and the senses would be to miss much of the power inherent to the aesthetics of horror cinema. The sensorium engages all categories of perception, ranging from the cognitive and intellectual to the sensory and carnal. But Carroll disallows the latter and understands it primarily through cognitive processes. As the examples from *Hills* 2006 highlight and as will be further discussed below, horror cinema (and New Horror in particular) drive home the centrality played by our sensory encounters with onscreen horror.

In her book *Carnal Thoughts: Embodiment and Moving Image Culture*, Vivian Sobchack reminds us of the early period of film theory that had not yet abandoned the relationship between intellectual and cognitive processes and "sensory thought" or "emotional intelligence": Sergei Eisenstein investigated the "synchronization of the senses"[27]; Walter Benjamin "speaks of cinematic intelligibility in terms of 'tactile appropriation,' and ... a sensuous and bodily form of perception"; and Siegfried Kracauer "located the uniqueness of cinema in the medium's essential ability to stimulate us physiologically and sensually."[28] Sobchack notes:

> This "still unclear sense" of the sensational movement that, "as if real," provokes a bodily response marks the confusion and discomfort we scholars have not only in confronting our sensual experience of the cinema but also in confronting our lack of ability to explain its somatism as anything more than "mere" physiological reflex or to admit its meaning as anything more than metaphorical description ... but despite current academic fetishization of "the body," most theorists still don't quite know what to do with their unruly responsive flesh and sensorium. Our sensations and responses pose an intolerable question to prevalent linguistic and psychoanalytic understandings of the cinema as grounded in conventional codes and cognitive patterning and grounded on absence, lack, and illusion.[29]

What, Sobchack asks, does it mean for the human body to be "touched" or "moved" by the movies, and how do somatic experiences the "unruly responsive flesh" figure in this encounter? The fact is that the process of watching films like *The Hills Have Eyes* is more like a ping-pong match with multiple balls in play at once — each ball representing a different way of "being touched" by what's onscreen: picking up on a generic reworking or allusion to other horror films; recognizing the social critique embedded in the narrative; feeling one's skin crawl; laughing at or recoiling from the over-the-top displays of gore and body desecration; empathizing with characters as they deal with abominable horrors; feeling a thrill deep down in that mysterious place called the "gut." So many cognitive and sensorial ping-pong balls. Yet New Horror endows the senses with an intelligence of its own: in worlds where meaning and culture collapses, the senses become a powerful — and often horrifying — method of communication. As cultural theorist Paul Rodaway explains in his book *Sensuous Geographies: Body, Sense, and Place*, the senses play an important role in mediating the experience of the world around us.[30] "The senses," he states, "are not merely passive receptors of particular kinds of environmental stimuli but are actively involved in the structuring of that information and are significant in the overall sense of a world achieved by the sentient."[31] In addition to our cognitive and evaluative skills, when we watch horror films — or any other film for that matter — we also rely on our senses to give meaning to the fictional geographies created by film. For the rest of this chapter, I'd like to explore what Rodaway calls "sensuous geographies" in order to understand the kind of experiences the senses mediate and give meaning to in our encounter with contemporary horror cinema.

The Case of the Living Dead: Synaesthesia and Sensuous Geographies

> When there's no more room in hell, the dead will walk the earth.—
> *Dawn of the Dead* (1978)

In 1968, George Romero's *Night of the Living Dead* hit the screens and altered the directions of the contemporary horror genre. The film's style stripped back the more atmospheric and mannered lighting, cinematography and music scores that typified horror films prior to the '60s. Instead (barring a few deliberate references to the early Hollywood Gothic-horror style), the film confronted the viewer with an in-your-face objective approach that was more typical of the documentary film. This sparse style all the more powerfully delivered the film's story, which was about the recently dead who had come to life (probably—but never confirmed—as a result of radiation emanating from a Venus space probe that exploded in the Earth's atmosphere). Not only had the dead been reanimated, but their only drive was to eat living human flesh. The raw style of the film also impacted on the sensory responses elicited from the spectator both to the narrative action and to shocking acts, which more often than not centered on the living dead munching hungrily away at still-living humans as well as not so living corpses. In addition to the film's sequels (*Dawn* and *Day of the Dead* [1978 and 1985], which were followed more recently by reboots [in 1990, 2004, 2008]), the film spawned the popular living dead or "zombie" subgenre of horror. In the 1970s and '80s, the subgenre underwent another transformation in the hands of Italian filmmakers like Lucio Fulci, Lamberto Bava and Bruno Mattei, all of whom pumped up the volume on the gore- and splatter-factor that had already been present in the living-dead films. The result was a subgenre that assailed the audience with extreme sensory experiences.

In *The Material Image: Art and the Real in Film*, Brigitte Peucker draws attention to the reciprocity that exists between the film spectator and the image, a relationship that she sees as generating an interface between the representation and the real.[32] Peucker expresses her interest in what she calls "the physiological perceptual" and argues a case for "the spectator's somatic responsiveness" to the projected image. Drawing on Sobchack's concept of the "cinesthetic body"—a concept that embraces "the complexity and richness of the more general bodily experience that grounds our particular experience of cinema, and ... also points to ways in which the cinema uses our dominant senses of vision and hearing to speak comprehensibly to our other senses"[33]— Peucker stresses how "the image itself is granted the semblance of materiality"[34] because of its capacity to incite our senses in very real ways. Peucker is correct in claiming that this reciprocity between the image and the real may be most apparent in genres such as the horror film, a genre that derives its very name from "the affect it seeks to elicit."[35] Like many film theorists of recent years, Peucker condemns film and art theory for prioritizing the visual to the detriment of other sensory experiences.

There's a scene in the film *Zombi 2* (Lucio Fulci, 1979[36]) in which the character Paola Menard (wife of the mad doctor partially responsible for the zombie epidemic) tries to escape the clutches of a zombie. Hearing a noise, she walks through darkened rooms that evoke an oppressive atmosphere, triggering in the spectator a sense of growing fear in anticipation of what the darkness may hide. Running to a room, Paola tries to lock the door, only to find it won't shut. The reason soon becomes clear to both Paola and the spectator — the zombie is pushing against the door. Eventually, his decaying fingers pry their way through the crack between the door and the door frame and, against the backdrop noises of the howling wind, Paola's moans of horror and suspenseful music, we look on as she pushes against the door, causing the delicate, putrefying flesh on his fingers to ooze blood, before the fingers finally snap free from the hand and release the door in the process. As Paola slides a chest of drawers against the door, the zombie's arm crashes through the wooden door, grabbing her viciously by the hair and, in an act that's torturously slow, Paola's head is pushed towards splinters of broken wood (fig. 4). The resistance of her body against this movement was translated in my own body as I watched the scene with a tension that mimicked Paola's; the combination of sweat and water (remnants of a shower previously taken) triggered in me a mental image of my own hand reaching up to brush my flesh and wipe away droplets of imaginary water from my neck. Unable to halt the movement forward, I looked on as Paola's right eye was pushed slowly, teasingly toward a shard of wood; the anticipation of what was about to happen played itself out forcefully in the pit of my stomach. Unable to turn away, I looked on in awe at Paola as she looked on — eyes filled with terror — at the initial, almost delicate touch of wood as it pressed against the cornea, a delicate touch that was almost immediately replaced by a vicious plunge into the eyeball that proceeded to ooze and squeeze its way out of the eye socket that contained it. Intense stuff — but you can expect nothing less from a film that sees a zombie challenge a shark ... *mano-a-mano*!

This entire scene plays on a key premise of horror: the tug of war that occurs between wanting to look and not wanting to look. Many horror films punish their viewers for looking at scenes like this one: introducing the device of the doubled audience, the events that take place onscreen are mirrored reflexively in the "real" domain of the audience. But the mirroring doesn't only occur through imagery centered on the eye. As Peucker explains, the contemporary horror film (she stresses the American horror film, but I'd widen this out to include other examples — in this case, from Italy) "supplements the activity of the eye with that of touch, taste, and sometimes even smell ... [and] engages its spectator in a multisensory and aesthetic experience"[37] — and to this I'd also add sound.

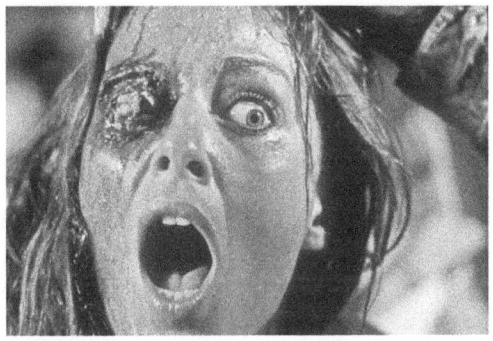

Figure 4: Paola (Olga Karlatos) from *Zombi 2* (Fulci 1979) is victim to a zombie attack; her eye has been plunged into a wooden shard (Kobal Collection).

While not an example of New Horror cinema, this scene from *Zombi 2* highlights the significant role that Italian directors of this generation would have on the aesthetics of New Horror. While certainly influenced by the splatter tradition of American horror as it developed after the apocalyptic wave of 1970s horror (for example, the *Evil Dead* films, *Dawn of the Dead, Braindead, Re-Animator*[38]), New Horror directors like Eli Roth preferred the less comical or openly carnivalesque splatter favored by the Italians in the wake of Dario Argento. It comes as no surprise, therefore, that the infamous Ruggero Deodato, director of the equally infamous *Cannibal Holocaust* (1980), was asked by Roth to make a guest appearance in *Hostel 2* (Eli Roth, 2007), wherein he played a creepy client eager to whet the appetite of his cannibal tastes. By adopting Italian horror's obsessive focus on splatter-gore, New Horror Cinema would return to a hardcore expression of body-horror and, by extension, would draw attention to the sensory power of the cinema and the cinesthetic body.

Drawing attention to the synaesthetic potential inherent in film spectatorship, Peuker, like Sobchack, recognizes how one sense — vision or sound, for example — can set off the perception of others through inter-sensorial exchanges. While most of us are born synesthetes "perceiving the world as a primordial soup of impressions,"[39] as we grow the senses begin to specialize and connections between sense modalities are lost; the cinema has the capacity to mimic the synaesthetic encounter. While I may not perceive like a "true" synesthete, my experience of *Zombi 2* reveals the synaesthetic dimensions of spectatorship. Consider this scene: as Paola's horror at the knowledge of what awaits her builds, and as the zombie forces her eye closer and closer to the sharp splinter of wood, my perception responded physiologically to what I saw onscreen, triggered by the memory not of being attacked by a zombie, but of corresponding sensory and somatic responses. Mesmerized by her eyes as they widened in horror, I also felt the tremors that vibrated across her body, and the tiny trickles of sweat that exited the pores of her skin. But my most intense moment of somatic reaction was felt while viewing the defilement of her eye. It's this moment of pure disgust that kicks my senses into full gear. As her eye was forced into the wooden stake I felt every squishy, repulsive, skin-crawling sensation that accompanied the ooze of damaged eye-flesh as the wooden shard sank deeply into her skull. In turn, the gooeyness and the soggy, sucking sounds of the eye responding to the entry of wood further suggested texture and tactility while the jelly-like substance had a haptic quality associated with food, as well as its taste and smell. Szaloky explains that the "metaphorical aspect of synaesthesia implies an inner hearing that, independent of immediate physical stimuli, relies on memory, imagination, and inference-making on the basis of lived experiences."[40] While not "real," this action was materially brought to life for me though my multi-sensory response to its disgusting properties.

Peucker directs her attention, in particular, to the earlier tradition of living-dead films and apocalyptic horror, claiming that horror's "imbrication of the senses ... promotes and encourages a spectrum of spectatorial responses to the image, including tactile and gustatory experiences, with the result that disgust is one of the central affects that horror films produce."[41] I agree. Disgust is at the core of these films and, even more so, at the center of New Horror. But the disgust doesn't simply function as a trigger to sensory overload; its underlying logic has a deeper social purpose.

Corpse Contagion and Disgust

> Thanks to George Bush, Donald Rumsfeld and Dick Cheney we have this whole new wave of horror.—Eli Roth

In his writings on disgust (originally published in the 1920s), the philosopher Aurel Kolnai stated that disgust is an aversive response that functions as one of the body's protective mechanisms against objects of impurity and threat, and here he includes corpses, open wounds, and creepy crawlies—all of which are iconic images in the horror film. Unlike many other theorists concerned with affect and the senses, Kolnai understands disgust as serving a cognitive function[42] that conveys information about "features of the outer world not readily available by other means and which also reveals something about the complexities and shadows of our inner psychic life":

Disgust helps to ensure the safety of the organism by inhibiting contact with what is foul, toxic and thereby dangerous.... But for all of its engagement of bodily responses, disgust is also an emotion that is at work in creating and sustaining our social and cultural reality. It helps us to grasp hierarchies of value to cope with morally sensitive situations, and to maintain cultural order.[43]

For Kolnai, disgust — as displayed in objects that include the corruption of living bodies, phenomena associated with putrefaction, decomposition, dissolution and the odor of corpses — occupies a borderline between life and death.[44] Reflecting Julia Kristeva's later study of the abject, the disgusting is, according to Kolnai, "pregnant with death."[45] It reminds the living of what they will become — the dead. This is made quite literal in the living dead films in which the horror associated with moral and physical disgust comes quite literally from the fear of the contagion of death.

In her book *Phantasmagoria*, Marina Warner examines the nature and function of zombies. For Warner, while manifested differently in both the voodoo and post–Romero film traditions, zombies embody a vision of human existence that's about slavery — a slavery that involves the theft of a soul.[46] By aligning zombification with the voodoo tradition, the films *White Zombie* (1932) and *I Walked with a Zombie* (1943) assign the state of zombification to a master voodoo practitioner. In the post–Romero tradition, however, the living dead are often masterless and, instead, are products of a faceless, social infrastructure.[47] While the reanimation of the dead may be given narrative rationale (exposure to radiation, bioengineering, biochemical experimentation etc.), once the dead come to life, they're left to their own devices as they plod around the world, sometimes influenced in their actions by residual memories of themselves as social beings, but always driven by a primal desire to devour living flesh. The source of horror in these films is the literal contagion of death that's embodied by the figure of the zombie. And the expression of this contagion is at its most disgusting and intensely sensory when the dead are caught in the act of consuming the flesh of the living.

The intense disgust that envelops us when watching these films radiates around the acts of cannibalism that motivate the living dead, and this cannibalism becomes the ultimate symbol of the nihilism and apocalyptic vision in which these films are steeped. In the case of cannibalism, according to William Arens the most generally used taxonomy includes: endocannibalism, which refers to eating a member of one's own group; exocannibalism, or the consumption of outsiders; and autocannibalism, which entails ingesting parts of one's own body.[48] To this system, Arens adds the motives for the act, which include: "(1) gastronomic cannibalism, where human flesh is eaten for its taste and food value; (2) ritual or magical cannibalism, which involves an attempt to absorb the spiritual essence of the deceased; and (3) survival cannibalism, a normally prohibited behavior that takes place during a crisis."[49] The living dead partake in the worst possible combination — that of "gastronomic endocannibalism," where human beings are eaten for their taste and to satiate hunger.

What I find bizarre about almost everything I've read about the living dead films and the act of cannibalism central to these films is the fact that it's the dead who eat the living and not the living who eat the dead (which is the case in *The Hills Have Eyes*). This fact is totally elided by horror critics and theorists. Peucker, for example, discusses the cannibalism in *Day of the Dead* (where the dead feed off the living) and *Texas Chainsaw Massacre* (where the living feed off the recently murdered dead) as similar acts. Yet, this cannibal reversal speaks to the core of the moral and physical disgust that's central to the subgenre. This form of cannibalism signifies the ultimate collapse of language and society, and our disgust is both physical and moral. It will result in total chaos and the end of civilization. In *Disgust: the Gatekeeper Emotion*, Susan Miller states the following:

> When we contemplate cannibalism, most of the emotion stirred is about the cannibal (the victim is simply meat). We think of the cannibals' perverse appetite and ability to rob the Other of human identity and consume a human body as mere food. Our emotion about such ingestion (even in desperate situations, where death by starvation is imminent) is overwhelmin.... The revulsion is ultimately about the cannibal's ability to strip the Other of human identity and make of him or her meat.[50]

The disgust experienced by the cannibal act is about confronting what Bronislow Molinowski calls "the supreme and final crisis of life — death."[51] When the subject and object of cannibalism are flipped over, as they are in the living-dead films, the "gastronomic endocannibalism" still signifies "the ultimate collapse of language and society" but with added emphasis. The fear of death is now symbolically represented in the figures of the living dead who literally come back to devour the living and force them to embrace the same fate: death. However, the bodies of the living dead serve another symbolic function. One of Romero's reasons for adopting the term "living dead" was to draw on the parallels that exist between the dead who are living, and the living who are living as if they're dead — empty, repetitive, unfulfilling lives that lack depth and emotion. This state of being speaks to Warner's idea of the "theft of a soul," but in the contemporary living dead films, it's society en masse that's been robbed — or has robbed itself— of a soul. The physical and moral disgust we feel, especially in the New Horror reboots, is callous and brutal. The extreme violence and visceral carnality that hammers itself insistently across the surface of these films generally act as metaphors for the violence and lack of humanity that riddles the world of the living.

Discussing the splatter aesthetic of New Horror and, in particular, the group of films that have been dubbed "torture porn" (for example, *Hostel, Saw, Wolfcreek, Human Centipede*), Phoebe Fletcher explains why the term "torture porn" has been applied:

> Dubbed "torture porn" by critics who highlighted the verisimilitude between the violent images leaked from Abu Ghraib and the torture of ordinary Americans in these films, this association mobilized a narrative that linked the rise in popularity of the splatter film to audience's unconscious fears of the "Global War on Terror." This discourse, repeated by journalists, critics and the industry itself, positioned the post–9/11 horror as an avatar for debates over the limits, use and justification for state violence.[52]

According to Fletcher, the splatter film (which is what she calls New Horror) has quite consciously and conscientiously become a "means of asserting and debating nationalism."[53] While technically not torture porn, other examples of New Horror, including *The Hills Have Eyes, Texas Chainsaw Massacre*, the *Living Dead* reboots, and the numerous examples of zombie horror, reflect similar concerns. Focusing on *Hostel*, she explores how many examples of New Horror critique imperialism through the figure of the "fucking American"—a phrase often literally heard in New Horror films, or a concept indirectly implied.

In the film *28 Weeks Later*, Americans do, indeed, take a beating but the social critique is explored through the logic of the living-dead film conventions. Financed by British (DNA Films, UK Film Council, Figment Films), Spanish (Sociedad General de Cine [SOGECINE] S.A.) and U.S.(Koan Films) companies and distributed by 20th Century–Fox, the film tackles the topic of global culture on more than its production level. The story takes place six months after the events depicted in *28 Days Later* and the U.S. Army has been brought in to secure an area of London which is kept under constant surveillance. At the beginning of the film, the spectator is introduced to the human inhabitants of a farmhouse, which is, soon into the story, invaded by the living dead. Sticking with the living-dead-on-'roids convention initiated by Danny Boyle in the first film, those infected with the "rage virus" violently prey on the occupants. In one heart-wrenching scene, the character Don selfishly leaves his wife, Alice, behind and, in a state of panic, escapes the farmhouse, abandoning Alice to her fate. Soon after, Don is safe at the U.S. Army camp in London and is joined by his kids who had previously been sent to Spain for safety. Believing he'll never be caught out in the lie, he informs his kids that he tried to save their mother but wasn't able to because the infected got her first. Well, of course, no sooner has Don lied to his kids than Anna is discovered and not only is she alive and survived an attack, but she carries a natural immunity against the rage virus. In one of the most sensorially explosive scenes, Don sneaks in to see his wife who's being kept in a medical installation. Apologizing for his reprehensible behavior — and unaware that Anna may be immune but is also a carrier of the virus — Don bends to kiss her.

Figure 5: In *28 Weeks Later* (Fox Atomic, 2007), after exposure to the rage virus, Don (Robert Carlyle) undergoes a violent transformation.

As the camera lingers on the visible exchange of saliva that occurs during the kiss, I remember preparing myself for what was sure to be a shocking and bloody transformation. But nothing could have prepared me for the display that would follow. Within seconds, Don transforms (fig. 5) and his face and eyes contort under the strain of the change. Like a rabid animal, saliva foams out of his mouth and his body gears itself up for going into berserker mode. Throwing his body violently and repeatedly on the floor and against the walls and windows of the room, blood flies in every direction, painting every surface they touch. Every action is amplified by the speeded-up shots, extreme close-ups, and images moving at high speeds. The audible and vicious blows inflicted on his thrashing body cease after what feels like a very long time and he approaches his wife. Turning her head away in terror, she presents her neck to him like an offering. He pauses, then plunges in, ripping chunks of flesh from her throat in a bloody feast that appears to have no end. Anna's final destruction is achieved through a method that seems to be straight out of an Italian horror film: standing over her and holding her trembling head down fiercely with his hands, Don ruthlessly plunges both thumbs into her eye sockets and his thumbs push downwards, entering her head so that thick streams of blood ooze out. The scene finally makes literal Don's betrayal at the beginning of the film; what had been an action that he believed facilitated his wife's murder now becomes an actual murder by his own hands. Don's horrifying and cowardly betrayal is all the more forceful because of the sensory overload that dominates in this scene. I felt his moral, and then physical, transformation from human into monster in the very pit of my stomach and across every pore of my skin.

Aside from the sensory and emotional sensations that the scene evokes, it's also a turning point in the film. From this point on, themes dealing with individual and social horror accompany the scenes of body destruction that are thrown at the spectator. When Don escapes from the medical center, a fast-paced montage sequence reveals the speed with which he spreads the virus throughout the safety zone. And as Don seeks to bring closure to his personal agenda — the destruction of his children and, by extension, his family — the social crisis is also thrown into the foreground. Survivors flee in panic while the American military watch through security cameras. In one scene, hundreds of innocent people are attacked by the infected, and the camera cuts to the camera room where military personnel look on. The orders of the commander to the military snipers looking down on the bloodfest are clear: "Abandon selective targeting. Shoot everything. We've lost control." And the snipers let loose on the crowd below. If Don is a man who's been robbed of his soul, then what are these men who control human life with the squeeze of a trigger? The reality of the Gulf War and U.S. military presence on foreign land clearly bubbles uncomfortably beneath the surface of *28 Weeks Later*, waiting to erupt like Don's viral-induced rage. The spectator is asked a moral question about the state of actual events occurring in our world, and my response to this question approached rage. And yet, despite the reflexive use of horror as a metaphor for real world politics, my response wasn't just a cognitive one; the extreme violence in this scene attacked my senses allowing me to experience the abomination taking place to the fullest degree. In doing so, the scene and the film reflect a key strategy of New Horror: the spectator's understanding of the ideological issues is reliant on targeting the spectator through the senses.

Earlier I referred to Bruno's description of the film experience as a psychogeographic journey that elicits affective and sensory responses from the audiences; these are also modes of travel that take the spectator to fictional places and embroil them in the lives of characters who travel their own life journeys onscreen. Like most New Horror Cinema, the psychogeographic journey we're forced to travel in *28 Weeks Later* is a traumatizing one that assaults the sensorium from all directions. In the following chapters I'll be turning to video games and theme park rides as media experiences, but in considering other horror media, the application of Bruno's model needs to be adjusted. As many of the examples in this chapter have shown, our perception and haptic visions that touch us have the potential to give way to sensory reactions and a "type of kinesthetics"[54] that activates the senses and creates for the "viewer" a corresponding offscreen response to the onscreen events. In the shift from spectator to player and participant, however, video games and theme park attractions involve a more literal engagement, both of the senses and kinesthetics. It's to these alternate psychogeographic journeys that I now turn.

2

Dancing with the Living Dead: Video Games, Avatars and Arms on the Brain

Survival Horror, Interactivity and Game Haptics

From the ancient legends of the Titan god Prometheus who molded human life out of clay to Dr. Victor Frankenstein who animated the flesh of human corpses with electricity to create his monster, myths that explore with the possibility of creating artificial life through dead matter are as old as human history. I turn to this theme in this chapter, which is a recurring one in the horror and science fiction genres. Artificial life is an abiding cultural fascination that's woven its way into our fictions and, in doing so, this monster in our media machines has rewritten these age-old myths and aligned them with contemporary fears, anxieties and belief systems. In the space of the diegesis, science fiction and science fiction-horror films imagine the reality of the cyborg body and artificial intelligence systems; and horror films fictionalize the revival of the dead through scientific experimentation and supernatural means. Beyond the realm of fiction, film and video game special effects rely increasingly on artificial intelligence (AI) technology that was once the stuff of science fiction; and robots are being created by the thousands by companies like Sony, Toshiba, Jetta, Aldebaran Robotics and Honda. In this chapter, however, I turn to video games as modern manifestations of age-old beliefs about the creation of artificial life. In particular, I explore how the myth replays itself through the technological mediation that occurs in the human-machine interface and, specifically, the relationship that's forged between the game player and their onscreen avatar. Focusing on *Resident Evil 4: The Wii edition* (Capcom, 2007), which is an evolution of the popular survival-horror genre, this chapter investigates how games rearticulate and complicate the Prometheus myth, transforming it into a theatrical performance whereby players, characters and game designers participate in this myth in wondrous and bizarre ways.

Like most games released since the 1990s, *Resident Evil 4* relies on AI programming that's a more literal manifestation of the creation myth come-to-life. AI programming makes it possible for non-player characters to perform and respond to "real" players in less predictable and repetitive ways.[1] Much like the emergent AI behavior used in virtual pet games like *Nintendogs* (Nintendo, 2005), *Spore* (Electronic Arts, 2008) and *Eye Pet* (Sony, 2009), the in-game characters adapt and learn from actions performed by the player and they modify their behavior accordingly, creating the illusion of intelligence and generating engaging and challenging gameplay. While fascinating as a topic in itself, it's not the technological manifestations of life and intelligence that concern me here, but rather a more metaphoric expression of the myth of artificial creation. Unable to escape the lure of the living dead, the iconic figure of the zombie weaves its way back into this chapter, appearing both in the narrative of *Resident Evil 4* and in the way I attempt to articulate the player's interaction with their avatar.

Resident Evil 4 (known in Japan as *Biohazard 4*) was first released in 2005 on Playstation 2 and Gamecube consoles, and a modified version was released and, dare I say, brought back to life in 2007 for the Nintendo Wii. Despite its misleading title, the game is the sixth in the popular *Resident Evil* series,[2] which has also spawned numerous successful film and comic book spin-offs. Playing an important role in solidifying the conventions of the survival horror game genre, which involves third-person action (but can also be first person) "where the vulnerability of the player character is played out through not so powerful weapons and limited ammo and health,"[3] the narrative premise of the series revolves around the spread of the T-virus, a contagious mutagenic biological agent developed by the pharmaceutical company called the Umbrella Corporation. Those infected with the virus resemble the reanimated corpses brought to life by George Romero in his films (and many also mutate into a range of monstrous antagonists) but, like the "zombies" in the films *28 Days Later* and *28 Weeks Later*, they're products of mad science gone wrong. And like their living dead cousins, they all have a penchant for the taste of living flesh.

In *Resident Evil 4,* our initial exploratory and less masterful gameplay sees us adopt the role of Leon S. Kennedy (the previous rookie cop from *Resident Evil 2* and now a U.S. Secret Service Agent) who is on a mission to rescue the president's daughter (Ashley Graham), who's been kidnapped under mysterious circumstances. With and via Leon, we've made our way to a small village "somewhere in Europe" and the attempt at mastering the game as our

Figure 6: Leon S. Kennedy, the player's avatar in the survival horror video game *Resident Evil 4: the Wii Edition* (Capcom, 2007).

avatar begins isn't an easy thing to keep under our control. With Leon (fig. 6), we take in the details of our environment: the colors and textures of the landscape that bare the marks of autumn, the rundown huts that conjure an air of the primitive, the old-style architecture of the town square that's burdened by the weight of the past, and the peasant villagers who go about their daily duties in a strangely plodding, almost zombie-like manner. Well, of course, they *are* zombies or, more precisely "los ganados" ("the cattle") who have been infected with a mind-controlling parasite known as *Las Plagas*.

Figure 7: *Los ganados,* the zombie-like parasitically controlled humans from the survival horror video game *Resident Evil 4: the Wii Edition* (Capcom, 2007).

Through Leon, we must expand our experience of this eerie place in order to increase our mastery of and ability to affect the fictional world we've entered. If we don't, Leon won't survive and gameplay will end.

Resident Evil 4 reflects the ways in which video games layer the Prometheus myth without always deliberately meaning to. While in the game story, humans are transformed into *los ganados* (fig. 7) through scientific experimentation, beyond the diegesis, through science, game technology has also made possible a game that animates non-player characters to virtual life: the dead matter that exists in the form of electronic and computer hardware and software is programmed to give expression to game worlds that are populated with characters, objects and environments that react to the player's presence *as if alive*. But beyond this, via the game designers the player is also granted the power of animation of inanimate forces through gameplay. Focusing on the horror games *Resident Evil 3* (Capcom, 1999) and *Undying* (Electronic Arts, 2001) Tanya Krzywinska explores the differences that emerge when comparing horror film and horror game experiences:

> The aim of these games is to defeat the manifestation such forces [of evil], and the games are structured to aid this quest. Both games deploy surface story lines and concomitant aesthetic strategies that reference the good-versus-evil format

of many horror films; however, in the games this dualism is more deeply embedded in the infrastructure that shapes the dynamic nature of interactivity.[4] Whereas horror films bargain on the audience's disempowerment and inability to affect the unraveling of story events — and the moral disorder these events unleash — video games demand the player's interaction with the story world. In order to effect "satisfying gameplay," the player needs to experience the outcomes of what Krzywinska calls the "moral occult" firsthand. The moral occult, according to its originator Peter Brooks, is "the hidden yet operative domain of values that the drama, through its heightening, attempts to make present within the ordinary."[5] In the case of melodrama, Brooks's subject matter, the excess and overstatement that typifies the form, confronts protagonists with dilemmas and choices and, in doing so, asks that they make moral and ethical decisions with regard to their existence. A similar process of decision-making is in operation in the horror film, which carries its own codes of excess in the concrete form of the monstrous that embodies a threat to society's moral and social codes. Krzywinska is correct in claiming that, in horror video games, the act of decision-making is passed on to the game player who enacts the role of protagonist through interface with the game avatar, but crucial to this interface is the sense of touch.

Discussing the haptic nature of film spectatorship, Giuliana Bruno states that "site-seeing partakes in a shift away from the long-standing focus of film theory on sight and toward the construction of a moving theory of site."[6] The conception of haptics and a moving theory of site becomes all the more overt and potent when transferred into the world of video games where, via their avatars and through the intensely haptic relationship to game controllers, players are responsible for movement through virtual sites. For Bruno and Marks, in the act of haptic visuality, "The eyes themselves function like organs of touch."[7] While video gaming shares this haptic visuality with the cinema through the player's sensory and affective connection to the fictional world, it also involves a literal haptic connection through the player's interaction with the controller and, in turn, in the way command of the controller translates onto the body of the avatar who then participates in a haptic experience of the virtual space that surrounds it. At the core of any understanding of game haptics is the process of interactivity, a process that's necessary in order that the player can engage with the experiences games offer. Yet, the word "interactivity" isn't simply about technological mediation; it carries with it emotive power and a mysterious quality — a moral occult. Yet my use of the term "moral occult" takes Krzywinska's meaning to a different place, one that speaks to the actual act of the union of player and her avatar; this is in addition to the moral decisions the player makes in response to the moral dilemmas that a game narrative may offer. As Diane Carr explains,

Given the role performed by avatars it is arguable that any uncanny resonance potentially generated while we watch a body move on film is amplified when, as players, we operate and navigate avatars. We use avatars as embodiments or vehicles, as our agents in the gameworld. The player hits a button; the avatar jumps, somersaults or flicks a switch. Every player, surely, has found themselves flinching when their avatar bangs their head, has felt themselves lean over with pseudo-centrifugal forces, or felt their stomach lurch when their avatar plunges over a cliff. Avatars are our emissaries and, at least to a degree, our doubles.[8]

In many respects what we need to do as players is learn to become comfortable in the avatar that we adopt. Like the living dead as players we struggle to gain control of avatar bodies that plod and waddle their way through the game space as we struggle to attain mastery over the body we partially possess. We don't just "interact," we actually undergo a state that's akin to entering someone else's skin and, in the process, we *animate* previously inanimate matter. Here we find a dramatic difference between the way we experience horror games (or any game) when compared to watching a film. Through tools fired by the power of electricity the player gives life to inert matter and gameplay generates the uncanny appearance, movement and action of a virtual being onscreen. When it comes down to it, the avatar and the modern variation of the zombie aren't that different. Both are products of human creation, and technology has brought them to life. In *Resident Evil 4*, the two come together and are brought to life through Leon, our digitally created avatar who simultaneously stands as a metaphor of the zombie while also battling fictional zombies. In addition, Leon is both the living dead and a form of artificial intelligence. It's not only technology that animates him. He is technology.

Dancing with One's Own Creation

In *When Toys Come Alive*, Lois Rostow Kuznets makes observations about the presence of animated toys as characters in literature, and the comments equally apply to game characters who similarly appear to "come to life" in game spaces. A recurring motif in such narratives is one that involves anxiety regarding the creativity that animated the toy in the first place. Whether fueled by the artistry of Geppetto in Carlo Collodi's *The Adventures of Pinocchio* (1883) or by the scientific know-how that creates a little girl's robot in "Robbie," (1950) the short story by Isaac Asimov, the anxiety that returns is one regarding a "creativity in competition with the gods."[9] For Leonard Mendelsohn, toy making exemplifies art and the toy maker becomes the "consummate artist, who experiences great joy when toys take on life," because this initiates an experience that's like "dancing with one's own creation."

Mendelsohn continues: "Endowed with life, it becomes a force that dominates and determines those who come under its spell, acting as a creator in no less a fashion than the individual who formed its existence."[10] Considering this from the perspective of video game creations, the metaphor of dancing is a more complex one. Game designers, like toy makers, may dance with their creations in the process of game production but ultimately it's the gamers who truly bring them to life through gameplay.

From the myths of Pygmalion and Prometheus to the realities of mechanical creations throughout human history, the artistic and scientific animation of dead matter into the resemblance of life has smacked of magical — even diabolic — purpose. The game designer may adopt the role of Dr. Frankenstein in creating life through the manipulation of computer hardware and software, but in hands of the player this life takes on a more magical and uncanny purpose: the player's dance with the characters of *Resident Evil 4* is more like the dance of that old-school mad scientist, the necromancer who, like Charles Lee Ray (better known as "Chucky," the infamous, voodoo-literate killer from the *Child's Play* films) enters the skin of his avatar and views the world through different eyes. My avatar, Leon, is a kind of "matter formed by artificial means" that appears to move of his own volition — matter that also seems to be endowed with spirit. But, like a puppet whose puppeteer releases hold of its strings, if I abandon my hold of the controls, Leon stalls in space and, in the process, creates a dead space out of the world he inhabits.

As I directed Leon towards the mysterious village in the distance for the fourth time, searching for an alternate access point that wouldn't send packs of zombified villagers after him, I felt like a necromancer who had special skills in summoning dead, digital flesh to life — a necromancer who then entered the body of Leon to view an alternate world through another's eyes. There's an awkwardness about this possession as I attempted to become accustomed to the feel of the controllers: the selection of buttons on the Wiimote and Nunchuk, the fact that movements of *my* body affect and translate into the movement of Leon's body onscreen. Yet, no matter how familiar I become with the interface process, no matter how much I master the game, Leon and I will never be like the samurai and his sword — a single entity. As player-necromancer I will always be a visitor in another's body, always aware of the duality that's taken me over.

Unlike film spectatorship, the psychogeographic journey we travel in games is one that involves a digital journey through virtual space. Game narratives have been discussed as spatial experiences — and they are; they rely on players using their avatars to explore and travel through landscapes: cityscapes, forests, motorways, outerspace and spaces of abstraction — these are all the player's experiential geographic spaces. But this psychogeography also has a double logic that includes both the real space the player is physically located in and the virtual world in which they play. Immersed in *Resident Evil 4*, I play a game (and produce a narrative) in space and time (virtual and real). In real space and time, my narrative may be a mundane one (my fingers are cramping because I've been playing *Resident Evil 4* for hours, or the cat may be meowing because he wants me to open the door so he can get out), while in virtual space and time my purpose may be somewhat grander: to save the world from a contagious invasion that threatens human kind. In their book *Landscape Narratives: Design Practices for Telling Stories*, Potteiger and Purinton state that "we live within worlds of stories, and we use stories to shape those worlds."[11] Games are precisely such worlds, virtual worlds that can affect us in very real ways. In *The Practice of Everyday Life*, Michel de Certeau argued that the fundamental difference between place and space is that place is abstract; I take my cue from Henry Jenkins[12] who's developed this concept in relation to games. Viewing a world like the one I saw in the game's introduction, for example, I'm confronted with an abstract place. I have an idea of what events took place in Leon's past and what that experience may have been like, but these events remain at a distance because *I* have no experience of it. But, once I enter the game and engage with its places as a player via the avatar body I possess, this place becomes a space — *my* narrative space that surrounds me and immerses me in ways that leave marks of my experience and memories of it all around it.

This experience is further heightened by the technology I'm using. Projecting the game onto a screen that fills an entire wall, and with the lights out and the surround sound system doing its immersive *thing*, I creep with/in Leon along a side path I've found to the left of the main road that leads to the village. In the back of my mind, I (not Leon) wonder about what, if anything, occupies the pitch-black void that is my garden through the windows. My mind shifts from the little bit of nature that exists in my backyard to the creepy, atmospheric landscape through which Leon and I make our way in this forest "somewhere in Europe." We're quiet and careful — we remember the last time we came this way. Before I realize what's hit us, those dreaded creatures are upon us again. Yet, despite being aware of the presence of my body in my living room, and no matter how much I tell myself this "isn't real," I nevertheless feel the terror build up in me as I shoot and shoot at four ghouls and face up to the revelation that I've run out of ammunition. With a frenzy I've never experienced while playing other consoles, I wave my Wiimote arm up, whipping Leon's knife out with the action — and I slash and slash and slash through the air at the unrelenting and unforgiving *ganados* who attack and threaten to take the life of this body into which I've breathed life.

Designing Corporeality: Game Controllers and the Arm on the Brain

"Bodies in space design spatial fields, which, in turn, design corporealities."[13] While directing the comment to film spectatorship, the meaning underlying this statement by Bruno is all the more powerful when considering gameplay. My emotional, sensory and bodily engagement with the virtual world of *Resident Evil 4* is all the more palpable because of my connection to my avatar, but my experience of Leon's movement through space is made possible through my interface with the Wii controllers. Graeme Kirkpatrick makes a valid case for the "relationship between hands and aesthetic experience" in gameplay:

> The controller occupies a paradoxical position in computer game studies. Although it is central to gameplay experience — it marks physically the difference between play with a game and merely watching a screen — it goes largely unreflected on by gamers and in gaming literature.... No one talks about pressing "X," then "O." ... Good play is about feeling, and being able to feel what we are supposed to be feeling is, at least partly, a function of not looking at or thinking about our hands. At the same time, It is powerfully determined by what we do with them.[14]

Kirkpatrick's comment makes clear the fluid connection that exists between mind and body, intellect and senses: the flow of information between brain and body is instantaneous and in gameplay we often act with our bodies before thinking with our brains. In his analysis of the nature of perception, Paul Rodaway explains that not only are the senses and cognition linked in the act of perception, but also that perception is corporeal: "it is mediated by our bodies and the technological extension employed by the body."[15] The extensions Rodaway refers to are objects like "walking sticks, spectacles and hearing aids, even clothes," but the game console is also one such crucial extension to the corporeal, affecting and effecting the player's relationship to the game world and to gameplay. It's what facilitates the unraveling of action onscreen but it also serves the role of umbilical cord, connecting the body of the player to the body of the game space and to its affective potential.

I'm reminded of my first "I did it!!" moment when playing the game *Batman: Arkham Asylum* (Eidos, 2009). Here my avatar was none other than Batman himself—the greatest fictional character ever invented and my childhood and adult hero. At first, my mastery of the controller and, therefore Batman, was pretty bad and left a lot to be desired. I felt great shame because due to my actions (or lack of them) Batman had to keep restarting sections of the game (and action). My lack of skill in terms of thinking fast enough — almost instinctively — to select appropriate combinations of buttons on the

Figure 8: The avatar Batman displays his glide technique in the video game *Batman: Arkham Asylum* (Eidos, 2009).

controller translated itself across the body of my avatar: Batman was a lame-ass superhero! A few hours into gameplay, however, and after repeating many game scenes until I got it right, the magic finally began to happen. I still remember the thrill I felt when I managed to make Batman bust some serious moves. Stealth mode? A piece of cake! Using the bat-cape to glide (fig. 8) and the grapple gun to swing onto gargoyle statues? Sheer magic! Taking down an array of Arkham's crazed residents by stealthily swooping down on them and connecting them to a knock-out bat-fist? Indescribable joy! Words can't explain the delight I felt when I was finally working that controller with certain mastery. I was Batman and I was kick-ass! As Kirkpatrick notes, adept gameplay requires that the player stop consciously thinking about the combination of actions needed to be pressed on the controller. Instead, in an action that finds a close parallel to touch-typing, the player's mind focuses on generating the end product — gameplay. In the process, the sense of touch translates into sight, sound and movement, which then brings other senses into play. It's an act that combines the senses and cognition — an act that follows a two-way motion between player and game world. The player's sensorium becomes alert in response to the virtual actions being articulated in the virtual space and this space is animated by responses to a digital sensorium triggered by the player. The relationship operates like a feedback loop in that the player and gameworld depend on a unified interplay of each other's actions.

The Wiimote and Nunchuk add a new and more intense dimension to corporeality, one that differs to any experience of *Resident Evil 4* on the Playstation 2 or GameCube systems. Rather than simply relying on the touch and tap of my fingers on the controller, the Wii system demands a physicality that's new to gaming: my arms and body now have a central role to play as my movements in real space are translated across the body of my avatar. Influenced by the philosopher Maurice Merleau-Ponty and his phenomenological writings about the synaesthetic perceptions of the body, the Dutch poet Remco Campert (who was one of the self-titled *Vijftigers* or Group of Fifty poets writing in the 1950s) once wrote: "I have got arms on my brains."[16] In gameplay, the sensorially loaded acts of movement and touch that are attached to the hands and arms are always intimately entwined with the intellectual and cognitive processes that are associated with the brain. Through repetition and habitual practice my interface with the controller becomes almost second nature, and actions appear to require little thought. Reiterating Campert's expressive imagery, Merleau-Ponty stated that "habituality is neither a form of knowledge nor an involuntary action ... it is knowledge in the hands, which is forthcoming only when bodily effort is made, and cannot be formulated in detachment from that effort."[17] The recent introduction of Xbox 360 Kinect makes Campert's metaphor all the more potent. The Kinect requires that our entire body becomes the controller as our body motions are interpreted by the camera and, in turn, by the game to affect how our performance plays itself out in the gameworld. In fact, if we take on board current developments about the senses in philosophy and the cognitive sciences, the role played by the senses is even more dramatic.

Fiona Macpherson discusses how the original five sense modalities described by Aristotle in *De Anima* need to be revised in light of recent scholarship.[18] Some researchers have located over 20 senses, but the two most significant in terms of gameplay (and theme park rides, which is the focus of the next chapter) are proprioception, which is an "awareness of the position of the parts of the body, awareness of movement of the body and of how much force is required to move it" and equilibrioception, which relates to the sense of balance.[19] Even when using a controller, while our hands and arms are primarily the body parts involved in movement, it's very common for the rest of our body to react physically (jerks, startled jumps, frustrated motions) to the events unraveling in the game space. Add to this the Wiimote, the PS Move, and Kinect and the sense modality of proprioception comes to the fore further still. In all of these new generation controllers, while the hands are still key to the player's haptic link to the gameworld, the body now also plays a pivotal role. Consider the wave of dance and exercise games infiltrating the market: my foray into *Dance Central* had me busting some serious moves to Lady Gaga with hands, arms, legs, head and hips. Furthermore, the way I move my body in my attempt to mimic the professional in-game dancers is both an incarnate response that relies on my senses and a cognitive response that attempts to translate, understand and transfer the dance moves onscreen onto my own body. Levisohn states that the development of new sensing technologies such as the Wii have facilitated interactions with media that "are less mediated by physical equipment than ever before." He also makes a valid point when he affirms that "the body be considered as not merely the controller of multimedia systems, but as a component within these systems and a unique medium unto itself."[20] Likewise, in relation to equilibrioception, when I was a firstperson shooter virgin I suffered intense bouts of nausea and disequilibrium that affected my balance and my perception of how my body related to the "real" space around me. Repeated gameplay conditioned my brain to make sense of two realities — game and physical spaces — colliding. Whether conceived as "knowledge in the hands," "arms on the brain" or "body on the brain" the implied meaning is the same in that it acknowledges a unified relationship between mind and body, the senses and cognition — and this relationship is felt intensively in gameplay.

In the midst of such intense corporeal and sensorial action, the sensorium allows me to forget (for a while, at least) that the cat *is* meowing at the door, that my arms are in pain from too much repetitive motion, that I lose my sense of balance when I turn my attention away from the game space to my physical space, and allows me instead to immerse myself in my avatar and the spaces we experience together. Potteiger and Purinton explain that "it's through narrative that we interpret the processes and events of place: We come to know a place [or space, in de Certeau's terms] because we know its stories."[21] Because of the intense corporeal connection to the game world, playing *Resident Evil 4*, the emerging story very much felt like it was my story as much as it was Leon's. In fact, the intensity of the experience, true to traditions of horror, was so intense that there were moments I (almost) convinced myself that the stories *in there* would spill into the mundane world of my living room and into the dark and creepy recesses of what had been my cute suburban garden. *Mere* gameplay conjured grander narratives that dealt with monstrosity and horror and my own universe was affected in very real ways. And all of this was because my avatar Leon *appeared* to undergo a magical transformation, becoming matter endowed with spirit —*my* spirit.

The Machine as Virtuoso: Performing God

To return to the Prometheus myth with which I began this chapter, a century before Collodi wrote his story about breathing life into a wooden puppet, inventors attempted similar feats by creating automata — mechanical toys that were modeled on a variety of living creatures. While there are records of automaton creations prior to the 18th Century, it was during this period

Figure 9: In the 1731 etching "La Charmante Catin" by Charles-Nicolas Cochin, the automaton moves and appears to come to life, in the process astounding her audience (National Library, Paris).

that the art of the automaton reached its peak of technological mastery and popular curiosity; and the primary reason they became popular entertainment forms during this time was because, as their name (which comes from the Greek *automatos*) suggests, they appeared to be driven by their own determination. Barbara Maria Stafford explains, "The automaton was the machine as virtuoso.... Its anthropomorphic physiology of concealed pipes and pulsating liquids established a metaphorical connection between animated artifice and live audience."[22] For the audience, the virtuosity of the automaton manifested itself in the ways it appeared to animate its own form but, ultimately, the spectator was required to acknowledge the true virtuoso: the designer of the mechanical wonder who was the "dazzling producer of incantatory effects that magically captivated and controlled others by their showiness."[23] The machine as virtuoso was, therefore, eventually unveiled as the creation of human virtuosity.

Video games present us with a like-minded logic: they aim to dazzle through their technological prowess and, in the process, stand as embodiment (or not, depending on the quality of the game) of the mastery of their creators. In the 1731 etching "La Charmante Catin" by the French engraver Charles-Nicolas Cochin (fig. 9), a group of upper-middle class people look down at a small doll that, thanks to her internal clockwork mechanism, moves as if by her own volition. Candles light the living room, casting shadows that generate an atmosphere that captures the wonder that these spectators experience in what appears to be an almost supernatural act.[24] In 1738–39, a few years after Cochin's engraving was completed, the famous inventor Jacques de Vaucanson constructed three automata, a "flute player, a drummer, and a duck — prompting Voltaire to write that: 'the daring Vaucanson, rival of Prometheus, imitating the forces of nature, seemed to steal fire from heaven to bring his figures to life.'"[25] As Horst Bredekamp explains in his book *The Lure of Antiquity and the Cult of the Machine*:

> In 1748, the physician Julien Offray de La Mettrie maintained that in light of advances made in automaton production, exemplified so admirably by Vaucanson, it was only a matter of time until some particularly deft mechanic would succeed in constructing a synthetic human being.... By the 1770s his prediction seemed to have come true with the building of similar yet more complex figures capable of such activities as playing the piano, painting, or writing. Like a child learning to write, an automaton designed by Pierre Jacquet-Droz predicted the coming of age of this type of figure, by writing sentences such as "We are the androids" and "Cogito, ergo sum."[26]

In the 17th century, scientists and philosophers like Johannes Kepler and Rene Descartes began to associate the human ability to create technological beings with the power of creation once only assigned to the Christian God. Experiencing automata for the first time, in 1598 Kepler was inspired to produce a diagram that revealed the world to be five geometric solids that were driven by a clockwork mechanism; this made the mathematician Henri de Monantheuil try to convince Henri IV of France that God was a "mechanikos"— a mechanic much like the automaton creators Vaucanson and Jacquet-Droz.[27] And in 1647, the philosopher Descartes explained that he could see "no difference between machines built by artisans and objects created by nature alone."[28] Such observations, however, were also followed by immense trepidation: the desire to create *like* God was just one step away from the desire to *be* God.

It's easy to see how this association of artistic creator with a divine creator could carry through into an analysis of games. The creative teams behind game design literally create and populate worlds. Artificial life and social simulation games like *The Sims* series (EA Play), the *Animal Crossing* series (Nintendo), *Spore* (Electronic Arts) and *WolfQuest* (Eduweb) allow the player to interact with artificial life forms and their virtual communities. In addition, the implementation of artificial intelligence systems into games that allow for greater verisimilitude in the actions on non-player characters has become common practice. In some of the earliest examples of the post–*Space Invaders* era, games like the *Creatures* series (Cyberlife, 1996, 1998, 1999), created by Steve Grand who has now gone on to create robots,[29] we're responsible for overseeing the birth of artificial creatures. These creatures, known as Norns, have their own rudimentary DNA structure; we watch them grow, learn and die, or we can take them to a "scientific lab" and experiment with their DNA structure and mutate them. We can also trade them online for other creatures with alternative genetic structures, then crossbreed with our Norns to create new genetic mutations. In adopting the role of mad scientist, this character from science fiction-horror slips from the world of fiction and enters our reality. And in "god games" like the *Black and White* games (Electronic Arts, 2000, 2001, 2002, 2005), we simply *are* God. While I find all of these examples fascinating, it's the metaphoric articulations of the Prometheus myth to which I return.

In addition to the creation metaphors as played out through the player and avatar interface, the performative role of God takes on yet another dimension when we consider the unraveling of narrative that's specific to video games. Unlike the automaton predecessors that functioned to evoke wonder, the AI worlds of games present the player with geographies and landscapes in which densely rich narratives and experiences unravel. While the player may experience amazement when confronted with a wondrous special effect or realistic 3D environment, one also needs to snap out of this state in order to make some reasoned decisions. The player makes choices when journeying through game spaces. Some of these decisions are informed ones that are further supported by skillful gameplay that allows for the successful completion of tasks, solution of puzzles, or destruction of ugly bogey-beings that attack our avatar. Other decisions may not be as informed and this has repercussions for the development of gameplay. In *Resident Evil 4*, for example, I can choose to follow a number of paths into the *ganados*-infested village; depending on the path I take and my proficiency and familiarity with the actions that I'll confront there, I may live to continue playing or I may die. If I die, the game level restarts and I have to perform the gameplay again. I can take a different route and fight off a different sequence of enemies; or take the same route but defend myself with greater agility thus altering the way my avatar interacts with the space; or take the same route and die early in the game again, but at the hands of a different *ganados;* and so on. The combinations of replayed gameplay and spatial unfolding are multiple, and with every variation comes a different version of Leon's (and my) experience of the narrative of the game world that is *Resident Evil 4.* Like someone who's thrust into one of Escher's *Relativity* worlds, several distinct narrative events can play themselves out in alternate ways depending on the choices we make as players, with the result that multiple worlds become possible.

In this respect, gameplay performs a role that's uncannily similar to that outlined by baroque philosopher and mathematician Gottfried Leibniz. Leibniz argued that multiple versions of possible realities existed and God selected the one that would eventually come into existence. Paralleling and influencing what would later become quantum theory and the hypothesis of the coexistence of many worlds,[30] in his *Discourse on Metaphysics* (1686) and *Monadology* (1720), Leibniz expounded a theory of multiple possible worlds that progress as a series. Leibniz's argument regarding the Identity of Indiscernibles posits a God who generates multiple possible worlds but, ultimately, reduces this multiplicity to a singular, actual world that finally comes into perfect existence as a "compossible" world.[31] For Leibniz, the compossible embodies the ultimate power of "God who conceives and chooses the world"[32] and who makes choices with regard to following one series of paths over another. By "positing an infinity of possible worlds," however, Leibniz perceives our world to be the only existing world because, given that it constitutes God's final choice, it's considered to be the best of all other possible scenarios — known as the "incompossibles" that are finally rejected. In games the player performs the role of *Leibniz's* God, but with a difference. In playing *Resident Evil 4* I leave behind me, quite literally, a world of multiple original story scenarios that intersect at certain points and diverge at others. Each of these unfolding worlds is imprinted across my body in the memories of my repeated experiences of them; in addition, the place where my created worlds exist — the Wii console — also stores imprints of these narratives in the form of saved games. But unlike Leibniz's model of a world of compossibles, in the digital realm of the video game, the game-player-as-God (and it is the player as God rather than game creator because it's the player who generates each possibility in the digital universe) gives reality to each possible world, in the process making all incompossibles worlds compossible. Compossibles and incompossibles aside, one thing I know for sure is that on that night I danced with my dead creation ... and he danced with me.

3

Dark Rides, Hybrid Machines and the Multisensory Experience

The Horror Ride and Its Influences

"Click here if you dare!"

So begins the warning on the website to Universal Studios' Revenge of the Mummy — the Ride. It continues:

> It's a psychological adventure that will tap into your most primal fears like ...
> Lysgophobia ... Fear of the Dark
> Entomophobia ... Fear of Insects
> Tachophobia ... Fear of Speed
> Acrophobia ... Fear of Heights
> Demonophobia ... Fear of Evil Spirits
> Necrophobia ... Fear of Death.[1]

On the back of the success of the films *The Mummy* (Stephen Sommers, 1999) and *The Mummy Returns* (Stephen Sommers 2001) the 2004 ride at Universal Studios presents itself as upping the ante on the film horror experience. Participants begin by entering the Museum of Antiquities, which is, in "actuality" the set location for the next Mummy film sequel. Surrounded by cameras, lights, statues, and scaffolding, video monitors soon inform us that the curse of the Mummy Imhotep may be more than a fabrication. Brendan Fraser, Arnold Vosloo and other actors from the films are interviewed in a mockumentary and express concern about a real curse that has haunted the latest production. To add to the backdrop of the climaxing calamity, the deeper we enter the ride, the more we realize that the set for the new Mummy film is on location. The Museum of Antiquities, in fact, houses the underground catacombs of Imhotep. Walking through what looks like a temple, we eventually enter the loading bay where ancient Egyptians (ride operators) help participants into a ride buggy. And so it begins. All the classic signs of horror are here: a darkness that harbors the unknown, eerie whispers, passages that appear labyrinthine, stolen souls, blazing fires, and a monstrous mummy that threatens to bring about our demise. Like the films that influence this ride, the audience shares an experience that's common across horror, regardless of the medium — an experience that Noel Carroll calls being "art-horrified."[2] As Carroll stresses, the horror genre is affect-driven: it seeks to elicit an emotional state from its audience — a shudder, a scream, a feeling of threat or terror. Yet, the process through which being "art-horrified" is achieved differs markedly across different media; in theme park attractions the art of horror impacts on the body and the senses far more directly and with an immediacy that's absent in film spectatorship. Through an analysis of Revenge of the Mummy — the Ride, this chapter looks at the horror ride in the contemporary theme park and explores the role such attractions play within the context of an entertainment industry that relies on diversification and media crossovers, but also on sensory experiences. I'll also look at amusement park predecessors of such horror rides, focusing on the shifts that occur in the sensorium when moving from horror film to horror ride experience.

Horror has made a lucrative market across a variety of media, including films, television shows, computer games, novels, and theme park attractions over the last two decades. Perhaps the environment in which it has shared one of its strongest and longest connections is as part of the amusement park and fairground. The ghost trains, magic phantasmic illusions, tunnels of love, and freak shows that first scared audiences in exposition midways and fairgrounds have continued to make their presence felt in amusement and theme parks today. As will be outlined below, these attractions were predecessors of contemporary horror rides like Revenge of the Mummy—the Ride. Most famously, Coney Island's attractions from the turn of the 20th century included the latest in cutting-edge examples of horror rides that would persist in inciting the fear factor decades later: the indoor scenic railway at Luna Park called the Dragon's Gorge (which included a brief trip to Hades and its River Styx), the Ghost House and Tunnel of Laffs at Steeplechase, and Dreamland's Haunted House, Haunted Swing, Hellgate and Freak Street with its "40 human monstrosities."[3] Authors that include Wolfgang Schivelbusch, Tom Gunning, Vanessa R. Schwartz and Miriam Hansen have all argued convincingly that the period of Modernity, along with the rise of electricity, consumer and mass culture, and new forms of mechanization (such as film, railways, amusement-park rides) gave rise to new relationships between the body and sensations.[4] This altered relationship was most dramatically felt in the amusement parks, where the body and perception were assaulted with new experiences that included the roller coaster and Ferris wheel, and which added to meaning centered around the corporeal response, a response already favored by the horror themes in the amusement parks. Variations of similar rides continued to attract audiences in fun parks throughout the 20th century, and many popular seaside and other holiday destinations even developed horror as an attraction theme. In the 1970s, for example, entrepreneurs developed the pier sector in New Jersey to include a series of popular "haunted attractions" that included Castle Dracula, Brigantine Castle, and the Haunted Mansion.[5] The attractions tended towards the hokey and corny — an aesthetic that didn't necessarily reduce the scares and frights that were on offer. As William Paul has so convincingly argued in relation to horror films of the 1970s and 1980s, the carnival origins of such experiences are concerned with a playful theatricality that generates the affective state of "laughing screaming."[6] As the opening quote from the *Mummy* ride website suggests, the narrative and cognitive levels of engagement take a back seat to more primal mechanisms that place the senses at full attention. The only thing our intellect needs to acknowledge is that our bodies may be under threat and that something scary may be out to get us!

Over the last three decades horror rides have undergone a renaissance, returning to the hi-tech and grand-scale attractions of the earlier amusement-park tradition, but this time within the context of the theme park: Scooby Doo and the Haunted Mansion opened at Paramount's King's Dominion in Doswell, Virginia; new versions of Disney's Haunted Mansion have opened in the Paris and Tokyo Disneylands, and in the Orlando parks visitors can experience the Twilight Zone, Tower of Terror Ride; Revenge of the Mummy, Van Helsing: Fortress Dracula, and Terminator 2: 3D scare audiences at Universal Studios in Los Angeles, Orlando and Osaka; and The Labyrinth of the Minotaur and Pyramid of Terror rides attract crowds at Paramount's Terra Mitica park at Benidorm, Spain. The horror-ride business has become so lucrative that it's sprouted a booming special effects-rides industry, one of the most successful being the Sally Corporation which specializes in horror rides such as the Challenge of Tutankhamen (Six Flags, Belgium), Zombie Paradise (Geopolis, Tokyo), Mine of Lost Souls (Canobie Lake Park, Salem), Haunted Hotel (Pavilion Amusement Park Myrtle Beach, South Carolina), Frankenstein's Castle (Indiana Beach, Monticello, Indiana) and Ghost Blasters (Knott's Camp Snoopy, Mall of America, Minnesota; Castle Park, Riverside, California; Santa Cruz Beach Boardwalk).[7]

Since the 1950s, the themes and experiences offered by horror rides most often draw upon a consciousness that horror films have burned into audience's minds over the last century. Increasingly, the exchange of character types, settings, sound effects, stories, and themes that are present across a variety of horror media reveals the complex interchange that occurs between contemporary entertainment industries. At first glance, this exchange seems to involve the simple transfer of codes and conventions from one medium to the next, but on closer analysis it becomes evident that each medium adapts common generic conventions to create experiences required of their own media form. In an era when mainstream films are being described as being more like roller coasters, and roller coasters as being closer to films, it comes as no surprise to discover that the overlaps between the two media are deeply connected on a systemic level. Today, film production is only one component of the economic drive behind the conglomerates that run the industry. As a result, the aesthetics that emerge support an industry that has multiple media investments. Some of these economic strategies and the ways they affect horror media will be the focus of this chapter. In addition to exploring the financial benefits of media crossovers, attention will be given to the formal overlaps found between the horror ride of the theme- and amusement-park industry and horror cinema. In particular, attention will be drawn to the "dark ride"—also known as the "laff-in-the-dark-ride"—which has been common to the amusement park since its beginnings at the turn of the 20th century. In dark rides, participants board a buggy, train, or boat and enter a dark, enclosed space. The space is themed—a ghost train, a haunted house, a trip to the moon—and the vehicle (on a track) allows the designers some control over the ways the "story" unravels.

Diversification and Transmedia Horror

Returning to the opening example the Revenge of the Mummy ride reveals the complex relationships that currently exist between entertainment structures. The crossover between popular media (such as films and theme park rides) tests the clear separation between diverse media forms, and this overlap has ramifications for genre analysis, which tends to contain and homogenize an understanding of genre within specific media. A more flexible account of generic development and the production of meaning should acknowledge the dynamic interchange between media. The horror genre is not a closed system that draws solely on examples of its kind within a specific medium. Its "meaning" also crosses into other media. Clearly, audience familiarity with genres from related media is economically advantageous to entertainment companies. Genre and media hybridization is crucial to creating a larger crossover market. The blockbuster Mummy films, for example, were produced by Universal and have proved especially successful crossover variations. The Mummy films — *The Mummy, The Mummy Returns, The Mummy: Tomb of the Dragon Emperor* (Rob Cohen, 2008) and *The Scorpion King* prequel (Chuck Russell, 2002) and its prequel *The Scorpion King 2: Rise of a Warrior* (Russell Mulcahy, 2008) — have found new media environments, the theme park attraction Revenge of the Mummy being only one of them. In an attempt to extend its audience by reaching out to the comic book audience, the release of *The Mummy Returns* was accompanied by a three-part comic book series called *The Mummy: Valley of the Gods*.[8] The comic book includes the films' main characters, but takes them on different adventures. Chaos Comics, the highly successful horror and fantastic comics publisher, negotiated a licensing deal with Universal in order to make this possible. Also, coinciding with the success of the first two Mummy films, *The Mummy: The Animated Series* (2001–03) was shown on Kids' WB, and collectible trading cards — *The Mummy Returns* — were released by Inkworks, a trading card company specializing in entertainment products.[9] This transmedia extension of the Mummy franchise also included the video games: *The Mummy* (PC and Playstation 2: Konami, 2001); *The Mummy Returns* (Playstation 2: Universal interactive, 2001); *The Scorpion King: Sword of Osiris* (Game Boy Advance: Universal Interactive, 2002); and *The Scorpion King: Rise of the Akkadian* (Playstation2: Universal Interactive, 2003).[10]

When considering the formal and aesthetic properties of genre, it's also crucial to consider the socio-economic context that has informed and nurtured its production. In contemporary culture, the formal properties of entertainment have responded dramatically to the contexts of globalization, conglomeration and postmodernism. The ailing film industry that emerged in the post–1950s was one that eventually recognized the competitive nature of a new, conglomerate economic infrastructure that increasingly favored global interests on a mass scale. Entertainment industries — film studios, computer game companies, comic book companies, television studios and theme park industries — expanded their interests by investing in multiple interests, thus combating growing competition more effectively and minimizing financial loss or maximizing financial gain by dispersing their products across a diversity of media forms. Horizontal integration, therefore, increasingly became one of the successful strategies of the revitalized film industry. To continue with the example of Universal, at the time of the ride's production and unveiling, the parent company that owned the Mummy franchise was Vivendi Universal Entertainment, which was a major leader in media and telecommunications, with entertainment interests that cross into film, television and games. (In 2004 Vivendi Universal was bought out by General Electric, the parent conglomerate of NBC; in 2011, General Electric merged with the cable company Comcast, forming General Electric–Comcast.[11]) Subsidiaries of Vivendi included Universal Music Group, Vivendi Universal Games (studios and publishing labels include Blizzard Entertainment, Fox Interactive, Massive Entertainment, Universal Interactive and Sierra Entertainment[12]), Canal+Group satellite and pay-TV company, and the mobile companies SFR Cegetel Group and Maroc Telecom. In addition, Vivendi Universal was at the time part owner of NBC Universal, whose interests are in television, film and theme-park operations. Aside from funding arrangements made with independent specialist companies like Chaos Comics and Inkworks, the diversity of its own subsidiary interests meant that Vivendi Universal was able to distribute the Mummy franchise — as an example of the horror genre — across a range of media. Indeed, it was in their financial interests to do so. Crossmedia (the duplication of one "story" across multiple media) and transmedia (the continuation of a story franchise across diverse media) production allows for the stabilization and standardization of some costs: Universal Interactive and NBC Universal, for example, could use sequences from the films in the production of their games and theme-park attractions; Decca Records, a subsidiary of the Universal Music Group, benefited from the release of the film soundtracks; and the Canal+Group satellite and pay-TV company had first access to the release of the films to television audiences. While ensuring that profit is distributed across a variety of media, this strategy also operates on the "don't put all your eggs in one basket" principle. If your film flops, maybe your games and rides will be a success. The key drive behind the diversification of products and company specialization is to reach as diverse an audience as possible, but also to offer a range of ways audiences can experience the franchise through different media. As will be discussed below and again in Chapter Seven, each medium brings with it specific demands on the sensorium.

Justin Wyatt suggests that the "relationship between economics and aesthetics" has become crucial to the formal properties of entertainment media.[13] Of course, the same may be said of the relationship between aesthetics and economics that eventuated during the classical Hollywood era. Universal Studios, which produced the early Mummy films, for example, did so according to the economic logic that drove the industry during the 1930s–1940s. The recent films regenerated what had been a very successful franchise during the heyday of Universal's horror output with the release of classics like *The Mummy* (Karl Freund, 1932), *The Mummy's Hand* (Christy Cabanne, 1940), *The Mummy's Tomb* (Harold Young, 1942), *The Mummy's Ghost* (Reginald Le Borg, 1944) (fig. 10), *The Mummy's Curse* (Leslie Goodwins 1944) and, of course, the later example of Universal's foray into the generic hybrid Abbott and Costello Meet the Mummy (Charles Lamont, 1955). Extension of the Mummy franchise was contained within the one medium — film. This was typical of a film industry that operated according to the logic of vertical integration[14]: the classical Hollywood studio structure specialized in one medium, and despite venturing into some cross merchandising, film was the primary business.[15]

Since the 1960s, however, Hollywood progressively changed from a Fordist mode of production, which relied on a system of vertically integrated and controlled film production, distribution and exhibition, to a post–Fordist mode of production reliant upon horizontal organization and great diversification. Early examples of this shift are reflected in attempts made by Universal during the time to extend their products beyond film production. Universal even toyed with attempts at migrating their horror franchises— Dracula, Frankenstein, the Wolfman, the Mummy— into comic book stories. In 1963, for example, Universal Pictures collaborated with Dell Publishing to release *Universal Pictures Presents Dracula—The Mummy and Other Stories* (September–November 1963).[16] The publication was publicity motivated, and the comic book coincided with the popularity of the television show *Shock Theatre*, which had appeared in various guises since the late 1950s and which showcased horror movies — including those of Universal — for television audiences. Clearly then, cross- and transmedia production and merchandising is definitely not a phenomenon specific to our times, however, horizontal integration has now become integral to the survival of the entertainment industry.

Figure 10: Lon Chaney as the Mummy in the film *The Mummy's Ghost* (Universal, 1944) (Kobal Collection).

Dark Rides and Haunted Mansions: Multiplying the Senses

To return to Wyatt's assertion, the economic context that was transformed in the late 20th century was also accompanied by transformed formal and

3. Dark Rides, Hybrid Machines and the Multisensory Experience 63

stylistic properties. By now, the basic premise of what Jay Bolter and Richard Grusin call *remediation* has been well rehearsed: remediation involves the refashioning or assimilation of one or more media conventions by another medium.[17] Perhaps more intensely than any other genre, horror possesses a rich and diverse media history that includes an array of sources — films, comic books, computer games, amusement park attractions, paintings, books, television — that survive by succumbing to remediation. The early amusement park ride, for example, drew upon a rich tradition of park and ride cultures and conventions that ranged from 18th and 19th-century pleasure gardens and rides aimed at the middle classes, the popular rise of the Gothic and horror novel, and magic lanterns (and other optical devices) that spooked audiences with their phantasmic displays in the 19th century. While borrowing predominantly from the theatre,[18] horror cinema of the pre–1940s also turned to the stories and affective states elicited by horror rides found in amusement parks and fun fairs, pulp and other novels and radio serials. Contemporary horror media are even more excessively engaged in this intertextual and intermedia logic. What's fascinating about the horror rides found in today's theme parks is that this intertextuality and intermedia tendency becomes literal: not only are multiple media referenced or alluded to, they're often literally incorporated into the ride experience. Contemporary horror is marked by an excess of self-referentiality and remediation that's as multifarious as the conglomerate structure that produces it. It gives rise to a hybrid logic that has significant ramifications for genres and the critical models used to analyze them and, in the case of the theme-park attractions, this is all the more so because of the excess media hybridity.

In addition to being influenced by the rich history of the recent Mummy horror films that preceded it, especially the more recent blockbuster films, the Revenge of the Mummy ride, for example, extends the parameters of the amusement- and theme-park ride by introducing into its structure a variety of media technologies. The roller coaster is given new life with the incorporation of cutting-edge technology that relies on a magnetic launch system. Single-sided, linear induction motors, or SLIMs, run under the track and magnetically propel the ride buggies during the coaster sections, accelerating riders from 0 to 40 mph before they have had time to catch their breath.[19] Reaching zero gravity has never been easier for ride technology — a fact that takes the haptic experience to a whole new level, especially when compared to competing media such as film and video games. Furthermore, digital animation and film are called upon to add to the illusion of the horror images that cause such terror in the dark. Images familiar to the Mummy films are strategically projected onto screens and the interior space of the ride. Film projections of the Mummy (including one of Imhotep's digitally animated sand-face with its cavernous mouth as it reaches to swallow the riders) and scarab beetles that emerge by the thousands from wall cracks and threaten to invade the space of the ride participants. Again, when Imhotep rises to draw us into his gaping mouth, the ride buggy follows the path of escape by plummeting what appears to be hundreds of meters downwards. This effect is produced by falling between two screens on which are projected images that create the illusion of movement through space at an extremely high velocity. The advanced robotics that Disney made famous in theme parks in the form of his animatronics again push technological boundaries in the attempt to thrill and frighten. The larger-than-life animatronic version of the Mummy and the four mummy warriors that lunge at the participants were produced by hi-tech hydraulics that give the impression of greater realism when compared to the electric or pneumatic systems that have been used in theme-park animatronics in the past. Add to this theatrical effects, such as explosions of fire and sprays of water, and the architecture that gives life to the ride, interior and exterior, and it can be said that the Revenge of the Mummy ride (like the Adventures of Spiderman Ride at Universal's Islands of Adventure theme park in Orlando)[20] is emblematic of the hybrid and multi-remediated theme-park attractions of recent years. In addition, these effects further speaks to the intense and immediate corporeal demands that are placed on the participant; narrative is significant only as a sketch or basic story premise and even that flies out the window when the attraction rider find themselves plummeting through space backwards, forwards, sideways and even upside-down in what often appear to be warp speeds that could puncture a hole in the space-time continuum!

One of the strongest influences on *Revenge of the Mummy* is that of the "dark ride." Within the ride, participants journey in darkness only to be exposed to a series of lit "scenes" that are created through props, figures in costumes, animatronics and sound effects. An early version of the dark ride (possibly the first) was "A Trip to the Moon," the cyclorama created by Frederick Thompson and his partner, Skip Dundy, for the Pan-American Exposition held at Buffalo, New York, in 1901. Here, viewers were taken on a trip to the moon by a giant ship. As the cyclorama revolved around them, revealing images on a painted canvas, the travelers met the moon people before soaring back to earth. The popularity of the ride attracted the attention of George Tilyou, who owned Steeplechase Park at Coney Island, and by 1902 this hugely popular ride was entertaining audiences there before moving to the nearby Luna Park (fig.11), where it also transformed into a roller coaster. It was in the Luna Park version that the horror themes emerged: the moon dwarves (the Senelite), led participants to a dragon's mouth that opened and allowed them to move into its stomach. Navigating the rocking stomach cavity, they made their way to their seats before the ride proceeded.[21]

The transformation of the dark ride experience along the more hybrid

3. Dark Rides, Hybrid Machines and the Multisensory Experience 65

Figure 11: Luna Park at Coney Island, New York c. 1902.

lines typical of our era was to come along in the 1960s with the opening of the Haunted Mansion at Disneyland in 1969.[22] Originally intended as a walk-through attraction in the haunted house amusement/fun park tradition, the ride became a turning point between old and new dark ride technologies. In the Haunted Mansion, the montage of various disjointed horror stories epitomized Walt Disney's lack of interest in narrative development and greater concern with immersing the audience into an "experience" that radiated around the senses. Entering the house on foot, a ghost host guides the crowd through a gallery of bizarre portraits that transform — a goddess becomes Medusa, a woman becomes a hag — in a room where solid walls and a ceiling appear to distort, stretch, and finally disappear. From here, the visitor is guided to the "Omnimovers" or "Doom Buggies." The buggies revise the ghost train tradition but, in addition to the buggies being able to travel on a track, they're also capable of moving forward, tilting in every direction, and performing 360-degree turns, the range of movements ensuring that the riders' view is controlled by the creators at every point in the ride. From the moment the visitor enters the Haunted Mansion, they're confronted with many remediated media illusions whose aim is to engage the participant in as many sensory experiences as possible. But the participant no longer relies on the haptic and synaesthetic possibilities inherent to sight and sound as they do in the cinematic experience; they're now also immersed through an experience that requires body movement: they walk into and physically navigate the spaces of the Haunted Mansion and the gallery and then sit on Omnimovers that plummet their bodies through the mansion's architectural spaces. The haptic is literal and, because more senses are called into action, the synaesthetic transference from one sense modality onto another isn't as active as it is in film spectatorship.

Figure 12: The Pepper's Ghost effect. *Spectre de Robin* (1863) (Galerie Gerard-Levy).

In the 19th century, John Pepper, a professor of chemistry from the London Polytechnic, popularized an illusionistic technique involving an image projected onto a piece of glass at a 45-degree angle by presenting it to audiences on a grander scale as public education and amusement. Using a mirror and directed lighting techniques, Pepper's Ghost (fig.12) made objects (most often ghosts) seem to appear or disappear, or to make one image metamorphose into another. While John Pepper was primarily interested in the technique as an experiment in optics and science, it was the entertainment displays of this technology that brought science to the people — as made evident by Pepper's first and most famous public demonstration, which occurred during a Christmas performance of Charles Dickens's Haunted Man in 1862. As Secord explains:

> Announced by the Liverpool engineer Henry Dircks at a British Association for the Advancement of Science meeting in 1858 and developed by Pepper for practical use, the technique involved placing a huge sheet of plate glass on stage at a 45-degree angle, together with screens and special lighting.... Pepper took the spectacle as an opportunity to explain some of the underlying principles of optics.... Skeptics used Pepper's highly public stage ghosts to argue that mediums claiming to raise the spirits of the dead were fakes. The famous "Ghost Show," then, was an integral part of a wider attempt by Pepper to inculcate a sense of rational wonder by bringing the public's fascination with spirits, alchemy, and magic to the service of science (1648–1649).[23]

While separated by a century, the Pepper's Ghost technique was used for many of the ghost effects in Disney's Haunted Mansion. The reflection of the psychic Madame Leota's face in a crystal ball, the appearing and disappearing spooks that float, dance, and hang off chandeliers in the ballroom during a birthday ball, and the hitchhiking ghosts that appear to be sitting with us in the doom buggy as we exit the ride — these illusions are all due to the Pepper's Ghost effect.

This wasn't the only earlier optical technology that Walt Disney and the Imagineers remediated. Other optical technologies that had been used in the past to conjure horror illusions also resurfaced: one of these was the magic lantern. Its origins hark back at least to the late–16th century, but it was in the 19th century that the magic lantern became one of the essential tools of the magician and was used primarily in the ghost or apparition shows that involved phantoms suddenly appearing "out of nowhere." Unlike Pepper's Ghost, which required the physical presence of the illusion off stage, the magic lantern conjured its illusions by projecting images onto screens. The most famous and most duplicated was the *Fantasmagorie* by Étienne Gaspard Robert (known as Robertson). Robertson was a Belgian inventor, physicist and student of optics who improved the technology of the magic lantern, including its capacity to enlarge and decrease images. In 1797, Robertson performed a live horror theater in a Paris cemetery. Crowds flocked to the dimly lit tombs to see magic lantern effects that included skulls, atmospheric lighting, sound effects, and the appearance of ghostly apparitions in an effects display concerned with what Terry Castle calls an "optical explosion of the senses."[24]

Similar illusions are present in the Haunted Mansion: the disappearing ceiling at the beginning of the ride was created by projecting then ceasing projection of a painted ceiling onto a translucent screen — as were the bicycling and flying ghosts in the cemetery. These past inventions, however, are transformed into new experiences by also being combined with radically new technologies, both in the inclusion of the hi-tech Omnimovers, which Disney Imagineers had designed for the It's a Small World and Carousel of Progress rides at the New York World's Fair of 1964, and in the way the ride relied on a multitude of ghost performers who were animatronic in nature.[25] Disney's Haunted Mansion was, therefore, an important turning point for the horror ride: the attraction paid homage to past visual traditions and illusions but transformed them by placing them within the context of the theme park. The Imagineers refashioned multiple media experiences — phantasmagoria and magic lanterns, Pepper's Ghost, automata, film, the haunted houses and ghost trains of amusement parks — and redesigned them into the kind of hybridized, hi-tech spectacle that would come to typify the theme park of more recent times.

Universal's website states that Revenge of the Mummy cross-pollinates elements of past rides into a new theme-park hybrid, which the Universal marketing department has dubbed a "psychological thrill ride." Taking its cue from the hybrid heritage popularized by Disney, next-generation dark rides like Jurassic Park (Universal, 1996), The Amazing Adventures of Spiderman (Universal, 1999), the Indiana Jones Adventure: Temple of the Forbidden Eye (Disneyland, 1995) and Revenge of the Mummy typically rely on an excessive remediation of media old and the new and, as mentioned, often literally engage in an intermedia approach. Dark ride, roller coaster, film, television, theater, architecture, music — all vie for the sensory attention of the participant and seek to make the experience intensely physical. While the horror theme is not a prerequisite of the dark ride (for example, Disneyland's Peter Pan, Pirates of the Caribbean and It's a Small World are fantasy rather than horror stories), it is understandable why the majority of dark rides have primarily been horror dark rides. Like most horror films they involve an entry into an enclosed space — a journey into the dark that places the viewer in the passive role over the narrative that then unfolds in space. Interestingly, aficionados have not missed the horror associations that typify the dark ride. In the special issue on dark rides, the online journal *Skew* published an essay titled "An Age-Old Terror: The spirit of the Dark Ride has been around for centuries." Here, the author, Brandon Kwiatek, suggests that the "dark ride is a ride-through Halloween" that shares a great deal with the "Western imagination of death, the devil and hell ... [and] Christian beliefs with symbols of heaven and hell, good and evil." Like the famed heroic journeys by Gilgamesh, Odysseus and Orpheus into the underworld or the many biblical stories that depict "hell as, respectively, a pit, a gate and a mouth," the ride participant boards a ride buggy to partake in a descent journey, opening the way to the horrors that lie therein.[26]

The Startles of Horror

Ronald Simons argues that being startled is one of the experiences audiences desire of horror films; furthermore, the startle impulse is common to many species: "The essence of startle is that it is the mechanism designed to ensure that the startled organism responds to a potential danger as rapidly as possible, even before the eliciting stimulus is consciously classified and evaluated."[27] Startling is a reflexive response that protects the individual from possible danger. It's an "induced emotional state" that's "like the pleasurable arousal sought from roller-coaster rides."[28] There are a great many startles to be had when the visitor enters the labyrinth interior of the dark ride. The startles of horror are responses to the unknown that the world of horror opens up: death and the dead, phobias, the dark, confrontation with the monstrous, and moral decay. In horror films our responses are generated via the intermediary main characters and it's through them that we empathize with the threat posed to their moral universe and their material presence. In horror video games we come one step closer to the corporeal and sensory impact of horror in that we actively affect and interact with the virtual world; however, we still do so through an intermediary that is our avatar and the fictional world is virtual. In horror rides the intermediary is no longer present and it's we— the ride participants—who become the main character and enter "real" spaces that we can see, smell, touch, hear and even taste; the sensory experience is intense and immediate and relies less on the process of synaesthetic transfer. For the horror rider, the fear of death and bodily destruction is one step closer to being a real threat. Yes, the participant knows that the technology that drives the rides is supposed to be safe (even though numerous ride-related deaths and accidents occur annually) but it doesn't feel safe when, in the Revenge of the Mummy ride, the dread of being swallowed by an enormous vision of Imhotep is replaced by a new horror: the ride buggy plummeting backwards and downwards at hair-raising speeds that make one's body vibrate and shake uncontrollably from the sheer force of movement through space.

Bruce R. Kawin and J.P. Telotte have drawn attention to the significance of vision in horror films. For example, Kawin states that "horror films often present us with images that are painful, grotesque, awful—horrible to look at—but they regularly imply that these images somehow need to be looked at, that they will show us something we might be more comfortable not to see but ought to see nonetheless."[29] Telotte takes this further still by drawing attention to the way contemporary horror, especially since *Halloween* (1978), reflexively uses the point-of-view tracking shot, often interchanging its association with the look of the main protagonist (Laurie) and the monster (Michael). In such horror films, the spectator's view of the screen and the events it contains is further collapsed into those of the camera/protagonist/monster. The result of this association for the spectator is that it amplifies empathic concern for the protagonist, which, in turn, can trigger a further response of emotional intensity.[30] In dark rides this emotional intensity becomes far more intense. In horror films the spectator has intermediaries and, even when the intensity and graphic detail of the horror manages to have a corporeal impact on the spectator (as was discussed in Chapter One), the sense of immediacy differs when compared to rides. In horror rides what the participant sees requires no mediator figure or object (such as a camera or computer program) because what's sensed and experienced actually surrounds the ride participant in all its glorious materiality. As discussed in the previous chapter on video games, the expansion of the number of senses to include proprioception or the kinesthetic sense has ramifications for theme park attractions. In rides, attention shifts away from the cognitive evaluation that's integral to storytelling and, for the participant, it's the body and its position in relation to space that becomes crucial to perception. In these wild rides, the senses of balance (equilibrioception) and acceleration also play a greater role when compared to film viewing or game playing; our sense of balance is dramatically disturbed (a point attested to by the bodily response of nausea) through acceleration that not only disturbs the body's balancing mechanisms but which also affects the participants' muscles and internal organs. The sense of nociception, or pain, also kicks into gear as heads snap sideways, torsos lunge forward and backward, arms fly upward, and stomachs feel like they'll exit the body interior.[31] Of all entertainment media, it's only the theme park ride that can deliver such intense somatic and visceral effects on the body. Some dark rides, like The Amazing Adventures of Spiderman[32] at Universal's Islands of Adventure in Orlando, even engage the sense of thermoception, or temperature, when Doctor Octopus in animated 3D form lets rip a burst of fire in the riders' direction; animated fire is instantaneously replaced by actual fire that erupts in front of the buggy so that those inside feel its heat with undeniable intensity.

For horror critics like Carol J. Clover, Linda Williams, and R.H.W. Dillard, vision in the horror film unveils a moral commitment. The stories these films have to tell address themselves to the construction of individual and social identity and to the collapse or threat to that identity as symbolically embodied by the monstrous. While horror cinema's desire is to extract affective responses from its audience, as discussed in Chapter One, its form is also conducive to interpretation. George A. Romero's Living Dead films, for example, may make our skin crawl as a result of the overt presence of decaying, rotting dead bodies that refuse to stay dead, but they also have much to say about the state of contemporary society and the way it produces alienation and dehumanization. Horror rides focus less on the narrative, evaluative and moral interpretations and more on the affective and sensory assault on the participant. Carroll suggests that in horror films, via the character's responses, the spectator is often "counseled" to "the appropriate reactions to the monsters," which usually comprise "shuddering, nausea, shrinking, paralysis, screaming, and revulsion. Our responses are meant, ideally, to parallel those of characters. Our responses are supposed to converge (but not exactly duplicate) those of the characters."[33] In rides, however, there is no need for these parallels to invoke such affective responses. Leaving the story behind, dark rides that incorporate wild roller coasters, for example, have no need of a mediator to make them shudder, feel nausea, cry out in pain, or scream.

In horror rides, much more is invested in what's seen and felt. All the senses have a far greater role to play in the experience of a ride. When, for instance, the buggy plunged backwards at super velocity in Return of the Mummy, I felt the air as it pushed my body back and made my hair whip across my face; I felt, smelled and even tasted the heat of fire on my skin, nose and mouth as it erupted from the Egyptian temple above me; and I felt like I could touch the hundreds of scarab beetles as they ran across my hands, legs and throat (a simple yet clever effect actually conjured by fine sprays of water) while I hyperventilated in anticipation of what "effect" would confront me next. For Carroll, the monster of horror cinema is a violation of nature.[34] It could be argued that, regardless of the "story" content of the horror ride, the highly sophisticated, hybrid machines that make rides like Revenge of the Mummy, The Curse of Tutankhamen, and Jurassic Park possible can also be understood as violations of nature, violations that make monstrous mummies and tyrannosauruses occupy space alongside the visitor and appear to threaten their existence. The hybrid machines of the dark ride are also monsters, of sorts. Steffen Hantke has stated that

> we are not supposed to understand horror, to comprehend it as the critical discourse lays it out for us; we are supposed to experience it. We are supposed to experience it as a loud, crass, and almost instinctual sensation, rather than as a gray sense of dread.... Horror, here, means bodily exertion: to shudder, to sweat, to squirm in our seats.[35]

Horror rides like Revenge of the Mummy take us a step closer to this instinctual sensation. As has been established, many of the recent dark rides favor a hybrid structure that not only draws upon other media beyond the theme park (film, television, comic books) but also from within it. Expanding the boundaries of what constitutes the dark ride by introducing engineering feats like the roller coaster, these rides introduce the horror genre's fear of bodily threat into the experience and, along with it, bodily responses such as sweating, screaming, or cowering. While from a film genre viewpoint rides like Amazing Adventures of Spiderman and Indiana Jones Adventure are not horror, from the perspective of a body's reaction to being hunted, haunted and terrorized by the horror machine that drives the ride technology, such attractions come very close to being horror experiences. Perhaps the parameters that contain the term "horror" need to be expanded to account for the hybrid nature of the dark ride.

In her book *The Tactile Eye: Touch and the Cinematic Experience*, Jennifer Barker outlines the experience of what she labels the "tactile eye." Like Bruno's articulation of haptic vision, the eye has the capacity to see but also to synaesthetically feel and touch that which it sees. "Touch," she explains, "need not be linked explicitly to a single organ like skin but is enacted and felt throughout the body."[36] Considering cinematic tactility, she states that the spectator's body can be affected haptically "at the surface of the body," kinesthetically through the muscles and bones, and viscerally "in the murky recesses of the body, where heart, lungs, pulsing fluids and firing synapses receive, respond to and reenact the rhythms of the cinema."[37] As I argued in Chapter One in relation to New Horror Cinema, this cinematic tactility is felt in all three regions and plays a key role in the cinematic experience. Yet the horror video games that were the subject of the previous chapter, and the horror-theme park rides that are the focus of this chapter articulate this tactility in very different ways. In theme-park attractions, in particular, the eye is no longer mediator to the fictional space and the sensory delights or horrors it has to offer. The senses now come into play with a greater immediacy that actually takes its toll on the participant's body. The encounter with horror is slippery in nature. It can produce a gamut of emotional, intellectual and sensory effects and, when we also slip into and out of diverse media experiences of horror the fluidity and nature of the encounter can be all the more marked in its difference. In the next chapter I turn to a medium that's probably the least overt in terms of its sensory impact — the novel and, in particular, the horror-paranormal romance. But even this seemingly uncomplicated format that gives life to its fictions through text (on page or screen) has its own way of getting under our skin and stirring up the sensorium.

4

Paranormal Romance: Anita Blake, Sookie Stackhouse and the Monsters Who Love Them

Body Genres: Romance Meets Horror

Two vamps came for me.... One of them was rotting down to bones, the other was solid. I shot the solid one first because he, I was sure, I could kill.... The solid one fell to his knees in a spray of blood, face split in half like a ripe melon. The rotting vamp jumped me in a blur of speed.... The mouth stretched above my face, naked tendons straining between the bones of his cheeks, fangs came for my face.... I turned my head and the fangs sank through the leather jacket pocket and my backup cross. A rotted hand caressed my face, sliding over the wound above my eye.... The cross flared to life like a captive star.... I swung the cross by the chain into its bare skull. Smoke rose from the bone, and the vampire jerked its face back from me, naked teeth opened in a scream. I shoved the cross in its face.... There was a moment where even without most of the flesh left on the skull I could see surprise on its face. I flung my arms across my face and heard the dull explosion, the splatter of debris.[1]

Love Sucks. Sometimes it feels good. Sometimes it's just another way to bleed.[2]

These are the thoughts of Anita Blake, feared vampire executioner and necromancer, human servant to Jean-Claude the vampire and Master of the City of St. Louis, Lupa to Richard the Ulfric of the Thronnos Rokke werewolf clan, Nimir-ra to Micah the Nimir-raj of the wereleopard Blooddrinkers clan, and animator of human corpses for Animators Inc. Anita is the powerful heroine of the *Anita Blake: Vampire Hunter* series by Laurell K. Hamilton. She has fought, maimed and killed many a monster without hesitation and always with maximum amounts of bloodletting, horror and violence. Her physical prowess, metaphysical "talents" and cutthroat bloody mindedness make even Buffy the Vampire Slayer seem like a wuss. Anita began as a conservative when it came to sex and romance. Despite her tough exterior, initially she was more or less an old-school romance heroine. As vampire executioner,

Figure 13: Anita Blake, Vampire Executioner. The comic book version of the Laurell K. Hamilton novel *The Laughing Corpse*. From issue 3, 2009 (Marvel Comics).

she'd given up on fulfilling a dream she nevertheless believed could be possible: settling down with the man you love in a house with a white picket fence and a couple of kids to seal the deal. Since the first novel (*Guilty Pleasures*, 1993), and over the 20 novels currently in the series, which now also includes a comic book series (fig. 14), she has progressed to a stage in her life where she has a series of official lovers — Jean-Claude (a vampire), Asher (a vampire), Richard (a werewolf), Micah (a wereleopard), Nathaniel (a wereleopard) — and a series of subsidiaries that include vampires, werewolves, wereleopards, lions and tigers, all of which help Anita satiate one of her powers, *the ardeur*, which she partially inherited from Jean-Claude and Belle Morte, the vampire mother of Jean-Claude's bloodline. The ardeur's power is derived from feeding off sex and lust, but can also include Anita being satiated through the consumption of blood and flesh. So when Anita Blake says that "love sucks" and that "it's just another way to bleed" she means it both metaphorically and literally.

In Anita's world and, more generally in the world of horror-paranormal romance, which is the main concern of this chapter, the rules of more traditional romance fiction are tested, stretched and often totally subverted. Romance, sex and desire almost always converge with violence, blood and flesh. The latter can occur when heroines like Anita are on the job as detectives, vampire executioners, or plain old vengeance machines, as occurs in the passage quoted above, but just as frequently, and reflecting a convention that's existed since the beginning of the romance genre in the 18th century, sex and violence are explored as experiences that are intimately interwoven. This chapter explores the ways in which horror-paranormal romances like the Anita Blake series and Southern Vampire series, which follows the adventures of Sookie Stackhouse, and upon which the television series *True Blood* is based, express moments of passion, sensuality and seduction but, in particular, how this is articulated and affected by being placed within the context of the horror genre. What happens to our sensorium when the genres of romance and horror collide? As will be explained below, the generic hybridity also allows for fluid sensory shifts. Paranormal romances such as those written by Christine Feehan use horror characters and stories and reshape them to romantic ends, while hardcore paranormal writers like Laurell K. Hamilton overlay the romantic with stories and sensory experiences that are more aligned with horror; the result is a more complicated and challenging exploration of desire and sexuality, one merging pleasure, danger and horror. Paranormal romance exists on a continuum: at one extreme end the sensorium languishes in the embrace of love, sex and romance while on the other it simultaneously recoils from and takes illicit delight in the horror, darkness and chaos that can lie at the core of eroticism.

The success of genres dealing with the paranormal or supernatural have been present in the cinema and on television since the beginnings of both media forms, but paranormal romance erupted as a runaway success in the 1990s with the writings of Rebecca Paisley, Nora Roberts, Laurell K. Hamilton, Susan Sizemore, Christine Feehan, Maggie Shayne, and others, and has continued to grow ever since. More recently, perhaps following in the wave of successful of shows like *The X-Files* (Fox, 1993–2002) and *Buffy the Vampire Slayer* (The WB/UPN, 1997–2001)[3] and Anne Rice's vampire novels, which all in their own ways dealt with horror and the paranormal in combination with romance, paranormal romances have begun to migrate to the small and big screens. Tanya Huff's Blood Books (1991–97), which follow the adventures of Vicki Nelson, a private investigator, and her vampire beau, Henry Fitzroy, a vampire, author of historical romances, and illegitimate son of Henry VIII, had a two-season run beginning in 2007 as *Blood Ties* (Citytv/Lifetime Television). While *Blood Ties* wasn't successful, the transformation of Charlaine Harris's Southern Vampire series into the television show *True Blood* (HBO, 2008–) by creator and producer Alan Ball was a huge success, with season two averaging over five million cable viewers and 12.4 million across media platforms (Seidman, 2009).[4] And then, of course, there's Stephenie Meyer's Twilight series (2005–08), which has also achieved immense popularity as the blockbuster film series, beginning with *Twilight* (2008) and coming to an end with *Breaking Dawn: Part 2* (November 2012). Belonging to the domain of teen paranormal, the Twilight series succumbs to the conventions of Young Adult fiction, which centers on the liminal time that precedes adulthood and, as such, the primary focus is the transition from adolescence to adulthood.[5] This chapter is concerned more with adult paranormal romance, which deals more explicitly with issues regarding sex, eroticism and horror. As will be discussed below, partly because it belongs to teen paranormal fiction, *Twilight* breaks with many of the conventions associated, particularly, with the character of the vampire lover.

Discussing the depiction of sex in film, in *Screening Sex* Linda Williams states that it evokes the "sensual pleasure of embodied viewing"; what we experience onscreen reflects back on "our own immediate sensuality."[6] Stressing the carnal appeal of the senses, Williams explains that the paradoxical nature of viewing sex scenes in films lies in the fact that, while we as viewers may not be participating, we can, nevertheless be intensely aroused by what we see.[7] Romance fiction has a similar carnal effect on its readers. In an article about erotics, Jody Davies asks: "What makes someone 'fall in love'? ... What do we mean when we speak of 'the sexual,' 'the sensual,' 'the erotic,' 'the romantic'?"[8] Quoting passages on love by Euripides, Homer, Shakespeare and Dryden, she continues:

From these selections we are drawn to the extraordinary singularity of passionate romantic love. We drip, we yearn, we are bewitched — romantic passion as ecstatic, creative, transformative. Our eyes open into our souls and expose our desires, and our exquisite vulnerabilities. But desire is also inextricably linked with pain. Love holds murderous intent and steals the minds of those who fall under its spell.... Romantic passion emerges as the apotheosis of human existence, and our surrender to those unparalleled dangers of wild romantic passion and to the idealized others who steal our hearts and bemuse our minds emerges for many of us as the pivotal moments that mark our lives, organize our memories, and construct its assigned meanings.[9]

Romance fiction imagines scenarios in which women and men find their "idealized others." It explores how wild romantic passion, ecstasy and love are expressed, and how the pain that can accompany sharing one's love and desire can also test a person's sanity. Yet, while often teasing its readers with the torturous and painful encounters love and desire have to offer, romantic fiction stays firmly grounded in the domain of pleasure, satisfaction and happy endings. But what happens when romance meets horror? Does romantic passion express itself in the same way, or does it tip over into the realm of pain, exploring some of the darker aspects of sexuality? This chapter addresses how paranormal-romantic fiction writes itself across the reader's body. Where does the romantic end and the horror begin, and how and why are the two intimately bound? As will be discussed below, horror and romance have a long history. But over the last decade or so this paranormal romance hybrid has returned with a vengeance, favoring more explicit descriptions of the heroine's sexual adventures. This chapter focuses on the sensory power of those encounters and also analyzes how and why the iconic character from horror — the vampire — has served a crucial role in unleashing the expression of the heroine's desire. It also explores what happens when paranormal romance migrates to film and television, media whose capacity for mimicry heightens the spectator's sensory responses to actions that occur in fictional worlds.

In her influential article "Film Bodies: Gender, Genre, and Excess" (1991), Linda Williams discusses the parallels that exist between three "body genres," melodrama, porn and horror. These genres belong "in the realm of the 'gross'" and they create sensory pleasures that are marked by bodily excess, both on and off the screen. In all three genres, the spectacle of a body is "caught in the grip of intense sensation or emotion"[10]: the bloodied, tortured and pained bodies in horror; the tormented, weeping bodies that are victims of desire and denial in melodrama; and the writhing, naked bodies caught in waves of sexual ecstasy in porn. Blood, tears and sexual juices: these are the gross manifestations of emotions that are unleashed by these "sensational film body genres" and they articulate their sensations across the bodies of their spectators.[11]

> Visually, each of these ecstatic excesses could be said to share a quality of uncontrollable convulsion or spasm of the body "beside itself" with sexual pleasure, fear and terror, or overpowering sadness. Aurally, excess is marked by recourse not to the coded articulations of language but to inarticulate cries of pleasure in porn, screams of fear in horror, sobs of anguish in melodrama.[12]

The sensory and emotional excesses performed across the bodies onscreen are echoed in the body of the spectator who is "caught up in an almost involuntary mimicry of the emotion or sensation of the body on the screen."[13] Williams continues:

> Whether this mimicry is exact, e.g., whether the spectator at the porn film actually orgasms, whether the spectator at the horror film actually shudders in fear, whether the spectator of the melodrama actually dissolves in tears, the success of these genres seems a self-evident matter of measuring bodily response.[14]

Williams's analysis of the sensations in which body genres immerse us is at the core of this chapter, but where Williams explores these body genres as distinct entities, my emphasis is on the way all three collapse into each other. A hybrid mix of horror-porn-melodrama/romance is paralleled by hybridized sensations of horror, ecstasy, and desire, and each explores the relationship one has with the other. Paranormal romances with horror leanings enmesh the bodily responses required of their generic fictional worlds. The horrific, the sensual, the erotic and, in the case of the later Anita Blake novels, the plain old pornographic often merge in the depiction of a single sexual act. The distinction that Williams makes between horror, melodrama and porn often collapses in paranormal romance. The sensations that are typical of traditional romance and which center on expressions of love and sensuality often combine with sensations of horror and revulsion. The "'ewwww' factor in sexuality" and "the incorporation of physical acts that revolt, disgust, and shame us"[15] find a whole new form of expression in paranormal romance — especially, as will be discussed below, when Anita Blake is involved.

Paranormal Romance: Romance, Horror and the Gothic

According to the Romance Writers of America, romance fiction branches off into numerous subcategories, which include contemporary romance, historical romance, Regency romance, novels with strong romantic elements, romantic suspense, young adult romance, and paranormal romance.[16] Paranormal romance is the most generically slippery and most difficult to define when compared to traditional romances such as the Regency, contemporary or historical.[17] Plots can deal with alternate realities, time travel, science fiction and settings in the future, and horror stories that involve shapeshifters, vampires, werewolves, witches, Greek gods and other paranormal beings.[18] The Paranormal Romance Writers website[19] even breaks the distinctions down further into paranormal creature types; for example, paranormal: devils and demons, paranormal: supernatural, paranormal: vampire, paranormal: dragons, paranormal: urban fantasy, and so on. In many of these subcategories (for example, urban fantasy) vampires, supernatural, werewolves, and zombies also intersect. To add to the generic complications, in addition to mixing horror, romance and fantasy, many examples of paranormal fiction (the Anita Blake series included) also draw on detective and investigative fiction. For this reason, I'll be using "horror-paranormal romance" to cover fiction that incorporates horror monsters into its romance world. In addition, some paranormal romances (and I focus on those with horror characters and plots) concentrate on self-contained stories that follow the "classic patterns" of other romances. For example, in *To Catch a Spirit* (Carrie Pulkinen, 2011), *Zombie Moon* (Lori Devoti, 2010) and *Devil of the Highlands* (Lynsay Sands, 2009), "The main plot centers around two individuals falling in love and struggling to make the relationship work" and it all comes to a head in "an emotionally-satisfying and optimistic ending."[20]

Predominantly, however, the horror-paranormal romance format favors two types of series: the first, which is exemplified by Christine Feehan's Dark Carpathians series and Susan Sizemore's Primes series, shares a similar narrative universe (a world that unveils the existence of the Carpathians, an ancient race that feeds on the blood of humans and who lose their souls and become out-of-control vampires if they fail to find their "life mate"; and a reality in which vampires exist and hot, male "Primes" struggle to keep their vampire families safe while developing romantic attachments to sexy, female heroines), but each novel follows the journey of new couples as they meet and come to the realization that they are meant to be together. The second series type follows an open structure: the couple, or, more precisely, the heroine and her dark hero (or sometimes expanding array of love-interest heroes), remains the same and the readers become embroiled not only in her journey but also in the paranormal universe she inhabits — its paranormal "reality," the creatures (human and paranormal) who populate it, and the struggles, horror, crimes, and relationships that take place in it. It is this type of paranormal romance that brings horror to the foreground. Given the focus on world building,[21] these series — which include Laurell K. Hamilton's Anita Blake Vampire Execution series, Kim Harrison's Hollows series (in which Rachel Morgan, a witch, grapples with her own powers and the "outed" communities of fairies, vampires, pixies, demons and werewolves), and Charlaine Harris's Southern Vampire series (whose reality revolves around Sookie Stackhouse, the community of Bon Temps, and the discovery of a synthetic blood that has allowed vampires to come out and be accepted as United States citizens) — focus as much on the romance between the gutsy female lead and her alpha male(s) as on the dense mythology that each novel creates around them. Because of their emphasis on mystery, monsters, violence, horror and action (usually the domain of the heroine) this type of series is sometimes also categorized as "urban fantasy" or "paranormal thriller." Fans and purists sometimes debate as to whether it even belongs to the romance genre. Yes, this category is slippery and its schizophrenic identity is reflected in how it's presented in bookshops. These books used to be found solely in the romance section of bookstores. Recently, their immense popularity has had an effect on their audience appeal with the result that anyone can now walk into a bookshop and not only find the Anita Blake novels in their very own paranormal romance section, but also under romance, horror, science fiction and fantasy, and crime — all in the one store! Even so, my interest here isn't with categorization but rather what happens when horror and romance meet.

Aside from paranormal romance's tendency to blend genres, the formulaic stability of the conventional romance, especially with regard to the inevitable coupling of the heroine and hero who are meant to be together, is unsettled in many paranormal romances. One of the reasons for this is the seriality and world-building structure that runs rife in this type of romance. Characters are placed in narrative universes that operate according to their own realities, morality systems and rules — vampires, werewolves, faeries and witches who have "come out" to the human world; secret paranormal underground cultures that are known only to a select few and who are contained by gifted slayers or executioners; vampire and shapeshifter myths that are rewritten into new mythologies as creatures of a different race or victims of viral diseases. In book after book within any given series the heroine, who is always an active character who propels the narrative action forward, is often in a tug-of-war relationship with one, two, or, in the case of Anita Blake, numerous lovers, and the happy closure that's reserved for conventional romances refuses to manifest itself. All the while, the fantasy settings and the characters that populate them become more complex. While the paranormal universe may expand and shift its focus, two things remain stable: the heroine and the hero. The female protagonist takes different forms: she may be human but also have special abilities (as private investigator, vampire hunter, necromancer, telepath) or be a paranormal creature herself (shapeshifter, faerie, witch), but she is always a tough, independent, woman of action who is capable of getting herself out of the often horrific scenarios that are thrust upon her. The male protagonist, whether vampire, werewolf, shapeshifter, or (at times even) detective, is pure alpha male.

Romance fiction has been around a long time. Tania Modleski (1982),

Janice Radway (1984), Jayne Krentz (1992), Pamela Regis (2003), Deborah Lutz (2006), Eric Selinger (2007), Kathleen Miller (2010) and other writers on the genre have all noted that while mass culture romances are products of the 20th and current centuries, their origins go back further still. Most often, the genre is linked to the 19th century romance writings of female authors such as George Eliot, Elizabeth Gaskell, and Anne Brontë. But it's the romances of Jane Austen (*Pride and Prejudice*, 1813), Charlotte Brontë (*Jane Eyre*, 1847) and Emily Brontë (*Wuthering Heights*, 1847) that are seen as setting in place many of the conventions: all three introduced strong female heroines characterized by independence and intelligence, and the sexy, mysterious Byronic hero who has become a favorite staple of the genre (Mr. Darcy, Mr. Rochester and Heathcliff).[22]

It's no surprise then that in recent years, propelled by the success of *Pride and Prejudice and Zombies* (Jane Austen and Seth Grahame-Smith, 2009) many of these classic romances have more directly merged with horror and the supernatural, pushing romance further into the domain of horror. *Pride and Prejudice and Zombies* (fig. 14) merges Austen's Regency romance text with the horror text of Grahame-Seth, in the process transforming the Bennet sisters into refined ladies who were also trained in the "deadly arts of the Orient" by Master Liu in the Shaolin Temple in the Henan Province of China. As such they're more than equipped to defend themselves against the zombie (or, the "unmentionables") invasion that has befallen Great Britain. Elizabeth Bennet is eventually coupled with her soul mate Mr. Darcy, who also showed great "proficiency with both sword and musket,"[23] and

Figure 14: The cover for *Pride and Prejudice and Zombies* (Philadelphia: Quirk Books, 2009) by Jane Austen and Seth Grahame-Smith.

the novel ends like many horror-paranormal romances: with the union of a powerful couple who are in love, with a world of subsidiary characters — good and evil — that help to paint a rich picture of the mythology of the world they occupy, and an opening for further adventures in the future.

> The dead continued to claw their way through the crypt and coffin alike, feasting on British brains. Victories were celebrated, defeats lamented. And the sisters Bennet — servants of her Majesty, protectors of Hertfordshire, beholders of the secrets of Shaolin, and brides of death — were now, three of them, brides of man, their swords quieted by that only force more powerful than any warrior.[24]

So ends *Pride and Prejudice and Zombies*. While poor Charlotte succumbs to the rotting of the flesh and dulling of the brain that is the curse of being a zombie, the Bennet sisters continue to fight the hero's quest, but now are under the spell of love.

Given the parallels that exist between both romance traditions, it's no surprise that *Pride and Prejudice and Zombies* was followed by a wave of classic romance revisions that merged romance and horror. The titles speak for themselves — *Jane Slayre* (Charlotte Brontë and Sherri Browning Erwin, 2010), *Little Vampire Women* (Louisa May Alcott and Lynn Messina, 2010), and *Wuthering Bites* — yes, Heathcliff is a vampire (Sarah Gray, 2010). But without doubt it's Jane Austen's novels that most inspire the paranormal conversion: *Pride and Prejudice and Zombies: Dreadfully Ever After* — the sequel (Steve Hockensmith, 2011); *Sense and Sensibility and Sea Monsters* (Jane Austen and Ben H. Winters, 2009); *Mansfield Park and Mummies: Monster Mayhem, Matrimony, Ancient Curses, True Love, and Other Dire Delights* (Jane Austen and Vera Nazarian, 2009); *Emma and the Werewolves* (Jane Austen and Adam Rann, 2009); and *Emma and the Vampires* (Wayne Josephson, 2010). Other authors have taken even greater artistic license in transforming Austen texts into paranormal romances that transform the romantic alpha male into a vampire. For example, *Mr. Darcy, Vampyre* (Amanda Grange, 2009) continues the story of *Pride and Prejudice*, but with a twist! Mr. Darcy is a vampire and must now share his dark secret and dangerous life with his new wife, Elizabeth Bennet. And again, in *Vampire Darcy's Desire: A Pride and Prejudice Adaptation* (Regina Jeffers, 2009), vampire Darcy returns. As the book jacket tells us:

> Tormented by a 200-year-old curse and his fate as a half-human/half-vampire dhampir, Mr. Darcy vows to live forever alone rather than inflict the horrors of life as a vampire on an innocent wife. But when he comes to Netherfield Park, he meets the captivating Elizabeth Bennet. As a man, Darcy yearns for Elizabeth, but as a vampire, he is also driven to possess her. Uncontrollably drawn to each other, they are forced to confront a "pride and prejudice" never before imagined — while wrestling with the seductive power of forbidden love. Meanwhile, dark forces are at work all around them. Most ominous is the threat from

George Wickham, the purveyor of the curse, a demon who vows to destroy each generation of Darcys.
Written in authentic Austen style and faithful to its Regency-era setting, *Vampire Darcy's Desire* retells the greatest love story of all time in a hauntingly imaginative fashion.

Given the predominance of "horrified" but "authentic Austen style" reboots, the series now follows the labeling format of paranormal series (The Anita Blake Series, The Sookie Stackhouse/Southern Vampire Series, The Rachel Morgan Hollows Series) but rather than taking the name of the series' heroine, this takes the name of the author as heroine and is titled The Jane Austen Undead Series. In fact, in *Jane Bites Back* (Michael Thomas Ford, 2010) — a parody of the Austen paranormal spin off craze — Jane Austen is herself a vampire, having survived a vampire attack early in her career and now living in a 21st-century small town, running a bookshop, selling Austen novels and marketing paraphernalia but not making a cent of profit. And yes, her adventures come complete with a dark love interest who just happens to be the one and only Byron, great Romantic author, *and* the vampire who turned her. As a paranormal romance, *Jane Bites Back* not only flags its heritage but also includes some of the writers who made it possible as its key characters. Not only are Byron and Jane Austen now vampires and 21st-century romance writers, but Charlotte Brontë (who Byron also foolishly made into a vampire) is a deranged romance critic/fan blogger out to destroy (as in *destroy*) Jane. While the Jane Austen reboots are a very small trend in the genre, they're significant in that they highlight the range of pleasures that readers (and viewers) extract from paranormal romances in general. In addition to the visceral and sensory delights they offer, the reflexive awareness both of romance and horror traditions being drawn upon become a form of cerebral or intellectual play that has its own pleasures.

Romance fiction and, in particular, paranormal and suspense romances also reveal the Gothic connection with classic Gothic romances like *Wuthering Heights* and *Jane Eyre,* while also revealing links both with early and later Gothic traditions: Horace Walpole's *The Castle of Otranto* (1764), Ann Radcliffe's *The Mysteries of Udolpho* (1794), Mary Shelley's *Frankenstein, or The Modern Prometheus* (1818), John Polidori's *The Vampyre* (1818) — all paranormal romances in their own way — would open the way to Sheridan Le Fanu's *Carmilla* (1872) and, of course, Bram Stoker's *Dracula* (1897), which went on to inspire what would become a mass-culture love affair with things paranormal and, especially things vampire. Discussing Deborah Lutz's essay "The Haunted Space of the Mind," Eric Selinger agrees that, while Gothic romance was popular in the 1950s and early 1960s, it's returned with a vengeance in the 21st century "as a brooding undercurrent in many paranormal romance novels."[25]

> "In an age peculiarly engaged in arduously knowing the self, in uncovering and illuminating all the dark demons," writes Lutz, "the Gothic provides a countermovement. The excessive popularity of the self-help book, the soul-searching memoir, the therapeutic relationship, shows a need in our culture ... to *know* the mind, to shine a bright light on interiority. The Gothic draws on another desire, one that crosses boundaries of historical periodization, gender, and class — that of peering into darkened rooms, stepping into haunted spaces not merely to expose them and banish all their mystery, but to keep the darkness in play, to fall in love with it even."[26]

Paranormal romances such as the Anita Blake series, the Rachel Morgan/Hollows series, the Sookie Stackhouse/Southern Vampire series and the Women of the Otherworld series (Kelley Armstrong) all delve into the darkened rooms and haunted spaces, both literally and figuratively, in that the heroines of each series turn into themselves, battle with the dark demons inside them, and struggle to understand the nature of their humanity in what is a supernatural and often horrific world. Significantly, this new Gothic heroine that populates horror-paranormal romances provides a new twist to the 18th-, 19th- and even 20th-century formula. Many of the vampire, werewolf and demon love interests are dark, violent, and mysterious alpha males. Comparing the alpha male of paranormal romance to the Byronic lover of 19th-century romance classics, Sarah Frantz explains,

> The domineering, emotionally remote alpha-male hero of modern hero-centric romances embodies patriarchal power in all its glory. Sarah Wendell and Candy Tan argue that romance heroes' "hypertrophied masculinity" is what proves that they "have the Biggest and Best Schlong of All in both figurative and literal terms." ... These heroes, according to Wendell and Tan are "strong, dominating, confident," but they are "often isolated" and have "a tortured, tender element within themselves that they rarely let anyone see."[27]

But in the continuing series type of paranormal romance (especially those often labeled "paranormal thrillers") often the alpha males parallel or sometimes don't even come close the alpha females who propel the narratives. The Byronic hero in these romances now tends not only to be the male but the female.[28] It's as if Mina of *Dracula* has now been given weapons with which to kill the monster (in the form of hardware or supernatural abilities) but she's also been given a dark soul and an intense attraction to the monster she seeks to destroy. It's these heroines who now "have the Biggest and Best Schlong of All," but unlike their male counterpart, it's a figurative "schlong," a fact generally considered to be a positive, rather than a negative.

Alison Milbank makes a valid point regarding the presence of a specifically female Gothic tradition going as far back as the writings of Ann Radliffe, Mary Shelley and the Brontës, and associates with this a predominantly female authorship and readership, a fact shared with the romance novel.[29] Likewise, Kathleen Miller notes the parallels between romance fiction and the Gothic genre, drawing attention to Tania Modleski's damning analysis of both. Miller explains that Modleski "concludes that these novels reflect women's discomfort with the 'social and psychological processes which transform them into victims,' but she does not credit these novels and their heroines with offering any agency or empowerment."[30] Ultimately, in consuming these texts, women "participate in glamorizing their own oppression."[31] Milbank disagrees, as do I, especially when considering this new brand of gothic horror that typifies many paranormal romances. These fictions are about grasping and giving voice to the sensory and emotional expression of female desire. Horror-paranormal romance, in particular, turns to its heritage — classic romance, contemporary romance, gothic horror, contemporary horror — and mashes up its sources. The final result is a new form of romance fiction that explicitly explores questions of desire, eroticism, and love through the lens of horror. In doing so, paranormal romance gives voice not only to the ideal conception of romance and love (union with the soul mate) but also to its darker, more dangerous and, sometimes potentially destructive side. One of the major factors that accounts for romance being a top-selling genre — paranormal or otherwise — is because it confronts romantic passion head on, and it imagines a "surrender to those unparalleled dangers of wild romantic passion and to the idealized others who steal our hearts."[32] It's to this stealing of hearts by dangerous, yet sexy, monsters that I now turn.

Dangerous Passions: Touching the Monster

> Her nails dug into his shoulders, an exquisite pain. He leaned her against the wall for better leverage, his hips savage, relentless, frenzied. His teeth scraped, nipped. Then she cried out at the piercing pain, so sweet, so sensual, as his fangs buried themselves deeply, claiming her blood as voraciously as his body was claiming hers.... His mouth worked at her throat, taking her very essence as her body took his, dragging at his, tightening around him, clenching and demanding until he had to cry out with the intensity and pleasure. Ruby droplets trickled down the swell of her breast, and his tongue followed the trail.... The ferocity of Aidan's lovemaking should have terrified her, but she matched his intensity, beat for beat, her fists wrapped in his blond hair, her body wrapped around his tightly, her cries muffled against his shoulder.[33]

This is a passage from Christine Feehan's *Dark Gold*, one of the "Dark" or "Carpathian" series novels. Alexandra Houton finds herself mysteriously drawn to Aidan Savage. Savage in name and savage in nature, for Aidan is a Carpathian, an ancient race that have kept themselves hidden from the human world, existing only in legend through vampire myths. But the "real" vampires of legend are actually Carpathians who are unable to control their bloodlust, a condition often triggered when, after centuries of solitude, the males have failed to find their soul mate (this is a bond that's biologically recognized and impossible to resist). Vampiric love, bloodletting, violent passion, pain and pleasure all merge in a swirling mass of sensation that leaves its imprint on the reader. Reflecting Williams's argument regarding mimicry discussed above, Alphonso Lingis writes that "the essence, of the body and of a life are comparable to that of an artwork, where the sense expressed is not separable from the expression itself, the exteriorization, where the sense is accessible only through a direct contact, where the sensorial matter radiates its significance without leaving its temporal and spatial site."[34] Helen Bailie explains that in paranormal romances, the characteristics of the vampire that are typical of horror novels "are appropriated and transformed by popular romance writers into the essence of women's fantasy heroes.... The image of vampire as predator and, more importantly, the taking of blood or the blood exchange between the protagonists become the very elements that enhance, consolidate, and secure the couple's romantic relationship."[35] But more than this, the sensory and carnal pleasures described in this passage make contact with the reader so that, as Lingis states, "The sense expressed is not separable from the expression itself." The process of reading and comprehending the sensations that are evoked through the text are translated across the body of the reader who is touched by that which is read. Alexandra's and Aidan's carnal responses are shared in ways that move beyond the cognitive comprehension of the physical act of sex that's described, and beyond the themes about romantic coupling where "the sexual act between the vampire hero and heroine symbolizes a connection between them that takes place not only on a physical level but equally on an emotional and spiritual level."[36]

Desire, its expression and the discovery of a soul mate, one can lose oneself are at the core of passages like the one quoted above from *Dark Gold*. And the sense that has the greatest power in mediating the sensory shift from the body of the text to the body of the reader is not sight but touch — the touch of fingers, mouth, the flesh of the bodies as they rub against each other while in the throes of passion: desire and touch, the desire to touch and be touched. In the article "Cinema as Second Skin," Tarja Laine, drawing on the writings of Jean-Paul Sartre, states the following:

> Desire ... is a specific mode of bodily consciousness in which the desiring subject makes him, or herself flesh through touch (caress). By touching the other's shoulder, I discover the other body's tactility, but simultaneously I make myself tactile. According to Sartre, the touch is in no way distinct from the desire: to touch and to desire are one and the same.... "The [touch] is not a simple

stroking: it is a shaping. In touching the Other, I cause her flesh to be born beneath my [touch], under my fingers ... but by the same stroke I make my hand disappear as flesh ... to reduce my hand to a soft brushing almost stripped of meaning, to a pure existence, to a pure matter, slightly silky, slightly satiny, slightly rough — this is to give up for oneself being the one who establishes references and unfolds distances: it is to be made pure mucous membrane."[37]

Like Jennifer Barker, Vivian Sobchack and Laura Marks, Laine extrapolates on this description of the relationship between desire and touch in order to account for the nature of film spectatorship and its embodied reaction to the presence of the screen. I'll be elaborating on the specificity of the filmic and televisual experience below, but for the time being, I'd suggest that Laine's analysis is also pertinent to the act of reading and, specifically, to reading texts about the expression of desire. In reading about desire and bodies losing themselves in one another, we, in the words of Sartre, also lose ourselves in the textual references and what we read so that the distance between the sensations described in the text — the exchange of touches — unfold and collapse distances between the fictional bodies and our own. As Barker explains in relation to film, we don't "lose ourselves" in these fictional worlds, but rather, "We exist — emerge, really — in the contact between our body and the film's body." She continues (via Lingis): "The touch between our skin and another's bring our own perceptive and expressive act into greater relief. In pressing ourselves against the other, we can feel ourselves touching. We and the other render each other real, sensible, palpable, through mutual exposure."[38] Just as the Carpathian Aidan and his life mate "render each other real" through touch, we render the text real through the act of reading, which, in turn, makes the text press sensually against our bodies in ways that are akin to being touched.

Until recently, female desire for romance texts — paranormal or otherwise — has been condemned for ideological and feminist reasons. Continuing a tradition of critique introduced by Modleski and Radway, a tradition that ignores the sensory and carnal impact of the genre, writers on the romance novel persist in condemning its form because of the nature of the requisite "happy ending." Jorgenson, for example, who makes a direct connection between fairy tales and romance novels, argues that despite the rebellious heroines, the story "ends up in monogamous heterosexual marriage that conforms to patriarchal norms."[39] Furthermore, she states, "Fairy tales disempower women by granting them superficial pleasure while denying them any real agency."[40] This heterosexual coupling is definitely the case in Feehan's Dark series: all the heroines bond with their dominant Carpathian males and, in the end, live happily ever after. But to focus only on the narrative action and, in particular, the ending is to miss out on what these stories have to say about the agency of female desire, and how the expression of that desire is conveyed to the readers.

Lohmann, Jorgensen and others have drawn attention to the connection that exists between many paranormal romances and the *Beauty and the Beast* fairy tale, and especially to Bruno Bettleheim's "animal-groom theme" as outlined in his book *The Uses of Enchantment*. Many of these stories focus on the father-daughter relationships and the transference of the daughter's love to the animal-groom. In addition — and this is more pertinent to the parallel with paranormal romance — the journey for the heroine is one about accepting, rather than fearing, male sexuality and its King Kong–like associations with bestiality. The latter serves a dual function in that it also teaches the heroine, through the undying love she has for her beast-man, to accept and express her own sexuality and desire. As Lohmann explains, "Learning the power of love is the magic of the animal-groom narrative."[41] But beyond this, taking a leaf out of recent postmodern fairy tale revisions, which famously include those by Angela Carter and Marina Warner, paranormal romances also often "problematize the desires they represent."[42]

In her book *From the Beast to the Blonde* (1995), Marina Warner "examines women's longing for beasts"[43] in fairy tales like *Beauty and the Beast, Little Red Riding Hood* and *Donkeyskin*. She explains, "Like romance, to which fairy tales bear a strong affinity, they could create the world in the image of desire."[44] But the brand of fairy tales Warner discusses explore a particular brand of desire, one that focuses especially on the relationship between sex, violence and aggression, especially as explored through the character of the male beast and the heroine's relationship to him. Warner discovers in these stories, which, like romances, were often written by women for women, the capacity female characters have to subvert dominant ideology. According to Lisa Propst, Warner

> criticizes Bruno Bettelheim, for whom "Bluebeard" and "Beauty and the Beast" represent the initiation of young women into adult sexuality and assuage "the terror of defloration" by dramatizing it violently. She protests that this view "takes the exuberance and the energy from female erotic voices ... turning [the beast] ... into a mistaken illusion in unawakened female eyes." ... For Warner, sexual interpretations of these tales are most valuable for women if they address real danger or hint at women's own aggressive desires.[45]

Both traditional fairy tales and their postmodern variations celebrate "polymorphous perversity" and narrativize the "the potential eroticism of aggressive appetites."[46] Eroticism hasn't been traditionally associated with fairy tales, however, the feminist writings of Warner, Catherine Ornstein, Cristina Bacchilega and many others have revisited the infantilization of fairy tales and studies about them. Unearthing the rich history and older tellings of modern (and often de-eroticized variations of) fairy tales, these authors explore the erotic undercurrent that ran through even classic stories by the Brothers

Grimm, Charles Perrault and the French Conteuses. While explicit sex may not always be depicted (a feature that's redressed in postmodern fairy tales), the tales still operate like "ideologically variable desire machines."[47]

Linda Lee discusses how many romance novels consciously rework fairy tales: Christine Feehan's *Lair of the Lion* (2002), for example, is a retelling of "Beauty and the Beast"; Teresa Medeiros's *Charming the Prince* (1999) retells "Cinderella," while her *A Kiss to Remember* (2001) is a reworking of "Sleeping Beauty." While most romance novels aren't conscious revisions of fairy tales, many are still marked by fairy-tale motifs and conventions.[48] Paranormal romances "are often closer to their fairy-tale counterparts in that they frequently depict male protagonists who are literally beasts or monsters, often vampires, werewolves, or demons of various sorts,"[49] but unlike their fairy-tale animal-groom counterparts, the beast doesn't transform into a handsome prince in the end. He remains and is accepted for his "beastness" and the dangerous possibilities that connotes. Discussing Feehan's *Lair of the Lion*, Lee analyzes the passage in which Isabella Vernaducci offers herself to the lion shifter Don Nicolai DeMarco.

> During their first interrupted attempt at sexual intercourse, just at the moment of penetration she sees him momentarily appear as a lion. When they finally do engage in sexual intercourse, he seems to transform into the Beast when he reaches orgasm — he "roars" and draws blood when he grips her hip too hard, presumably from the transformation of his fingers into claws. In this dual penetration of the heroine's body, of her vagina and of her skin, the blood drawn echoes the more common smear of blood on the sheets that indicates loss of virginity. This scene inverts the standard transformation-by-love of "Beauty and the Beast"; here it is physical expressions of love/desire (that is, sex) rather than emotional love that is the catalyst for transformation, and the (momentary) transformation is from a controlled man to an uncontrolled beast.... The conflation/confusion of desire and danger, or eroticism and violence, persists throughout the novel, and it is a common trope of many popular romances. The not-so-veiled threat of sexual danger both heightens the eroticism of the popular romance and serves as a point of contention for feminists who are concerned with the larger cultural messages transmitted by the romance novel and what these indicate about women's fantasies.[50]

These alpha male "beasts" signify the problematizing of desire of which Warner speaks, especially in how they explore eroticism that can accompany the expression of "aggressive appetites"— male and female. Like Isabella, for example, rather than being terrified by the fact that Aidan tears open her throat, and feeds on her life force, Alexandra embraces the animalistic drives of his vampiric nature, and pain, danger and pleasure merge into an erotic frenzy that feeds her desire.

Nevertheless, despite the parallels with fairy tales, the fact remains that the male love interests in horror-paranormal fiction are creatures adapted from the horror genre and, as such, they often also succumb to the rules of horror. The function and characteristics of the vampire in literature, film and television have remained reasonably stable despite many surface transformations since their entry into popular culture. The vampires in the tradition of Count Orlok in *Nosferatu: A Symphony of Horror* (F.W. Murnau, 1922), Kurt Barlow master vampire in *Salem's Lot* (Stephen King, 1978), the monstrous zombie-like vampires in *The Strain* trilogy (Guillermo Del Toro and Chuck Hogan, 2009–), the Wamphyri of the *Necroscope* series (Brian Lumley, 1986–2009), and the Master from *Buffy the Vampire Slayer* (The WB/UPN, 1997–2003) all bring with them pestilence of potentially apocalyptic proportions and signify a society collapsing into a state of chaos. These bestial, primal creatures are driven by violent hunger, one that refuses to be reined in by social morés and taboos. The reaction they trigger in those confronted by them (character, reader or viewer) is one of horror. In turn, their terrifying guise and antisocial nature make them unconducive to romantic seduction. To put it mildly, they're anything but objects of desire.

The second vampire "type," as depicted by the "lead" vampires in *The Vampyre* (John Polidori, 1819), *Carmilla* (Joseph Sheridan Le Fanu, 1872), the multiple versions of *Dracula*, *Interview with the Vampire* (book and film), *Angel*, *True Blood*, the *Twilight* series (books and films), vampire chick-lit by Katie MacAlister (*The Last of the Red-Hot Vampires, A Girl's Guide to Vampires*) and Kerrelyn Sparks (*Vampire Mine, How to Marry a Millionaire Vampire*) and many, many other examples, are equally as capable of committing atrocious acts of bloodletting, but these vampires are first and foremost creatures of seduction. They're charismatic, powerful, attractive and, in more recent years, just downright "hot." This is the vampire who populates horror-paranormal romance fiction. Anita Blake's beau and "master" Jean-Claude, for example, has been branded by fans as one of the hottest vampires *ever*— an observation with which I have no argument. Even when there is a threat in these novels by a vampire or vampires to the social order (the berserker vampires in the Carpathian novels, the vampires who are able to rot their flesh in the Anita Blake series, the renegade vampires in the Twilight series), these vampires are subordinate to the more socially integrated (even if still outsider) lead vampire characters and are coded as the ones who need to be controlled or removed from the narrative universe they threaten. Typically, the vampire in horror is often a concrete symbolization of fears, failures, desires, or repression in the social "norm," and this can be played out on an individual level (Mina's fear of the sexual excess her husband and men represent in *Dracula*) or on a social level (the small-town community in a state of moral decay in *Salem's Lot*). The vampire signifies the potential collapse of social morés and ritualistic taboos that keep in tact the social order and "normality."

Monsters like the dangerous, seductive vampire carry with them heavily coded meanings specific to the horror genre and to horror-paranormal romance and, in turn, target the sensorium in distinctive ways. Like the beast of fairy-tale romances, the figure of the vampire makes possible the exploration of social boundaries relating to sex, passion and desire. They're seductive enough to establish intense attraction for both the heroine and reader/viewer but threatening enough to tip desire into dangerous territory. This undead being that savors and survives on the life force of the living also has the power to transform this thirst for life and blood into a game of passion that tugs painfully at dueling and seemingly opposite sensations and states of being: pain and pleasure, terror and passion, death and life. The vampire's unbridled passion as played out across a body that's part monster and part human opens the door to the heroine who is invited to explore her humanity and sexuality further, delving into a territory that's simultaneously dark and exhilarating. The *Twilight* series is interesting in the way its monster-vampire Edward Cullen (fig. 15) represents exactly this possibility of unbridled and dangerous passion, but denies giving it access to the heroine Bella Swan. As is typical of many heroines of paranormal romance, Bella desperately craves and desires her vampire lover; she even gives voice to her desire to have sex with Edward

Figure 15: Edward (Robert Pattinson) and Bella (Kristen Stewart) from the film version of Stephenie's Meyer's *The Twilight Saga: Eclipse* (Summit Entertainment, 2010).

numerous times throughout the series, but Edward fears the damage his unbridled, "monstrous" lovemaking can do. He fears his monstrosity. Even when they finally "do the deed" after they're married (in *Breaking Dawn,* 2008), the act most associated with the vampire, drinking and exchanging blood with his partner — only occurs as a means of saving Bella's life. Becoming pregnant while on their honeymoon, Bella discovers that her unborn child (Renesmee) is developing at an accelerated pace and, when the baby finally attempts to exit the womb, Bella's fragile human form can't withstand the birth. To heal her broken bones and massive loss of blood, Edward finally gives Bella the "gift" of vampirism, by feeding in the way of the vampire. Having denied Bella the blood exchange that symbolizes, combined with sex, the expression and celebration of "aggressive appetites" in paranormal romances, Edward chooses instead to exchange blood when Bella is in a state of extreme pain and her life is threatened. Jonathan Allan has argued that, whereas the virginal heroine is a norm in popular romance, the virginal hero is something of an aberration. While this sexy vampire who sparkles in sunlight is presented as anything but monstrous, he is nevertheless a "defiantly deviant vampire" in that he "contradicts the stereotypes of male sexuality" by adopting a virginal attitude towards Bella.[51] Edward enforces a boundary that keeps Bella within the domain of teen-paranormal fiction, but throughout the series Bella reveals a voracious appetite that craves the dark and dangerous sexual experiences offered adult paranormal heroines by their truly monstrous, anti-virginal vampire lovers.

With the vampire lover (perhaps even Edward post the Twilight stories) we enter the realm of what Davies calls "the darker side of eros" or "'the perverse,' with a small *p*"[52]; this is the space of intense passion and yearning that's fueled by erotic desire. Davies explains that she is using the term "perversion"

> to denote a kind of universal, polymorphous, powerful, almost always shame-riddled aspect of human sexual imagination, an aspect of sexual fantasy and behavior that may be experienced as deviant but that ... is anything but. These are the fantasies we think of as "a little dirtier," "a little rougher," and often "a little hotter." These are the fantasies that we all have and about which we are all ashamed to speak.... These are the fantasies that involve aggression, shame, domination, and submission, the power dimensions of who loves who more, who needs who more, the will he come, the will she stay, the must I tie her up, him down to hold, arouse, titillate, and drive to distraction and surrender. These are the fantasies that unite the self with a taunting, teasing, ever-alluring, bad exciting object.[53]

The vampire is the bad object par excellence. He or she connotes the kinds of eroticism of which humans are capable but are "ashamed to speak." In horror-paranormal romance it's the vampire in particular, followed by the lycanthrope as a close second, who embodies the license to give voice to dangerous passion and elicit eroticism. Their bodies trigger an eroticism that encourages the dirty, rough and hot.

Without directly meaning to, the passage quoted above from *Dark Gold* gives a symbolic representation to eroticism as discussed by Georges Bataille in his book *Eroticism: Death and Sensuality*. According to Bataille, human passion as it relates to eroticism is at the core of human identity. Discussing the relationship between reproduction and eroticism, he states that, while separate from it, the concept of reproduction is bound to eroticism through the act of sex. But while signifying life, reproduction also "implies the existence of discontinuous beings"[54] in that, to reproduce means to give birth to a distinct being from which we are separate. Our entire life is spent trying to bridge a gap between two beings — ourselves and another — we try and need to communicate, yet ultimately "no communication between us can abolish our fundamental difference"[55] and our solitude. Love, passion, and eroticism all, in their own way, present an illusion — or perhaps, a temporary reality — that the gap has been bridged; that two discontinuous beings have come together as one and that there is total communication between them. Two bodies merge and become one. This is that state in which Anita Blake loses herself when she describes a passionate and metaphysical exchange with Jean-Claude, Master Vampire:

> I might have pulled away, I might have not, but the moment the front of our bodies touched, it was too late. There was no going back, no saying no, nothing but sensation.... For one trembling moment we were pressed together, our energy breathing against each other like the sides of two great beasts. Then the boundaries that held our auras in place gave way. Think of it as if you were making love and suddenly your skin slid away, spilling you against your partner, into your partner, giving you an intimacy that was never imagined, never planned, never wanted.[56]

The bridging occurs through touch and Anita loses her identity (one of her fears throughout the series) as she and Jean-Claude meld into one. The seductive vampire concretizes this merging of bodies and identities through a union that's sensory: the tearing of delicate skin, the feeding on blood, its taste, its smell and the feel of its thick, liquid form as it trickles over sensate flesh. To drink the blood of a living being is to drink their essence. Anita Blake recognizes this and, unlike Alexandra (who savors the symbolic merging of her identity with that of Aidan through the exchange of blood) she fears it (even though she eventually succumbs to, as well as practices it).

However, Bataille also reminds us that eroticism is intimately tied to death. The association of sex and reproduction brings to mind the life cycle: the continuity of life but also the reminder of its eventual demise. "Eroticism gives us a glimpse of the continuity from which we emerge when born and to which we return in death: erotic activity to Bataille is a paradoxical exuberance of life which, at the extreme, is akin to death."[57] In horror the vampire is symbolic of this very process. This undead being is always a reminder of the eventuality of death, while simultaneously being capable of reproduction by "birthing" new vampires. But Bataille moves beyond this, posing the question, "What does physical eroticism signify if not a violation of the very being of its practitioners?" He continues:

> The whole business of eroticism is to strike to the inmost core of the living beings so that the heart stands still. The transition from the normal state to that of erotic desire presupposes a partial dissolution of the person as he exists in the realm of discontinuity.... The whole business of eroticism is to destroy the self-contained character of the participators as they are in their normal lives.... Eroticism always entails a breaking down of established patterns, the patterns, I repeat, of the regulated social order basic to our discontinuous mode of existence as defined and separate individuals.[58]

The act of vampire sex and blood feeding in horror-paranormal romance embraces this idea of the dissolution of the self. In fact, it celebrates and revels in it. Even though heroines like Anita Blake fear this dissolution of the self and her independence, so much so that for a long time she forbade Jean-Claude to feed on her, she eventually succumbs to its power. She and many of the heroines of horror-paranormal romance understand that "physical eroticism has ... a heavy, sinister quality"[59] and the vampire manages to balance the sinister and destructive with the pleasurable and seductive in ways that allow the heroines and readers to push their own erotic thresholds in satisfying ways. But the exchange also impacts on the body of the vampire lover. As Bailie explains,

> Through the taking of the heroine's blood, the vampire seeks redemption for past deeds and renewal through love that gives his life meaning and purpose.... While traditionally women's blood, specifically menstrual blood, has been associated with not only the unclean and profane, emphasizing, as Kristeva writes ... the sexual difference between men and women, in the vampire romance the woman's blood for the hero comes with the promise of a new life, a rebirth ... nothing is hidden so the lines of difference are blurred. The blood exchange in these vampire novels not only assures the couple of a prolonged life, it also symbolizes redemption and eternal love.[60]

But what happens when the lead romantic monster changes? Do all monster-beasts signify in similar ways? Change the monster and not only do different meanings come to the fore, but they're accompanied by different sensations, both diegetically across the body of the heroine and, in reality, across the body of the reader. The sensorium is a slippery creature in horror, and when different monsters replace the romantic vampire lead, the romance can quickly transform into something horrific.

Life and Death, Vampires and Zombies

Let's imagine the above seduction scene from *Dark Gold* not with Aidan as a vampire, but as another undead monster, the zombie. The highly charged and erotic touch of flesh and exchange of fluids takes on a whole new meaning.

> Her nails dug into his shoulders, and she felt the flesh give way, her fingers plunging inwards. She felt her fingertips touch a squishy, sticky substance and the first thing she noticed when she pulled her hands away was the rancid, nauseating stench. Peering over his shoulder she gazed at her nails, which had pulled out with them bits of torn, rotting flesh, and her fingers dripped with an oozing, green substance. He leaned her against the wall for better leverage, his wound-riddled hips savage, relentless, frenzied. What was left of his teeth tore and ripped savagely at the skin on her neck. Then she screamed at the intense pain, so unspeakably agonizing, as his teeth buried themselves even more deeply, claiming her pulsating and ravaged throat muscles as voraciously as his body was claiming hers. His mouth continued to ravenously gnaw away at her throat and she could hear the guttural sucking sounds he made as bits of her flesh ripped away from her body, making their way into his mouth and down his throat. The sound was terrifying. She could feel her very essence slipping away, and as her hands slipped down his shoulders, gliding over the multiple, putrid sores, she pulled quickly away when she also felt the clumps of rotting flesh detach from his body and hit the ground with an audible splat! His unquenchable hunger made him cry out with an animalistic intensity that demanded more. She looked down and saw a waterfall of ruby-rich blood trickling down the swell of her breast, and she watched in horror as his tongue followed the trail. Moments later, his tongue followed a journey all of its own. Having snapped out of his mouth, it rolled down, finding spaces between their bodies until it finally landed with a *thunk* onto Alexandra's right foot. The ferocity and horror of Aidan's attack was translated as terror across every cell in her body. Finally snapping out of her state of shock, she beat wildly against him with her hands until her fists wrapped themselves in his clumpy, pus-drenched blond hair and, using his body for leverage, she yanked and yanked until two chunks of Aidan's skull — hair, pus and bone — ripped free, exposing the throbbing brain matter beneath it.

Unless we enter this passage as individuals whose erotic identities have embraced Perversion with capital P, the seduction by an attractive vampire metamorphoses into an aberrant and horrifying rape by a putrid, decaying zombie. In Feehan's passage, touch, taste, sight, sound and smell unite to heighten the heroine and reader's sensual and erotic experiences and ignite desire. Alexandra's response is to want to lose herself in her lover, and the reader's desire mirrors that of the heroine. In my passage above featuring the zombie, touch, taste, sight, sound and smell unite to disgust, repel and horrify. Here, Alexandra desperately struggles for separation from the creature that signifies death. Again, the readers' senses and logic echo this reaction. What had been a desirable object — the vampire's body — is now something horrendous and the stuff of nightmares.

The vampire and the zombie have much in common: both are dead, both have a taste for human flesh and blood, and both cross a boundary that defines what is and what isn't human. Likewise, the living dead and the vampire also test the rules of human society, its laws, rituals and taboos. But both monsters speak to different drives, desires and fears. The lover vampires in paranormal romance tease with the possibility of disgust — or what society perceives as disgusting moral behavior (feeding off the blood of your partner) — and this becomes a powerful ingredient that fuels the erotic exchange and bond of the couple. It becomes something that's utterly desirable. The vampire connotes a "ravenous displaced sexuality" that represents both what we fear and desire; its "voraciousness and instability," in fact, speak to the very nature of desire.[61] Its undead nature brings to the fore questions about life, death and immortality[62] but, ultimately, its obsessive orality, hypersexuality, and lust for life place it firmly in the realm of the living. For the heroine, the vampire lover is an ideal man who fulfills her desire. The zombie, on the other hand, signifies anything but desire.

As discussed in Chapter One, the zombie or living dead in horror are putrid things to be avoided. The living being's aversive response to them functions as a protective mechanism: this bad object signifies impurity, decay, and a threat to the living. It threatens to overcome the living through contagion, a contagion that not only threatens the stability of the individual human body but, through the spread of its disease, humanity at large and, along with it, the social structures that give humans their humanity. "Disgust," explains Korsmeyer, "is an affective response that can be mustered to patrol social boundaries and norms, for instance, to reinforce proscriptions on what should be eaten or on sexual behavior."[63] Unlike the seductive vampire in these novels, who often represents passion and a lust for life, the living dead triggers a visceral disgust and "an affective state that is closely tied to involuntary physical responses such as the gag reflex, nausea, and even vomiting."[64] As Korsmeyer describes, "Disgust erects a protective barrier between subject and object, but the ultimate recoil is from our mortality and the recognition that, by being proximate to contamination, we lose our bodily integrity — die, decompose, and become the disgusting object itself.... The disgusting is, as [Kolnai] puts it, 'pregnant with death.'"[65] The romantic vampire in paranormal romance walks a the fine line between life and death, but this teasing ultimately favors erotic life and undying passion. The zombie, on the other hand, steps firmly into the realm of death and, through the carnal presence of its animated and putrefying corpse, is a reminder to the living (both diegetic and beyond the diegesis) of what awaits them when life comes to an end. The difference embodied by these distinct corporeal responses that the lover/victim and reader have to the vampire and zombie "attack" explains why there are no paranormal romances that cast the zombie in the lead love-interest role. While zombie paranormals have begun to appear over the last couple of years, most characterize the zombie as a social threat that has to be eradicated by the heroine or romantic couple (*The Loving Dead, Hollowland, Zombie Moon, Zombies Sold Separately, Married with Zombies*). Where a more sympathetic zombie is depicted, as in *Slow and Sweet: A Love Story, with Zombies*, which focuses on a human couple who protect a small town of non–brain-eating zombies, or, in *Deadtown*, where the zombie is the comic relief sidekick of the werewolf heroine, the extreme disgust associated with the conventional zombie is pushed into the background. Recently, the publishing house Night Wolf Publications put out a call for submissions. It read as follows:

> Ain't no lovin' like undead lovin'—it applies to more than vampires.
> Night Wolf Publications seeks the latest in paranormal romance: zombie romance. Whether your polished manuscript is light, dark, humorous, serious, gory & greasy, or carefully exfoliated, the staff at Night Wolf Publications wants to read it before Aug. 30, 2011.[66]

The ground may be shifting, but a romantic, seductive zombie is yet to make an appearance in paranormal romance.

Laurell K. Hamilton often explores the sensation of disgust in the Anita Blake books, particularly through Anita's choice of love objects. Through her werewolf lover Richard, Anita evaluates the relationship she has to her own humanity but, unlike Richard, who is disgusted by his monstrous side, Anita becomes more like Jean-Claude, eventually embracing her monstrosity while retaining part of her humanity. As human necromancer, through countless battles with paranormal enemies, over time Anita becomes infected with multiple viruses, including those of the werewolf, wereleopard, and werelion and weretiger, yet her body is immune to them and, as a result, while gaining many of their paranormal abilities, she doesn't undergo the requisite, painful shift into animal form. Likewise, her affiliation with vampires has given her vampire powers and desires, the most powerful being the ardeur, which, as mentioned above, is a libidinal drive that demands sex but is also susceptible to blood lust. Like the function of the beast in fairy-tales that Warner discusses, Anita's collection of monster-beasts allow her to understand her own desire, which is rarely expressed and thoroughly repressed in the early novels, and to give expression to it in ways that transgress social norms. In the process, her understanding and tolerance of objects that disgust also undergo a transformation, and the nature of her desire expands to allow for new expressions. Her initial experience of seeing Richard transform into a werewolf and then proceed to consume another alpha wolfman sent her fleeing in terror, her body responding to the disgusting sight by succumbing to waves of nausea and vomiting. But whereas Richard perceived Anita's response as proof of the disgusting and abhorrent nature of his monstrosity, Anita allowed the experience to alter her, so much so that she eventually embraced the horrific animal drives (and desire to violently rend people apart) that plagued her, subduing them to the will of her sexual desire. As Bataille explains, "There does remain a connection between death and sexual excitement" that sometimes spills over into the realm of "aberrant sensuality"[67] and it "takes an iron nerve to perceive the connection between the promise of life implicit in eroticism and the sensuous aspect of death."[68] During times of erotic play triggered by the ardeur, which, in turn, unleashes her inner paranormal "beasts," Anita often plays with the possibilities of death by biting, drinking the blood, tearing and even eating the flesh of those with whom she has sex; but, despite the desire to sometimes go further, and to cause irreparable damage, she always pulls back and, in the process, remains in the domain of erotic life. The Perversely disgusting (at least, where some readers' tastes are concerned) is held at bay.

"Perverse with a capital P" eroticism, however, does find expression in many of the Anita Blake novels, but tends not to have Anita play a central role as one of the participants. For example, regular appearances are made by vampires whose "special powers" aren't the ardeur, but who have the ability to rot and decompose, often gaining intense pleasure doing so while feeding and having sex. Jason, Jean-Claude's *pomme de sang* (on-site feeding partner) and one of Richard's werewolves had the displeasure of being victim to this aberrant form of sexuality. In *Bloody Bones,* Jean-Claude and his people meet with another vampire group led by the Master Vampire Serephina. As a result of vampire etiquette, Jason is forced into agreeing to have sex with two of Serephina's female vampires, but what he doesn't realize is that they both possess the power to rot.

> The brunette ran her fingers down his naked back. Her flesh sloughed away, leaving a trail of greenish slime behind. A tremor ran through his body that had nothing to do with sex.
> From across the room I could see Jason's chest rise and fall faster and faster, as if he was hyperventilating.... The brunette wrapped her decaying arms around his shoulders, leaned her rotted face next to his, and whispered something.
> Jason struggled away from them, crawling against the wall. His bare chest was covered in bits of her flesh. His eyes were impossibly wide.... A strand of some-

thing thick and heavy slid down his neck onto his chest He batted at it like you would swat at a spider that you found crawling along your skin.... The blonde rolled off her back and crawled towards him, reaching a hand out that was nothing but bones with bits of dried flesh. She seemed to be decaying in dry ground. The brunette was wet. She lay back on the floor, and some dark fluid rushed out of her to pool beneath her body. She'd undone her own leather shirt, and her breasts were like heavy bags of fluid.

"I'm ready for you," the brunette said.[69]

Needless to say, both rotting vamps get blasted by Anita's Browning as a result of wanting to give expression to their own special brand of erotic play. "Eroticism," explains Bataille, "is an infraction of the laws of taboos," and yet it remains "a human activity."[70] But there are taboos, and there are taboos. Anita Blake may expand her sensuality and sexuality by learning to break many taboos in the name of carnal pleasure, but she draws the line at corpses. Bataille states that the corpse, in all its putrefaction and decay, is a forbidden object that triggers disgust.[71]

> The horror we feel at the thought of a corpse is akin to the feeling we have at human excreta. What makes this association more compelling is our similar disgust at aspects of sensuality we call obscene. The sexual channels are also the body's sewers.[72]

Our disgust at this putrefying object, and the feelings and obscenity that decay arouses are grounded in a "desire [that] originates in its opposite, horror."[73] Desire, eroticism and horror — these are the foundations that underpin Anita Blake's world, and they often intermingle. Where as for the two rotting vampires eroticism is firmly wound up in their ability to decay and rot on their lovers while having sex, for Anita and her team this is an act of disgust that threatens life with death, sanity with insanity. Korsmeyer argues that "disgust can be the occasion for reflection for it provides insight about its objects."[74] The presence of this aberrant act serves a purpose in setting up boundaries for Anita and for the reader: when does the danger and violence explicit in Anita's eroticism transform into a thing that's repugnant and horrific? However, while the object of disgust — in this instance, the rotting vampire corpses — may incite aversion and the desire to look away, it can also fascinate and attract, resulting in what Korsmeyer calls "aesthetic disgust." It's to aesthetic disgust that I now turn.

From Text to Screen: Sookie Stackhouse, *True Blood* and the Aesthetic of Disgust

In an episode of *True Blood* titled "It Hurts Me Too" (3:3), the show's writers took the series' predilection for exploring the limits of human sexuality and eroticism to new limits. Held captive by Russell Edgington, the Vampire King of Mississippi, seemingly of his own free will but actually to keep his lover, Sookie Stackhouse, safe, the vampire Bill also reunites with his maker and ex-lover Lorena. In the final scene in the episode, Bill's hatred for the vampire who sired him collides with his attraction to her and unleashes itself in a sex scene that left some reviewers and fans outraged and others still wanting more. Against the backdrop of creepy, gothic non-diegetic music and a mise-en-scène dominated by blacks, reds and browns, I looked on as the scene unravels. Lorena taunts Bill about his obsession with his humanity, initially through wanting a connection with his wife and children (who he had to abandon in 1868 when he was turned by Lorena) and now with his relationship with Sookie. In a fit of rage, Bill rushes across the room in an act we see as speeded-up images that only just manage to capture Bill's motion. He grabs Lorena around the neck, squeezing tightly, and is met by eyes and a smile that greet his action with unabashed desire. The eerie gothic sounds become more abstract, and the combination of screeching horns and the plucking of violins heighten the anticipation of the disturbing action yet to come. Still squeezing her throat, Bill proclaims, "You have deprived me of my freedom, my home, my humanity. I will never, ever love you." His words drive home all the more forcefully because of the combinations of loss and anger that write themselves across his face, in the lines of his expression, the torture in his eyes, and in the force with which the words "never, ever" squeeze themselves painfully out beyond his clenched teeth. Lorena, turned on by Bill's violence and inner pain, grabs him in a kiss, and Bill responds by throwing her on the nearby bed. What happens next made my body tighten with expectation. Lunging on top of her, Bill plunges his teeth into her neck, his action made all the more powerful through the audible "crunch" of sharp teeth piercing flesh. "Never ... love you!" he repeats as he rips off her dress and plunges himself into her. And as Lorena murmurs the words, "Make love to me," Bill pounds into her relentlessly, the repetitive, aggressive motion accompanied by the sound of flesh slapping into flesh. Lorena grabs his back, ripping open his black shirt and exposing skin that's been ripped open by her nails. Bill rears back, screaming, his expression alternating between states of anguish, hate, and rage. The slap of his left hand is heard as it grabs the right side of her face, while the other reaches for the back of her head, then slowly, and working against Lorena's resistance, Bill begins to turn her head backwards. I hear bones cracking and crunching as her head is slowly twisted downwards and, with one final crunch, I look on in shock and horror as the head flops down towards the floor and Bill continues thrusting himself into her (fig. 17) In the midst of the frenzy, Lorena, blood trickling out her mouth, mutters the words, "William, I still love you." As Lorena's words and his actions dawn

Figure 16: Bill Compton (Stephen Moyer) and his vampire maker, Lorena (Mariana Klaveno), engaging in violent vampire sex. "It Hurts Me Too," *True Blood*, season 3, episode 3 (HBO, 2008–).

on him, Bill stops, runs his fingers painfully through his hair, and screams like a madman.

This scene, to put it mildly, is a sensory whirlwind. And it's all the more potent because of the fact that it finds expression on the screen, drawing on the impact of vision, sound and the corresponding connections between the senses. The rich, multi-tonal reds that decorate the walls of the room, the lush velvet fabrics that evoke the sensation of touch, the depth and range of facial expressions that trigger multiple emotions, the aggressive and violent touch of hands as they strangle and scratch, the sounds and texture of ripping fabric, the sight, sensation and taste of trickling blood on lips, the feel of flesh against flesh, and the smell of sex and blood — these are only a few of the sensory encounters evoked. There's no parallel scene in Charlaine Harris's *Club Dead*, upon which series three episodes of *True Blood* are based. In the book, Bill is held hostage by Lorena and is wrapped in silver chains (silver weakens a vampire's power and causes them great pain). There's no mention made of any sexual interaction between the two, even though it's implied after Sookie rescues Bill. Even if such a scene existed in the books, Charlaine Harris, like her main protagonist Sookie, tends to shy away from detailed gritty goriness, and so I doubt it would pack the same punch that it does on the screen. Not even Hamilton, despite her love of bloodlust, horror and gore, could describe this scene in a way that could affect the sensorium with such immediacy and force. This sensory feast is only achievable because of the power inherent to televisual and cinematic form.

According to Jeanne Deslandes, all fiction — "books, plays, screenplays, films, operas, interactive media, art installations" — has the ability to "stir up emotion"[75] that has an affective impact on the reader or spectator through their imagination. The paradox of fiction is that, while we recognize its fictional status we can still respond with "real emotions" to "virtual world experiences" as if they're real.[76] She argues, "An emotion stirred up by fiction is just as real as in real life. All emotions, in this view, are encountered, embodied and comprehended in the hermeneutic circle described by Heidegger: previous emotional experiences produce, via self-reference, new emotional experiences, whether virtual or not."[77] I agree; however, there is also a major difference. I'm reminded of Miriam Hansen's analysis of the different experience that film introduced into the media arena in the early 20th century, and her discussion holds true for most moving image fictions today.

> Hollywood films in relation to modernity may take cognitive, discursive, and narrativized forms, but it is crucially anchored in sensory experience and sensational affect, in processes of mimetic identification that are more often than not partial and excessive in relation to narrative comprehension.[78]

The cinema is an aesthetic and sensorial form that encourages "mimetic identification" in ways that differ radically from text or static image. Describing this sensory experience further still and directing it explicitly to the depiction of sex on the screen, Williams asks, "In what precise sense do we sexually feel when we screen sex? How are our bodies engaged through vision and sound in a kind of vicarious touch, taste, smell?"[79] Expanding on Sobchack's argument in *The Address of the Eye*, Williams asserts that the attraction isn't just directed to the eyes but to the flesh: "Our entire sensorium is activated synesthetically, all the more so ... when the moving image shows two (or more) beings touching, tasting, smelling, and rubbing up against one another ... in watching them [bodies engaged in sex] I am solicited sexually too."[80] Sensory contact is made between "the very body of the perceiver and the perceived"[81] so that through our eyes and ears, our other senses join in; the corporeal, sensuous, erotic events onscreen affect us and write themselves across and inside our bodies in very real and intimate ways. Williams's words take on more powerful meaning when considered in relation to the scene from *True Blood*. This scene explores a very dark, disturbing and violent side of sex and it does so by not holding back the darkness for the sake of the viewer. In fact, the viewer is forced to confront the commingling of expressions of desire, hatred, horror and disgust.

According to Benjamin Riley, this scene and, by extension, the show "had crossed a line."[82] While he understands a film like *Elephant* (Gus van Sant, 2003) as using extreme violence to "make a political statement," *True Blood* uses violence gratuitously "beyond its dramatic function": the emphasis is on "shock attacks" and acts that are plain old disgusting. For Riley, Lorena's proclamation that she loved Bill at the end of this scene "was the golden ticket." Deriding "collective commentary" on the episode for claiming "that obviously this is just what vampires do," Riley continues:

> The scene showed the most graphic act of sexual violence done to a woman by a man I've ever seen in mainstream popular culture. We should be discussing it in these terms, contextualising it in reality instead of mitigating its severity by trying to justify it in the context of the show.[83]

For Riley, the context of the scene in relation to the horror genre to which it belongs "*de*contextualises the scene's violence" and rips it away from its relationship to "sexual violence in reality." I'd argue that, in fact, it's the context of horror that makes possible the scene's significance to the context of reality. The context of horror makes possible the exploration of the dark and sinister side of eros. As a Bill fan, I couldn't help but feel a sense of thrill and excitement watching this scene that opened up a disturbing side to the character that hadn't been witnessed before this point. He was Bill, and he was still hot! I empathized with his pain, rage and sorrow but at the same time I was both excited and shocked at the way he gave physical expression to these emotions; and his final horrific act left me with a heavy weight at the pit of my stomach. What did I feel about what I'd just seen and experienced? How and why was I still attracted to this character who had performed such a disgusting act?

Korsmeyer argues that the artistic arousal of disgust "can be turned to political, social, religious, and aesthetic ends, and it may be mingled with horror, humor, sorrow, or satire."[84] She is interested in what she calls the "aesthetic of disgust." Turning to modern philosophy and, in particular, to the writings of Alexander Baumgarten, she defines "aesthetic" as a state linked to sensory experience which responds and gives insight to the object that triggers disgust. "Disgust," she states, "affords a powerful means by which difficult truths are conveyed with maximum aesthetic impact."[85] Observing that, commonly, the chief senses associated with disgust are considered to be taste and smell, with touch coming in a close third, she also reminds us that, according to Kolnai, vision also plays a crucial role. She agrees, but also wonders how art, film and other graphic representations dealing with disgust "do not directly stimulate the senses of taste and smell or even touch" yet still give rise to these sensations.[86] Vision and sound (she gives the example of someone retching) are capable of arousing the spectator synaesthetically but, because "they have less potent effects on the Viscera ... consequently disgusting things can be experienced in art that would be intolerable in reality."[87] Herein lies the power of horror in cinema and television. Horror-paranormal romance as experienced on the screen is able to thrust us into emotional and sensory states that are far more evocative and potent when compared to their text versions. I watch and listen to Lorena and Bill's violent sexual encounter and simultaneously draw upon my own sensory experiences to migrate the audio-visual across to other senses. I know what it feels like to touch, taste and smell, and my brain recodes what I experience onscreen into a sensorial encounter that's felt in very real ways across my body. But the experience of disgust is bearable because the primary triggers of disgust — touch, taste, and smell — are not actually present. It's this sensory mimicry that, according to Korsmeyer, gives rise to an aesthetic of disgust that allows critical distance, making it possible to analyze the object that is its source.[88]

Korsmeyer asks whether sex should be included as an object capable of triggering disgust: despite sexual fluids that include "semen and menstrual blood" or other "'unclean' emanations from the body that signal compromise of its boundaries," sex can also be understood as the antithesis of disgust given its association with attraction and desire.[89] Yet, drawing on the writings of William Miller, she stresses that "desire itself depends upon a prohibited domain of the disgusting." Desire, sex, love, hate and disgust often confusingly commingle[90]; add horror to the mix and we enter disturbing territory indeed. In his analysis of sexuality, Lingis states the following:

> Sexuality is not merely meaning-constitution, to be sure; it is behavior, caresses and orgasm, but the release of sexual functions depends on the emergence of a meaning-structure. The erotic significance of a person, and of a situation, is not produced by cogitations, and is not even a representation, but the way a perception itself is structured so as to accentuate the erogenous zones and address them immediately to kisses and caresses, to erotic gestures. Structuring the sensuous configuration itself, addressing it to the embrace of the witness, the carnal sense is an incarnate meaning.[91]

Yet, the scene from *True Blood,* like so many of the sexual exploits of characters in the series, and like many of Anita Blake's sexual encounters, gives expression to an eroticism that's dangerous, and the danger is all the more palpable because it's explored through the lens of horror. Lorena isn't turned on by kisses and caresses but by violence, pain and an obsessive desire to cause suffering to her lover, Bill. Bill denies that he loves Lorena and yet his intense hatred of her is transformed into an erotic passion that relies on hatred that's powerfully expressed in actions that unwittingly fulfill his lover's perverse desires, but also reveal Bill's equation of sex with violence. There's no logic that can explain the motivations that drive these characters to be sexually fueled by the ingredients of hate, violence, pain and the disgusting, just as there's no logic that can explain my simultaneous response of desire and shock while watching this scene. To this day, one of the most powerfully erotic scenes I've ever seen is in the *True Blood* episode "The Fourth Man in the Fire" (1:8). Presuming Bill is truly dead, Sookie visits his grave. As she turns to leave, and as the music warns ominously of impending horror, an arm erupts from the ground and grabs her by the leg, dragging her forward across the ground. We (and she) realize it's Bill and, as he emerges from the earth, his naked body covered in soil that begs to be brushed off, he and Sookie fall into each other's arms and make wild and passionate love. What is it about this scene that makes my insides quiver in ways that make me blush? Is it my love of vampires, or of horror? My fan-crush on Bill? My predilection for dirty, naked, well-muscled men who hang around in cemeteries? While psychoanalysis may try to understand and give meaning to what may account for locating the source of our desires, as Lingis says, the "erotic significance of a person ... is not produced by cogitations" but through erotic gesture and carnality: "The carnal sense is an incarnate meaning."[92] Our bodies have a language all of their own, a language that we can feel with intensity but whose significance we don't always understand.

This is the journey that the aesthetic of disgust in horror-paranormal romance takes us on; when it comes to eroticism and sexuality we often enter the realm of the unknown. Like horror, the thrill and power of eroticism comes from entering the realm of the unknown.[93] Horror-paranormal romance explores regions that are shadowy and it sends out an invitation to its main heroine, reader and spectator to explore the nature of these shadowy, unknown spaces. In tamer paranormal-horror fiction, the vampire or paranormal lover represents the thrilling entry into an erotic world where one lover merges his or her identity with a soul mate. Initially, the heroine fears beginning such a journey — a fear expressed through the body of her monstrous beast-man; but ultimately, the thing she fears facilitates the heroine's development as a vibrant and fearless sexual being. Paranormal romance with stronger horror leanings, such as the Anita Blake series and *True Blood*, push the association of eroticism with pleasure and danger further. This, in turn, offers more challenging sexual and sensory encounters for both heroine and audience. Anita, through her first-person narration, allows the reader access to her psyche, her fears, her horrors, her desires and her horrifying desires. What she and the reader come to understand is that desire is a complex and, at times, horrifying thing. How and why it takes the form it does can't fully be understood through any rational means, and yet it still exists and demands attention. The shift of paranormal romance texts to the screen in recent years has only served to intensify the allusiveness of what gives voice to desire. Despite film and television's direct access to only two senses — sight and sound — it has the capacity to ignite all the senses through mimicry and memory. We allow the cinematic and televisual body to wrap around our sensorium in very real and intimate ways. It's no wonder that Barker views the relationship between spectator and screen as "fundamentally erotic."[94]

Paranormal romance visibly flaunts its mixed heritage. Nineteenth- and 20th-century romance fiction, Gothic fiction going back to the 18th century, Gothic as filtered through screen horror over the last century, the rich tellings and retellings of mythic horror monsters such as the vampire, the zombie and the werewolf, the fairy tale, and the contemporary paranormal genre itself — all inform the rich and expanding conventions of paranormal romance. The paranormal romance's uniqueness is found in the way many genres, conventions and traditions have come together to provide an original variation of the romance genre. Unlike its romance predecessors, even the feisty "bodice rippers" of the 1980s, the collision of gothic horror, horror and romance has shifted attention away from the themes of romance and love (with lots of sex) and towards eroticism and desire. Horror-paranormal romance, in particular, tests the rules of traditional romance fiction by exploring the nature of desire, but a desire that delves into a dark and often sinister place. Not only do the various horror icons that infiltrate her world place intense sensory demands on the heroine, but her experience of carnal pleasure and pain also forces her to ask questions about the nature of her own desire, identity and psyche. Horror-paranormal romance's connection to contemporary screen horror has given rise to the expression of intensely visceral, erotic and challenging sexual encounters which are played across the bodies of heroine and reader alike. As has been discussed, paranormal romance can shift its focus, allowing the sensorium to wallow in the pleasures of sex and romance, but also delighting in the horror and aberration that can lie at the core of eroticism. It comes as no surprise that works like the Southern Vampire series have found a happy medium in the television series *True Blood*. Via Sobchack, Marks and Barker have both stated that the communication that occurs between the screen and the spectator is not only an exchange between two bodies, but also an erotic exchange.[95] *True Blood* taps into the power inherent in this erotic exchange by also touching the spectator's body with highly charged erotic action. The sensual and violent content of these actions carve themselves across the spectator's body with an immediacy that's incredibly potent and which demands that we ponder on the meaning and significance of what sparks the senses. In the next chapter I turn to a different kind of eroticism, one that is closer to Marks and Barker's understanding: the erotics of the screen/spectator relationship, but this is one that's driven by the more cerebral act of cinephilia, which brings with it its own sensory pleasures.

5

Payback's a Bitch! *Death Proof*, *Planet Terror* and the Carnivalization of Grindhouse Cinema

Gross-Out Horror, Grindhouse Cinema and the Carnivalesque

The story of *Planet Terror* (Robert Rodriguez), the first film screened in the *Grindhouse* (2007) double feature that also included *Death Proof* (Quentin Tarantino), revolves around the events that occur after a town full of people in Texas are exposed to a biochemical called DC2 (code name, Project Terror). Following the recent zombie film convention, due to exposure to a chemical agent, one by one the living lose their identity, their flesh begins to rot and they develop an unquenchable desire to feast on living, human flesh. In one especially grisly scene, the recently retired pole dancer Cherry Darling (played with great flair by Rose McGowan) confronts one of her captors, a soldier named Lewis (played with equally great flair by Quentin Tarantino). Lewis, who also happens to be infected with DC2, is part of a top-secret military unit led by Lt. Muldoon (Bruce Willis) who were first exposed to the DC2 biochemical in Afghanistan but who have also managed — through a partial antidote — to temporarily control the full symptoms of the infection. In this scene, Lewis holds Cherry at gunpoint and demands that she dance for him. Having previously had one of her legs ripped off by ravenous zombies, Cherry has only one leg — the other (thanks to the thoughtful ingenuity of her boyfriend, "El Wray") having been replaced by the leg of a wooden table. Hobbling, stumbling and shuffling through her clumsy dance, Cherry reaches the breaking point and roundhouse kicks Lewis in a move that would do Chuck Norris proud; and using the spike that now remains of her damaged wooden limb, she plunges her spike into Lewis's right eye. One would think that this horrifying assault (and the chunk of wood that breaks off and lodges itself in his eye socket) would be enough to curb Lewis's libido but his rage drives him on as he declares, "You gave me some wood, now I'm gonna give you some!" Pulling down his trousers Lewis displays his goods, but if he was aiming to impress, things don't quite go according to plan. The DC2 antidote in his body is spent and he looks down and, through the camera, the audience is invited to do the same. What we see is the stuff of men's nightmares: Lewis's penis and testicles begin to melt and slowly detach from his body. In a point-of-view shot from behind and between Lewis's spread-out legs, I remember seeing Cherry in the background, her face aghast and soon it was matched by my face which expressed a similar state of shock; I also remember groaning as I watched globs of what had been Lewis's sexual organs ooze from his body and hit the ground with audible "plops." And then? I laughed and groaned and laughed and groaned in response as his entire body continued to transform into a pulsing surface of throbbing, pus-filled wounds and rotting clumps of flesh, the abject spectacle culminating eventually in Lewis violently vomiting out all of his internal organs.

It would be logical to assume that the abject and grotesque actions presented in this scene would incite sheer horror and disgust from the audience; and they do, but they do so in combination with laughter. By taking the gory and gross conventions of the zombie film to an exaggerated, parodic level, this scene — and the film in total — succeeds in bringing together the seemingly antithetical states of horror and comedy. Yet Rodriguez is one of many directors of horror films since the 1970s to merge these two forms in a successful union. According to William Paul, the 1970s and '80s introduced new types of "gross-out" comedy and horror films that were "quite happy to present themselves to the public as spectacles in the worst possible taste."[1] *Planet Terror* is clearly aware of the debt it owes to gross-out films like *Dawn of the Dead* (George Romero, 1979), *Evil Dead* and *Evil Dead II* (Sam Raimi, 1981 and 1987). Gross-out films not only embrace bad taste but they transform "revulsion into a sought-after goal"[2] and more often than not the spectator is drawn into the film through physiological reactions to its content. Rather than aiming at the audience's intellectual talents, gross-out films target physiological responses — laughter, disgust, horniness, and horror. Paul continues:

> A gleeful uninhibitedness is certainly the most striking feature of these films — of both the comedies and the horror films — and it also represents their greatest appeal. At their best, these films offer a real sense of exhilaration, not without

its disturbing quality, in testing how far they can go, how much they can show without making us turn away, how far they can push the boundaries to provoke a cry of "Oh, gross!" as a sign of approval, an expression of disgust that is pleasurable to call out.[3]

In this chapter I extend William Paul's approach by understanding the gross-out horror tradition utilized in *Planet Terror* and *Death Proof* as modern expressions of the carnivalesque tradition as theorized by Mikhail Bakhtin. In a series of essays that were published originally in the 1930s and 40s ("Epic and Novel," "From the Prehistory of Novelistic Discourse," "Forms of Time and of the Chronotope in the Novel," and "Discourse in the Novel") and which were eventually published in English as the collection *The Dialogic Imagination*, Bakhtin develops his arguments regarding the generic logic of the novel, often as a point of difference to the epic and tragedy. As a more recent literary form, he argues, the novel hasn't remained static nor have its conventions become codified within a historical past. Instead, the novel is always caught up reflexively in the process of "becoming." In *The Dialogic Imagination* and his dissertation *Rabelais and Folk Culture of the Middle Ages and Renaissance*, which was eventually published in 1965 as *Rabelais and His World*, Bakhtin outlines key concepts that inform the writing and the readership of the novel. His concepts of dialogic processes and the carnivalesque have since impacted on film and media studies primarily because Bakhtin's concern is with the "language of the marketplace" and popular culture. According to Bakhtin this language is expressed most dominantly during the Middle Ages, but its form can also be traced back even further to the Hellenistic era (in the writings of philosophers Socrates and Menippus of Gadara) and the literature of the Byzantine era.[4] Remnants of the carnival tradition persisted after the Middle Ages, initially during the Renaissance in the form of commedia dell'arte, fairs, and traveling theater troupes but later were adjusted to meet the demands of new commercial needs in the form of amusement parks, penny arcades, burlesques, and film genres such as comedy and horror.[5] As Robert Stam notes (while for the most part viewing it as a watered-down version of the carnivalesque), the Hollywood film tradition reveals its historical affiliations with the "old-time carnival," given that its origins were developed side by side with the fairground, sideshow and amusement park.[6]

From a literary perspective, the writing of Rabelais, Cervantes and Shakespeare would introduce new expressions of the carnivalesque, which would again continue "with special force and clarity beginning in the second half of the eighteenth century," a period that witnessed the popular rise of the novel.[7] In *The Dialogic Imagination*, Bakhtin especially expresses his interest in "eras when the novel becomes the dominant genre. All literature is then caught up in the process of 'becoming,' and in a special kind of 'generic criticism.'"[8] For

Bakhtin, "generic criticism" doesn't exist beyond the text but is built into the very structure of the novel and is the result of the novel's inherent dialogic nature. The writings of Rabelais, Cervantes and Dostoyevsky all reveal a complex intertextuality that not only refers to external texts but which engages in a dialogue with them. As such, these texts not only contain their generic heritage but they also interact with it, reproduce it, reflexively engage with it, or radically transform it.

In his analysis of contemporary Hollywood genre films, Jim Collins locates similar characteristics to those outlined by Bakhtin and uses the term "genericity" to "address not just specific genre films, but genre as a category of film production and film viewing"; during a period when "popular entertainment is undergoing such a massive recategorization," our understanding of genre history, its engagement with its own history, its modes of production, and viewing experiences have all undergone radical transformations.[9] Collins recognized a process in operation in 1990s genre films that, by the end of the first decade of the 21st century, has reached fever pitch. In addition, the cult of the auteur has complicated these relationships further still, especially when considering that "auteurs" such as Robert Rodriguez, Quentin Tarantino, Tim Burton, Sam Raimi, Stephen Chow, Kathryn Bigelow and Takeshi Kitano adopt a meta-cinematic approach to their filmmaking that's also deeply informed by meta-genericity. As Collins further clarifies,

> The traditional relationship between genre and auteur — in which the former was synonymous with the formulaic and the mythic, and the latter synonymous with the intensely personal — no longer holds in quite the same way when directorial signature has become increasingly a matter of a distinctive style of generic reconfiguration.... Quotation is inseparable from narration, the former determining both the *range* of intertexts used to advance the "action," and their *register*, that is, the degree of ironic distance o empathetic involvement that the viewer is expected to mobilize from screen to screen.[10]

This chapter is concerned with the meta-genericity of *Planet Terror* and *Death Proof* and with the dialogic discourse that's generated within the films about generic process. Both films carry their generic history and evaluate it reflexively; by dialogically interacting with conventions of the horror — and other — genres, both films critically debate the nature of generic process and the production of meaning. In doing so, *Planet Terror* and *Death Proof* critically reflect on the fact that genre is always in a state of "becoming." In tackling a genre often considered to be antithetical to "serious" genres (for example, the drama, art cinema, the biopic, the war film), both films embrace the carnivalesque spirit as articulated in Bakhtin's *Rabelais and His World*. These films address the audience directly, demanding their critical participation in a game that's about the construction of the films' meaning. The films perform a ludic function in that they don't require the spectator to merely observe, but to also critically engage with the film universe mapped out before them. As was the case with traditions of carnival, the performance is one that involves everyone — director, actors and spectator — and crucial to the performance is the role served by laughter, which Bakhtin understands as being at the core of the carnivalesque.

According to Bakhtin, prior to the 17th century carnival festivals, written and oral parodies and abusive language were steeped in the voice of a folk culture that was intimately integrated with that of the official culture of the Church and feudalism. Spectacles that included carnival pageants that comically mimicked feudal rituals or ecclesiastical ceremonies facilitated a dialogue between folk and official culture that contested, ridiculed, laughed at, and overturned the serious and oppressive nature of the ruling culture, even if only for a limited space of time.[11] At the core of these spectacles was the festive laughter which, unlike "the satire of modern times" that aims at a private reaction, aims at the social: it is, according to Rabelais, an "ambivalent laughter" of the people in that it "expresses the view of the whole world; he who is laughing also belongs to it."[12] Turning the "world inside out," festive laughter simultaneously exposed the oppressive nature of official culture (of which the "folk" were still a part), while also having the power to renew and revive it. For Bakhtin, "Rabelais, Cervantes, and Shakespeare represent an important turning point in the history of laughter. Nowhere else do we see so clearly marked the lines dividing the Renaissance from the seventeenth century and the period that followed."[13] He continues:

> The Renaissance conception of Laughter can be roughly described as follows: Laughter has a deep philosophical meaning, it is one of the essential forces of the truth concerning the world as a whole, concerning history and man; it is a peculiar point of view relative to the world; the world is seen anew, no less (and perhaps more) profoundly than when seen from the serious stand-point. Therefore, laughter is just as admissible in great literature, posing universal problems, as seriousness.... The attitude toward laughter of the seventeenth century and of the years that followed can be characterized thus. Laughter is not a universal, philosophical form. It can refer only to individual and individually typical phenomena of social life. That which is important and essential cannot be comical. Neither can history and persons representing it — kings, generals, heroes — be shown in a comic aspect. The sphere of the comic is narrow and specific (private and social vices); the essential truth about the world and about man cannot be told in the Language of Laughter. Therefore, the place of laughter in literature belongs only to the low genres, showing the life of private individuals and the inferior social levels. Laughter is a light amusement or a form of salutary social punishment of corrupt and low persons.[14]

While expunged from religious, monarchical and other areas that represented official culture, significantly, the separation of official and folk voices facilitated the extension of festive laughter and the carnivalesque, from "the depths of folk culture" into "the sphere of great literature and high ideology."[15] For Bakhtin the writings of Rabelais, Cervantes, and Shakespeare encapsulate this shift and this new carnivalesque spirit is further seen in similar developments that took shape with the popularization of the novel in the 18th century. As mentioned earlier, Bakhtin's theories have since been extended to an analysis of film and television genres, particularly comedy and horror. But here, rather than finding expression in "quality" television and cinema, horror and comedy are still understood as Bakhtin describes them in the quote above: as examples of "low genres" that target "low persons." In that sense, many examples of these genres can be seen as updated, modern versions or continuations of this earlier tradition that marginalized what were considered to be debased voices of the marketplace. And gross-out horror, with all its foul humor and bad-taste depictions of bodily functions, does indeed find itself (critically speaking) very much at the bottom of the generic heap. The gross-out horror tradition is very much a part of the history of grindhouse cinema, which began to come to an end around the time that many of its "gross-out" conventions began to enter the mainstream.

Grindhouse films included a mixed bag of low-budget, exploitation films from a variety of genres including horror, blaxploitation, car chase or carsploitation films, "shock docs," martial-arts films, spaghetti Westerns, Italian giallo films, and sexploitation.[16] In addition to sharing low-budget production values, they also shared a distribution and exhibition practice that gave these films their nickname. While prevalent in cities throughout the U.S. it was Times Square and 42nd Street in New York that set the scene for the grindhouse theatres: post–World War II, the (in)famous bump-and-grind strip joints, which included theatres such as the Cameo, Lyric, Apollo and New Amsterdam, became film venues and the bump-and-grind action moved onscreen. While the exploitation tradition goes back to the beginnings of the cinema,[17] its post-war 1950s identity was kick-started by the likes of Roger Corman and William Castle and, in the 1960s, was developed further within a grindhouse context by exploitation mavens who included Russ Meyer (*Faster, Pussycat! Kill! Kill!*, 1965; *Vixen,* 1968), Herschell Gordon Lewis (*Blood Feast,* 1963; *Goldilocks and the Three Bares,* 1963; *Two Thousand Maniacs!*, 1964), David Friedman (producer, *Brand of Shame,* 1968; *Ilsa, She Wolf of the SS,* 1975) and Doris Wishman (*Bad Girls Go to Hell,* 1965; *Deadly Weapons,* 1973 — which starred the 73-inch busty stripper Chesty Morgan!). While many of the gross-out horror films that William Paul discusses did increasingly enter the mainstream, they also found a home in grindhouse cinemas, which in the 1970s and '80s continued to screen hardcore splatter-and-gore films directed by George Romero, Tobe Hooper, Sam Raimi, Lucio Fulci and Mario and Lamberto Bava. Importantly, despite the range of genres and stylistic approaches that were presented, as Mike Atkinson explains, for grindhouse those "elitist concerns such as acting, conviction, continuity and pacing were never issues — just the raw viscera, literally and otherwise."[18] In this respect, Eric Schaefer isn't far off in linking exploitation cinema's visceral concerns to the ballyhoo ploys of P.T. Barnum: "Ballyhoo, that noisy, vulgar spiel that drew audiences to circuses and sideshows, was a hyperbolic excess of words and images that sparked the imagination." The exploitation tradition has relied on the same hyperbole.[19]

The grindhouse tradition saturates the structure of *Planet Terror* and *Death Proof*: the original release of both films as a double feature, which duplicated the screening format of grindhouse cinemas; the focus on "raw viscera" and sensational gross-out action; the scratched and damaged film reels that look like they've taken a battering over multiple screenings; the hammed-up acting in *Planet Terror* that was typical of grindhouse films; and the insertion of Italian horror soundtracks in *Death Proof*, which include Ennio Morricone's "Paranoia Prima" from *Il gatto a nove code/Cat O'Nine Tails* (1971) and "Violenza Inattesa" from *L'uccello dale piume di cristallo/The Bride with the Crystal Plumage* (1970) — both directed by Dario Argento — and Stelvio Cipriani's song "La Polizia Sta a Guardare" from the film *Tentacoli/Tentacles* (1977), directed by Ovidio G. Assonitis. However, as I go on to discuss below, Rodriguez and Tarantino approach this tradition as elitist "auteurs." The gross-out and grindhouse tradition becomes, in their hands, a cinema of meta-gross-out and meta-grindhouse: the low becomes high. But both directors engage in a double inversion in that the ludic pleasure of these films also lies in their ability to invert "high quality" cinema by allowing the "low-ness" of gross-out/grindhouse to enter the realm of "quality" auteur cinema.[20] For many purists, this act may be perceived as a grotesque one but herein lies its carnivalesque logic, because for Rodriguez, Tarantino, and fans of the *Grindhouse* films, it's in this inversion of the rules that the pleasure is to be found.

While both directors perform a "grotesque" intellectual act by toppling cinematic hierarchies, their films are also literally brimming over with grotesque imagery that's as raw and visceral as those of their generic predecessors, but more reflexively and critically so. Rejecting official perceptions of beauty and "proper" social behavior, the carnivalesque's interest lies instead in the body and in "the lower bodily stratum": orifices, blood, sex, corpses, decay, obscenity, digestion, defecation — all have a role to play in shaking up the established order, and in *Planet Terror* and *Death Proof* the lower bodily stratum remains central to the films' dialogue with the generic universes they play with and unsettle. Both films test the limits of the human body by savagely — and humorlessly — exposing characters to the ritual bodily destruction that's typical of many contemporary horror films. But, whereas Rodriguez plunges his characters into the conventions of the zombie film, Tarantino takes his characters on a journey through slasher and car-chase films. As a result, in addition to critically evaluating the role performed by the human body within the diegetic worlds they construct, both directors are also interested in dissecting the bodies of genre and film: its conventions and the materiality of the medium itself.

The analysis of *Grindhouse: Planet Terror* and *Grindhouse: Death Proof* (the focus of this chapter) sets the scene for the next two chapters, which continue to explore the corporeal and sensory encounters we have with horror media, but also the more cerebral pleasures we can extract through intertextual encounters with media texts. Here I shift the focus on the sensorium away from the more immediate sensory and synaesthetic experiences that horror media can inflict on the spectator and towards the more critical and intellectual processes, which bring with them their own sensory delights. Rodaway makes the point that the tendency to create binaries of the sensory and cognitive processes that operate in human experience propagates a false understanding of perception. "An effective geographical understanding of perception," he explains,

> needs to recognise both dimensions of the term: 1. perception as sensation, and therefore a relationship between person and world, both kinetic and biochemical (here perception is grounded in the environmental stimuli collected and mediated by the senses); and 2. perception as cognition, and therefore as a mental process (here perception involves remembering, recognition, association, and other thinking processes which are culturally mediated).[21]

Perception, therefore, involves a "myriad of different stimuli" that engage both the senses and intellectual engagement simultaneously. It's precisely this interplay that concerns me in this and the following chapters. However, the meta-gross-out logic that gives meaning to these films more reflexively collides the sensory and the intellectual into two intertwined and inseparable processes: to become nauseated at the many graphically exploding or decaying bodies in these films also requires an intellectual consideration about that physiological response and with how that response was created.

Planet Terror and Grotesque Bodies

Early on in *Planet Terror* we're introduced to the chemical engineer Abby who, we soon discover, has a sexual fetish for collecting testicles; he even has an assistant who's responsible for holding the testicle jar. Of course, his sexual urges can only be realized through the violent act of castration. One of the group of men responsible for guarding three zombies held in captivity has unwittingly allowed them to escape, and Abby is not happy. As the group of men swarm around him, Abby proclaims, "I also want your balls" at which point we see one of the men whip out a nasty instrument that looks like a triple-bladed pair of scissors with long, sharp serrations. While we don't witness the act of castration we do see one of the poor victim's balls — freshly detached — thrown towards Abby, who orders his assistant to pick it up. The ball action is, however, interrupted when Lt. Muldoon and his soldiers arrive on the scene, demanding access to the escaped zombies. The meeting doesn't end happily: amidst gunfire and mayhem, Abby's testicle jar falls to the ground and breaks, setting the testicles free. Seconds later, Abby trips and finds himself lying flat on the ground, face down with his balls in his mouth. Such poetry! But this unification of the grotesque and hilarity was, for me, outdone later in the film when Cherry's wooden leg, which had seconds earlier been destroyed in the tangle with Lewis, is replaced by another leg — again, thanks to the canniness of boyfriend Wray. Ripping out the remains of the wooden stump, Wray affectionately tells Cherry how he feels about her and then shoves an automatic submachine gun into the hole in her stump. But do stumps have holes? In a masterful act of displacement that would do any limping patriarch from a film noir proud, this sexually charged act is soon put into action when Cherry tries out her revamped phallic member by pumping a mega-load of bullets into a group of attacking soldiers, ripping each and every one of them apart (fig. 17).

Figure 17: The ex-exotic dancer Cherry (Rose McGowan) tries on her new automatic rifle limb in *Planet Terror* (Dimensions Films, 2007) (Kobal Collection).

William Paul argues that in gross-out films (and I'd add the grindhouse exploitation tradition from which it emerged), "Aggression is the keynote ... as these films assaulted us with images of outrageously violent or sexual behavior, or violently sexual, or sexually violent."[22] Sex and violence figure prominently in grindhouse horror and not only do they frequently overlap, but they often become confused, and they always do so in bad taste. A similar confusion of sex and violence is explored in *Death Proof* in which Stuntman Mike's muscle car (first a 1970 Chevrolet Nova SS [fig. 18], later a 1969 Dodge Charger) is understood by its owner as an extension of his manhood; the use of his stunt car to stalk, terrorize and kill women is an act that he associates with his sexual potency. The film drives this point home savagely in the scene in which Mike drives toward a group of girls. In the buildup to the head-on collision, the camera repeats an action it's performed many times during the film: like Stuntman Mike, the camera lingers frequently and longingly along one of Jungle Julia's sexy, long limbs as it hangs carelessly out of the car window. But this sexualized shot is violently ripped from the spectator's vision as the two cars collide and Jungle Julia's leg is viciously torn from her body and is shown gliding in slow motion through the air until it lands shockingly on the road.

For Bakhtin, grotesque realism tests the limits of the body and our relationship to it. "Against the static, classic, finished beauty of antique sculpture, Bakhtin counterposed the mutable body" that's capable of change and which

Figure 18: The killer Stuntman Mike (Kurt Russell) in his 1970 Chevy Nova SS in the film *Death Proof* (Dimensions Films, 2007) (Kobal Collection).

is in continuous dialogue with the world around it. "The grotesque body is not a rigid langue, but a parole in constant semiosis."[23] The collision of sex and violence in these scenes speaks to this constant semiosis, in this case between states of life and death. Cherry's transition from sad pole dancer with two legs, to terrorized victim with one wooden leg, to triumphant killer of zombies with one submachine gun leg speaks about the literal and psychological shifts that have taken place in her body and sense of self. An act that represents the fragility of life (the violent removal of her leg) is transformed into a symbol of renewal. The gross act of Wray ramming first the wooden table leg and then the submachine gun into Cherry's stump is further paralleled by the hammy love scene in which the two engage in the Bone Shack, which eventually leads to the generation of new life in the form of the baby that Cherry carries on her back at the end of the film.

But none of this is expressed in a serious way. The narrative action is textured throughout with explosions of blood, revolting corpses, enormous erupting pustules, bodies that are torn to pieces, and disgusting beings that feast on living flesh. Even the schmaltzy love-making scene between Cherry and Wray occurs against the grotesque backdrop of J.T.'s Bone Shack[24] with its filthy surfaces and barbequed meats and sauces that resemble the surfaces of the decayed, putrefying flesh of the living dead. Bakhtin's argument regarding the dehierarchization of the senses is seen in full force here. The spectator isn't only assaulted by the excess audio-visual spectacle, the audio-visual senses also trigger synaesthetic alliances with touch, taste and smell. For example, seeing the disgusting pus-filled abscess on the bite-victim Joe's tongue and listening to the squishy, wet sounds as he squeezes his tongue and pops the contents gives way to taste and touch when he wipes the filthy, oozing matter onto Dr. William Block's face. Likewise, the entire interior of the Bone Shack with its emphasis on browns and reds evokes the smell and taste of J.T.'s barbequed meats and sauces, but the smells and tastes so easily slip to be associated with rotting zombie flesh. In fact, when the zombies finally invade the Bone Shack, it's hard to distinguish the meat sources — a point driven home in the scene in which J.T. is found lying behind the bar, presumably dead with his dog munching on what seem to be his intestines, and seconds later we discover that he was unconscious and the intestines were actually BBQ sausages and sauce! The hyperbolic nature of most scenes in *Planet Terror* sends our sensory engagement with the film into hyperdrive, but while we intensely respond with repulsion to the grotesqueness on display, we're also simultaneously overcome by the hilarious ludicrousness of what we're experiencing.

According to Bakhtin, "Pre-Romanticism and Romanticism witnessed a revival of the grotesque genre but with a radically transformed meaning. It became the expression of subjective, individualistic world outlook very different from the carnival folk concept of previous ages, although still containing some carnival elements."[25] Unlike the medieval and Renaissance grotesque, which possessed a ludic quality that encouraged the participation of the group, the Romantic (and, in most cases, the Gothic) grotesque "acquired a private 'chamber' character. It became, as it were, an individual carnival, marked by a vivid sense of isolation."[26] The laughter that was essential to grotesque realism was transformed into "cold humor, irony, sarcasm" with the result that it "ceased to be a joyful and triumphant hilarity" that possessed regenerative powers, which were at the center of the carnival spirit.[27] He expands by exploring the different attitudes in relation to terror:

> The world of Romantic grotesque is to a certain extent a terrifying world, alien to man. All that is ordinary, commonplace, belonging to everyday life, and recognized by all suddenly becomes meaningless, dubious and hostile.... If a reconciliation with the world occurs, it takes place in a subjective, lyric, or even mystic sphere. On the other hand, the medieval and Renaissance folk culture was familiar with the element of terror only as represented by comic monsters, who were defeated by laughter. Terror was turned into something gay and comic. Folk culture brought the world close to man, gave it a bodily form, and established a link through the body and bodily life, in contrast to the abstract and spiritual mastery sought by Romanticism. Images of bodily life, such as eating, drinking, copulation, defecation, almost entirely lost their regenerating power and were turned into "vulgarities."[28]

The gross-put and grindhouse traditions embrace the regenerative power of these "vulgarities" with "joyful and triumphant hilarity."

William Paul makes an interesting observation when he points out that, whereas Sigmund Freud argued that civilization itself is built on the repression of baser drives and desires controlled by the lower bodily stratum, Bakhtin celebrated the unleashing of that which, according to Freud, should be repressed.

> Because Bakhtin's concept of the grotesque reverses this formulation by assenting the ascendancy of the body, it in effect offers a challenge to the very foundations of civilization. For this reason it is at least understandable why works that aggressively elevate the low may be regarded as dangerous since in Freudian terms they celebrate the return of the repressed. In a sense these works are dangerous to the ways we think of ourselves as civilized people.... Grotesque humor as Bakhtin defines it is both less purposeful but ultimately more radical.[29]

According to William Paul, gross-out horror movies "make the audience laugh, make the audience scream, make it scream with laughter, make it laugh in terror, create a 'laff riot' or a 'screamfest' to stir up the pleasure of pandemonium. In short, these films seek to create a festive, communal atmosphere in the theater" and they have much in common with the fun house at the fairground.[30] Films like *Dawn of the Dead, Child's Play, Halloween, A Nightmare on Elm Street* and *Friday the 13th* aim at producing "a special kind of pleasure that derives from disruption, an abrupt challenge to the nervous system. This is a pleasure akin to what a child feels when a parent suddenly says 'Boo!' There is a jolt of surprise, followed by giddy laughter, and then a desire for the whole thing to happen all over again."[31] Comparing the experience to that in a fun house, the combined responses of laughter and horror are about trying to gain mastery over the scares that wait to frighten the participant within the fun house maze or the spectator within a film scene. Part of the pleasure of horror comes from the confusion of reality and representation or, rather, the interplay between the two. "These pleasures, then, present an undermining of our ordinary sense that we can process reality in a way that makes us certain of our place in it," and comedy becomes key to this undermining process.[32] The audience lets loose and celebrates the anti-social and uncivilized within a controlled environment and, for a contained amount of time, making possible a "regenerated" return to the social sphere. Ultimately, then, the liminality of the carnival space — despite its potential for radical change — is seen by Paul as reinforcing the social status quo.

Since the 1970s the contemporary horror film has become a highly ritualized form. Films like *Night of the Living Dead, Halloween* and *Friday the 13th* have inspired an endless stream of highly formulaic sequels and knockoffs — some good, some not so good. As Vera Dika explains in her study of the stalker film, part of the pleasure for the audience of these films comes from their literacy regarding the conventions, which are formulaic in the extreme. According to Dika, the most distinctive element of the audience's relationship to the stalker film comes from their familiarity with the subgenre's highly formulaic conventions and the way these films then tease the audience with this familiarity by hiding the presence of the psycho-killer.

> This manipulation of expectations has been known to elicit a voiced response from the audience. Viewers shout warnings to the film's victims, but, strangely, they do not seem to be overly concerned for the victims' welfare. Instead, the young spectators greet the gruesome events on screen with open enthusiasm, cheering and laughing, and dividing their support primarily between the heroine and the killer.[33]

However, like Paul, Dika also attributes this enthusiasm and laughter to the deeper cultural function that's provided by the stalker film's formulaic structure. For Dika, the conventions serve a ritualistic, unconscious function that's associated with the mythic structures outlined by the structural anthropologist Claude Levi-Strauss: such repetitions are understood as addressing the unconscious fears and drives of the social group and, in the case of the stalker film, its "greatest success" is achieved "at a transitional period in American history" that follows the loss and guilt of the Vietnam war which was proceeded by the faltering economy, the failure of the Carter administration and the Iranian hostage crisis.[34] These films are seen as the audience rehearsing an attempted mastery over that which is socially threatening, both within and beyond the film. What both Dika and, to a lesser extent Paul, fail to recognize about many examples of contemporary horror is that the laughter can also be about the audience's celebration of their familiarity with the conventions, the way horror can also undermine those expectations, and the thrills and scares the genre can offer them. The pleasures offered by gross-out and grindhouse films aren't necessarily about addressing deeper cultural or psychic needs and desires. Most often, these films direct themselves to an audience whose pleasure derives from horror-philia.

Discussing the ultra-gore torture porn or "gorn" subgenre, Brenda Cromb considers the audience's reaction to films like *Saw*. "If anything," she explains, these films are

> reinforced by constant references to earlier films of which most horror fans would be aware.... It is my position—backed by suggestions in both scholarship on comedy and horror—that the real unease produced by these films is in the desire to laugh at the clear visceral pain in what remain, frankly, ridiculous situations, a desire fed by the films' frank and unapologetic refusal of good taste.[35]

Seeing a link between the 1970s and '80s gross-out horror films, she reiterates Paul's position and suggests that "the line between 'body horror' and 'body comedy' is very fine." Cromb's point is that "while the films individually can certainly be mobilized in terms of political meaning, the impact of the cycle as a whole has to be understood in terms of its visceral impact and the way this impact functions. This ability to disgust and willingness to aesthetically transgress the boundaries of good taste—without necessarily being ideologically transgressive—is both the reason for gorno's critical failure and its central appeal."[36] I'd extend Cromb's observations to an analysis of both the stalker and living-dead subgenres, both being the focus of Rodriguez and Tarantino's films, respectively. But both directors bump this reflexivity regarding viscerality and transgression up a notch.

Meta-Genericity: "The one who writes is the same as the one who reads"[37]

In a scene in *Death Proof*, soon after we and the film's psycho-killer Stuntman Mike have been introduced to all the main female protagonists of the first part of the film, Mike loads up his first victim into his car and, as the second group of victims get into their car and drive off, Mike casually takes a final drag from his cigarette and watches them go. Before getting into the car he turns, looks directly at the camera/spectator and smiles. Not only does he know, but he acknowledges that we also know that the game is finally on. Like the *Saw* and *Hostel* series, horror films like *28 Weeks Later* and *Halloween* can be understood as critiquing and signaling the destruction of the social order, While *Planet Terror* and *Death Proof* acknowledge the "serious" narrative dimensions of the living-dead and stalker/slasher subgenres and make them into theatrical performances that are about the carnivalization of the horror genre. As will be discussed in the next chapter, much in the same way that Sam Raimi toys with the generic rules of horror in the *Evil Dead* trilogy and *Drag Me to Hell* (2009), Rodriguez and Tarantino are interested in bringing generic conventions to the surface so they may be investigated, undermined, laughed at and rewritten. For Bakhtin, the carnivalesque is inherently revolutionary: "It is the oppositional culture of the oppressed, a countermodel of cultural production and desire. It offers a view of the official world as seen from below — not the mere disruption of etiquette but as a symbolic, anticipatory overthrow of oppressive social structures."[38] If we understand many of the examples in the grindhouse and gross-out tradition as operating like modern-day carnivals, we can definitely see how their chaotic response to social rules and bodily decorum are indeed disruptive. But the *Grindhouse* duo engages the spectator in a carnivalesque game that's about the body of genre itself: how it produces meaning and the intense sensorial responses that remain central to that meaning. The chaos and destruction occurs not in relation to the social but in relation to the "oppressive" and formulaic rules and conventions that are specific to both genres.

Above, I discuss how, according to Bakhtin, a radical shift occurred in the culture of laughter and carnival. While expunged from the official culture of the Church and aristocracy, the carnival spirit continued along two paths: the first belonged to the low genres of folk culture while the second saw the carnivalesque enter "the sphere of great literature and high ideology."[39] Contemporary horror cinema has taken a journey along both paths: it's a genre that is critically placed amongst the lower stratum of generic forms, but it's also a genre that's attracted many an auteur — John Carpenter, Tobe Hooper, Wes Craven, George Romero, Sam Raimi — a fact that also shifts it into the "higher" domain of, if not great literature, then great cinema. This ambivalence inherent to the genre is attested to by the schizophrenic attitude that met one of the most influential modern horror films, *Night of the Living Dead*. On its release is 1968 it was critiqued as bringing a new low to the exploitation film. A review in *Variety* in the same year called it an "unrelieved orgy of sadism." The film was doing its run in grungy grindhouse theaters, while simultaneously being shown at the Museum of Modern Art in New York. As is explained on the MoMA website, "MoMA was one of the first institutions to screen *Night of the Living Dead*, honoring Romero in a Cineprobe program in 1970, years before the film achieved commercial success via its cult status" and in 1980 the film entered MoMA's collection.[40] In *Grindhouse,* Rodriguez and Tarantino clearly wanted to present an homage to this earlier exploitation tradition of horror by reviving it for modern-day audiences, but both directors were also aware of the fact that, as cult auteurs, their films would appear in both mainstream and art-house cinemas. It's from this vantage point that's the equivalent of "the sphere of great literature" that Rodriguez and Tarantino facilitate a dialogue with the grindhouse and gross-out horror. The inversion of the rules of generic hierarchies and transference of the "low" into the realm of the "high" becomes a source of über-cinephilia; the directors and spectators take gleeful delight in the recognition that both *Planet Terror* and *Death Proof* acknowledge the artistic merit and critical reflexiveness that's always been integral to the contemporary horror film.

As indicated by Bakhtin, it was the 18th-century genre of the novel (for example, the works of Dostoyevsky) that continued the efforts of Rabelais and Cervantes in transferring the methods of carnival culture into "the sphere of great literature." The key strategies he focuses on relate to the inclusion of "extraliterary heteroglossia" and "layers of literary language" that become "dialogized, permeated with laughter, irony, humor, elements of self-parody," all of which emphasize an openendedness that stresses process.[41] Intertextuality, or what Bakhtin calls dialogism, becomes integral to a practice that's about the generic process of the novel and how its meaning is constructed: external texts it brings into its universe through allusion and external references that are introduced so they may be altered or questioned — all engage in a dialogic process that resists the static and the fixed. In the words of Bakhtin. "Only that which is itself developing can comprehend development as a process."[42] But the novel not only generates a dialogic relationship with other contemporary and past examples external to it, it also relies on a dialogic relationship with its reader: "Understanding comes to fruition only in the response. Understanding and response are dialectically melded and mutually condition each other, one is impossible without the other."[43]

Bakhtin's ideas about the dialogic process that's both internal to the text and external to it in the relationship forged between text, writer and reader have a great deal to tell us about the intertextual practices that operate in *Planet Terror* and *Death Proof* between the directors, films and audience. Roland Barthes famously proclaimed that all texts are intertexts and there is much value in understanding genres in this way. Genres rely on audience familiarity with their conventions and rules; when particular formulas are repeated the viewer recognizes their meaning, and when expectation of a formula is introduced in order to be undermined, the generic pool of conventions expands as a result of the introduction of a new convention. As mentioned, genericity, eclecticism and intertextuality have become key to understanding the saturated and self-aware nature of contemporary genre films, but contemporary horror films allude to and draw attention to the rituals and conventions of their form far more self-consciously when compared to other genres. This is a highly theatricalized genre that directs itself self-consciously to its spectator's horror-philia. Extending the ideas of Bakhtin, Julia Kristeva has observed that the carnival

> is a spectacle, but without a stage: a game, but also a daily undertaking; a signifier, but also a signified. That is, two texts meet, contradict, and relativize each other. A carnival participant is both actor and spectator; he loses his sense of individuality, passes through a zero point of carnivalesque activity and splits into a subject of the spectacle and an object of the game.... The scene of the carnival, where there is no stage, no "theater," is thus both stage and life, game and dream, discourse and spectacle. By the same token, it is proffered as the only space in which language escapes linearity to live as drama in three dimensions.[44]

Planet Terror and *Death Proof* bargain precisely on this spectacle that is theater without a stage (a form of spectacle to which I'll return in the final chapter on transmedia, where the stage quite literally vanishes). But extending the theatrical nature of horror, these films display a meta-genericity that's central to the spectator's horror-philic and, even more broadly, cinephilic desire to play. The audience is drawn into a game about generic signification and this becomes, for this spectator at least, the source of ultimate pleasure. The game is an intellectual one that also happens to rely on conventions that display visceral thrills as well as textual signifiers. So many sequences in the film draw attention to generic signifiers that are loaded with signification about the diegetic world, about the living-dead film conventions, about narrative rules, about special-effects conventions, about character types and their function.

Earlier in this chapter and in Chapter One I discussed the social subtext that often underlies the zombie film, and *Planet Terror* is no exception. Near the end of the film, Wray meets Lt. Muldoon, leader of the infected military group. Muldoon exclaims in an abbreviated style that could only be performed with such punch by Bruce Willis: "You want the story? I'll spin it for you quick," and so he does. While he and his team were on the Afghan border they found Bin Laden and "put two in his head" but the victory turned sour when they were exposed to the chemical weapon that was DC2. No sooner has he finished his heart-wrenching tale than he begins to transform into a deformed mass of decaying, bubbling flesh. Wray points a gun at him and proclaims, "God bless you and your service to this country!" before popping him one. Responding to the convention typical of many living-dead films, Rodriguez provides the monster's appearance with a social rationale, in this instance U.S. military involvement in Afghanistan and the war against Bin Laden. Films like *Dawn of the Dead* (Zack Snyder, 2004), *Day of the Dead* (Steve Miner, 2008) and *Land of the Dead* (George A. Romero, 2005) suggest that the emergence of the monster is the symbolic manifestation of global terror and religious fanaticism, government corruption and experimentation with biochemicals, and out-of-control corporatization; and the narrative actions and characterizations sustain this reading. In the case of *Planet Terror*, the convention that stresses the theme of society in a state of disorder is brought to the surface, but only to parody the convention. In doing so, Rodriguez draws attention to the social rationale for the appearance of the living dead as a convention and nothing more. The zombies' metaphorical link to "actual" social reality is introduced in order that its function within the subgenre can be examined. As Kristeva explains, the signifier becomes the signified.

In an earlier scene, Cherry and Wray participate in a cliché-to-the-max love scene that comes equipped with corny dialogue ("Why'd you leave?" "'Cause you didn't believe in us anymore") and formulaic editing that weeds out everything but the "special" lovemaking moments. Soon into this sequence, however, the film shutter jams and the film burns to nothing, soon to be replaced by this text: "Missing Reel. Sorry for the Inconvenience. Theater Management." Such mishaps involving damaged or missing reels were typical of grindhouse cinema experiences but this scene both serves to draw attention to its cinematic heritage and to film-narrative conventions. On returning to the story, the audience is forced to fill in the narrative gaps that they should have seen in the missing reel and it becomes very clear that viewer expectation fills the missing gaps very effectively: the transformation of Earl's invalid wife into a zombie; the accidental death of Dakota's son, Tony; Dr. Block's transformation into a zombie and his attack on Dakota; the revelation that Earl is Dakota's father — none of these new bits of story information are continued because their introduction presents the viewer with the essential bits of story information further details would only clutter the narrative (which isn't, let's face it, the main concern of this film). So out it goes with the missing reel and when the next reel continues all survivors magically find themselves holed up at the Bone Shack. In addition, up until this point the narrative had placed emphasis on Wray's dark and mysterious past but had provided no details about that past; it was also made clear that Sheriff Hague and Wray had a history because the sheriff makes no secret of his hatred for Wray. When we jump to the next reel, we realize that the answer to these questions is missing. As the sheriff's wounds are tended to (he was wounded in the missing reel), the following exchange occurs:

> *Sheriff*: Thank you for telling me about ... you know ...
> *Wray*: Don't mention it. That's an order!
> *Sheriff*: If I'd known you were "El" Wray I wouldn't have given you such a hard time about it.

Asking one of the assistant sheriffs to return "El" Wray's weapons, El Wray shows his gratitude by putting on a show with some hifalutin gun action, and J.T. caps it all off by hilariously exclaiming: "That boy's got the devil in him!" Who is El Wray? Why does he have the devil in him? We don't know and it doesn't matter. All that matters is that we know he's a badass with a history and that he'll get them through the zombie invasion.

Planet Terror revels in its evocation of both a narrative and stylistic materiality that suggests it belongs in the 1970s. The narrative premise, the acting styles, the comedy/horror focus, the mise-en-scène, the film scratches and dust on the film surface, the fake preview trailers showing classic grindhouse fare such as *Machete* ("He was given an offer he couldn't refuse!" "Set up, double crossed and left for dead") — all evoke a time gone by. But the nostalgic fetishization of a film materiality that existed over 30 years ago is a deceptive one. The intertextual referencing that harks back to the 1970s is present so that it can then be scrutinized and commented on: Rodriguez consciously sets up a dialogic relationship between past and present in the film and invites the audience to enter the dialogue. For example, in a scene early in the film we're introduced to Dr. William Block (Josh Brolin) and Dr. Dakota Block (Marley Shelton) — their home décor appears to be straight out of the 1970s, as do the enormous hair rollers in Dakota's hair, but time jumps three decades when Dakota, surrounded by the mise-en-scène of her retro kitchen, reaches for her cell phone and sends a text message to an ex-lover. This act thrusts the film forward into the first decade of the 21st century. (Tarantino uses the cell phone as a prop that evokes the current era in a similar way in *Death Proof*.)

But Rodriguez pushes this dialogue between past and present further still. In fact, he sets the scene in the opening-title sequence, which intercuts Cherry Darling's pole dance with the film titles. "Our feature presentation," complete with noisy and scratched film frames sets the scene for *Planet Terror*. The Dimension Films logo appears out of focus and is then refocused, giving the impression that someone in the projection booth is responsible, while all the while we can hear the sound of the film running through the projector gate and shutter. The words "A Robert Rodriguez Film" appear onscreen and falter through the shutter, the motion affecting the focus. More titles follow, all scratched and damaged, appearing to have suffered the wear and tear of grindhouse repeat screenings, and are soon intercut with the figure of Cherry Darling as she dances to the theme music of *Planet Terror*—written by

Rodriguez and intertextually referencing the music of horrormeister John Carpenter. As Cherry dances, her kicks often signaling the entry or exit of further titles, the shots are intercut with quick snatches of burning celluloid as if, as Caitlin Benson-Allott states, her fiery dance sets the film itself aflame.[45]

This opening sequence isn't merely an homage to a cinematic past, it's also a comment on the materiality of film itself and to the nature of the cinematic apparatus in the early 21st century. Here the audience is confronted with a grotesque carnival that's about the body of film as a medium: what we see is an illusion — a point further echoed in Cherry's doubling in the reflected mirror. Despite its heavy emphasis on a 1970s exploitation film aesthetic, nothing "filmic" is actually present in this scene or any other scene because the entire film is the product of digital technology: the burning celluloid, the film scratches and dirt, the shutter that stalls and traps the film sprockets, the jump cuts that connote jumps in the projector or sections of damaged film that were spliced out — everything was created by the special-effects division (Troublemaker Digital) of Rodriguez's Troublemaker Studios. This fact is even more playfully exposed during the film's end titles where film celluloid is frequently layered, film sprockets are visible and, projector's light shines through them — physically impossible states if they were the product of film technology.

Addressing herself to the status of the film as an example of a new digital cinema, Benson-Allott states that "this sequence acknowledges the significance of apparatus in the creation of affect, and Rodriguez repeats the move elsewhere in his film to add meaning to his ostentatious use of CGI."[46] She continues:

> *Planet Terror's* insistence on its cinematic history is also the *raison d'être* of its special effects, turning the latter into a digital homage to both a bygone platform (celluloid) and a bygone genre (the exploitation film). In fact, these digital excesses celebrate a specific subgenre of exploitation film, namely splatter cinema, a derivative of Italian art horror. Like early splatter, Rodriguez's film wants to look at what the flesh can do (as opposed to *Death Proof's* interest in what it can withstand), the various fluids it can ooze, ways it can break, and decays it can manage ... *Planet Terror* is not actually particularly interested in frightening its viewer (as *Death Proof* will); rather it pursues the uncomfortable sensation an audience might experience when shown potentials in the human body that they have never seen before. What matters is showmanship and the way humor can emphasize the mortification of the flesh.[47]

Yes, the film is concerned with exploring and exposing the grotesque limits of flesh and the human body, but it's also fascinated with exploring the grotesque limits of the flesh that is the film medium and that of the digital medium. The final product that is *Planet Terror* is like a zombie that's consumed both a film heritage and film itself; cannibalizing its predecessors, it vomits out a digital reincarnation that signals a new era of digital cinema. To reframe Bakhtin's terms, *Planet Terror* carnivalizes its sources — all of which represent the "official" voice of 1970s exploitation horror — and creates a new being that uses the living dead in order to present a dialogue about genre, the film medium and the digital era. In the process, it is both homage and virtuoso performance that outdoes the past — a point delivered with great mastery when one of the sheriff's assistants is literally pulled apart by three zombies. The assistant is played by Tom Savini, one of the guru "old school" special effects and make-up experts who reigned in the 1970s and '80s, producing the body explosions and horrific effects in films that included *Dawn of the Dead* (1978), *Friday the 13th* (1978), *Creepshow* (1982) and *Day of the Dead* (1985). Savini stands as representative of an earlier tradition of special effects technology in horror cinema and the de(con)struction of his body becomes a carnival act that also marks the de(con)struction of the ruler that was film and "old school" special effects.

In "Heteroglossia in the Novel," Kristeva elaborates on Bakhtin's arguments regarding dialogism and the novel, explaining that this is an active process that circulates between author and text, text and other texts, text and reader and author and reader. A heteroglossic dialogue is set in place and produces multiple voices that interact with, complement, contradict and even deconstruct one another. From the perspective of generic process and reception, the implications are significant in that genre is understood as a state that is always dynamic and its dynamism relies on an audience that's aware of the significance of generic conventions.

> The relationship of the author to a language conceived as the common view is not static — it is always found in a state of movement and oscillation that is more or less alive (this sometimes is a rhythmic oscillation): the author exaggerates, now strongly now weakly, one or another aspect of the "common language," sometimes abruptly exposing its Inadequacy to its object and sometimes, on the contrary becoming one with it, maintaining an almost imperceptible distance, sometimes even directly forcing it to reverberate with his own "truth," which occurs when the author completely merges his own voice with the common view.[48]

Rodriguez relies on a common language that radiates around the grindhouse horror and zombie film tradition and then invites the spectator to participate in a game about that common language; but he also makes clear that no matter how nostalgically he plays with and reproduces the formulas and repetitive formal structures of the 1970s films, his film can never turn back the hands of time and fully "belong" to that period. Genre, as Bakhtin puts it, is always in a process of "becoming" and in the case of *Planet Terror*, the "becoming" is grounded in the current period of digital filmmaking and special effects.

Über-Cinephilia, *Death Proof* and the Slasher Film

In *Death Proof*, Tarantino has a similar agenda to that of Rodriguez: his primary concern is to expose the ever-changing, dialogic process of genre. But rather than being interested in CGI and digital film (upon which he refuses to rely) Tarantino is interested in exploding the narrative logic of the slasher/stalker from within. The film examines and teases the audiences with its conventions — its "common language" — and then injects new elements taken from other exploitation genres, especially rape-revenge, carsploitation and girl-gang films. The result is that *Death Proof* stands as a reaction against and rewriting of the slasher convention that places the girl as passive victim of the psycho-killer. Tarantino's intention is supported by interviews where in he expresses his interest in Carol Clover's classic text on the slasher film — *Men, Women, and Chain Saws: Gender in the Modern Horror Film*. Like Jean-Luc Godard, whom he admires immensely, Tarantino isn't interested in producing films that offer commentary on reality: he makes films that are about film — film reality is the only reality. In an interview he explains:

> One thing that shows that I'm a film professor or student is that you are not gonna find many other filmmakers looking at this kind of thing. I love subtextual film criticism, especially when it's fun, when a guy knows how to write in a readable, charming way.... In a weird way this goes back to Death Proof, because one of the biggest inspirations for the film, especially the first half of the movie — the more slasher-oriented section — was Carol Clover's book Men, Women and Chainsaws. I really truly think that her chapter on the "final girl," the role that gender plays in the slasher film, pins down the best piece of film criticism I've ever read. It gave me a new love for slasher films and one of the things that I was doing when I was watching that movie was applying her lessons.[49]

Tarantino develops a dialogue about the conventions of the slasher-horror film tradition; hybridizing the conventions by injecting elements of car-chase and girl-action films, he takes the slasher film into entirely new directions. In a very real sense, *Death Proof* is emblematic of the slasher film subgenre, but is also anything but a straight genre film: instead, it's a film about generic process and about filmic reality.

As is the case with *Planet Terror*, the film is brimming over with references to the grindhouse tradition and to the cinema in general. The walls of the Taco Bar, for example, are littered with film posters (mostly Mexican), some having direct connections with *Death Proof*, and others having none: *El Car-*

naval de la Muerte, the Spanish version of *The Hanged Man* (1964), a revenge film directed by Don Siegel for television, which alludes to *Death Proof*'s link with vengeance plots common to action and horror cinema; *King Kong* (Merian C. Cooper, 1933) an early horror film that transfers the female character's fear about male sexuality onto the body of an actual beast; the low-budget classic *Robot Monster* (Phil Tucker, 1953), whose plot involves a robot monster that's used his death ray to destroy all but eight humans on Earth who are immune as a result of an antibiotic — presumably an allusion to the plot of *Planet Terror*; and a poster for *Las Tres Elenas* (Emillo Gomez Muriel, 1954), a Mexican melodrama about three women named Elena, hangs behind the three main female characters as they sit drinking in the Taco Bar. Grindhouse references riddle the film: from the soundtrack that plays themes from horror films; to characters who wear T-shirts that feature Tura Satana's character from the girl-gang film *Faster Pussycat! Kill! Kill!*; to characters who mention the car-chase classics *Vanishing Point* (Richard C. Sarafian, 1971), *Death Race 2000* (Paul Bartel, 1975), *Dirty Mary, Crazy Larry* (John Hough, 1974) and *Convoy* (Sam Peckinpah, 1978), whose main character Martin "Rubber Duck" Penwald inspires the duck hood ornament on Stuntman Mike's car; to the nickname of Lee's boyfriend "Toolbox" that refers to the exploitation horror film *Toolbox Murders* (Dennis Donnelly, 1978).

The contemporary horror context also fills the mise-en-scène of the film and the films *Wolf Creek* (2005), *Dawn of the Dead* (2006), *Saw III* (2006), *Scary Movie 4* (2006), *Pan's Labyrinth* (2006), *The Texas Chainsaw Massacre: The Beginning* (2006), *The Grudge 2* (2006), *The Hills Have Eyes 2* (2007), *Pumpkinhead: Ashes to Ashes* (2006), *28 Weeks Later* (2007) and *Resident Evil: Extinction* (2007) are discussed, appear on the cover of magazines, or are seen on billboards — and gorn guru Eli Roth even appears as Dov, one of the girls' male friends. Beyond the grindhouse and horror references, intertextual references are also made to Tarantino's films — *Reservoir Dogs* (in the 360-degree tracking shot that circles Lee, Zoe, Kim and Abernathy in the café); *Pulp Fiction* (Stuntman Mike refers to the Big Cahuna Burger from *Pulp Fiction* [1994]); and the character Earl McGraw the Texas Ranger appears in *Planet Terror* and *Kill Bill vol. 1*, while also appearing as the same character in Rodriguez's *From Dusk Till Dawn* (1996). Rodriguez makes similar, but not as obsessive, allusions to the fictional worlds of other films. In one scene, for example, Dr. William Block treats one of the zombie bite victims, Joe, and his wife, Dakota, is asked to fetch the needles. At this point in the film we're already suspicious that he's unbalanced and dangerous. Dakota enters her office and grabs the needles, at which point I noticed (on my third or fourth viewing) a notebook on her desk. Freezing the image I noted that this was Dakota's "To do" list, and it listed the following:

- Get cereal for Tony
- Crickets for Tony's pets
- Kill BILL

Of course the "Bill" mentioned refers both to her maniac husband, and to the Tarantino double *Kill Bill* (2003–04).

Discussing the Kill Bill films, Maximilian Le Cain states:

> In *Kill Bill* ... the audience is constantly, winkingly reminded that what it is watching is "only" a movie. This postmodern distance gives rise to if not exactly a critical distance, then a pedagogical one. What *Kill Bill* offers is a lesson in cinema history that unites several genres in a loving, mannerist monument to the films that made Tarantino's cinephilia as powerful a driving force as it evidently is for him. We are not looking at an alternative reality, but an actual existing reality or, rather, realities — those contained in the history of certain movie genres, each with its own folklore and ethical procedures.[50]

Death Proof typifies the level of media literacy that's required of contemporary audiences and, as director and film fan, Tarantino ups the ante on this media literacy, in effect making this a film about film. His films reflect on the inherent dialogical nature of their form, creating a game out of the fact that all films rely on intertextual processes. In addition to curating a mini-exhibition of films that influenced him by displaying their images and music across the mise-en-scène and soundtrack, *Death Proof* is also an exploration of cinematic styles. At numerous points in the film Tarantino establishes a dialogue between the low-budget aesthetics that typified both the French New Wave and grindhouse cinema and, in doing so, invites the audience to ponder on the aesthetic parallels that connect the two. He frequently uses the jump cut — a technique favored by Jean-Luc Godard — but in *Death Proof* it takes on a double significance that creates a dialogic loop between grindhouse and early art-house cinematic styles. For example, in one of the scenes in the Texas Chilli Parlor the girls sit around talking and drinking and Arlene tells them she's going outside for a smoke. In the same shot, she grabs one cigarette from the packet and her lighter and the shot cuts to what appears to be a reverse jump cut: the action has rolled back a few seconds and we see Arlene grab her cigarettes and lighter again. And yet, this isn't the film simply reversing and replaying in time, as if trapped in the projector, jumping and replaying the action. In the second version, Arlene takes the entire packet of cigarettes and her lighter. This simple yet masterful act (the existence of two instances of the same event that occur in separate spatio-temporal realities) collapses art cinema and exploitation into each other. The scene can be interpreted as an art-cinema strategy — à la Godard — that reminds us that what we're watching is a representation that's controlled and manipulated by the filmmaker in order to produce a semblance of reality. Or it can be interpreted as bad continuity editing — a common practice in grindhouse exploitation films. Probably more so than *Planet Terror*, engagement with *Death Proof* exists on two levels: on one level we can immerse ourselves in its story, while on another we follow a story that's about the creation of meaning in film.

The same applies to the way the film establishes an exchange with the genres upon which it draws. *Death Proof* is an exploration of the slasher film, but this exploration occurs in dialogue with other generic conventions, in particular, car-chase and rape-revenge action films. Know little about these genres and film history and you'll only be able to engage with the film on the level of story and the gut wrenching sensory thrills on which the story takes you. Know a great deal about these traditions and you'll be offered an intellectual puzzle to be solved, one that requires you to actively untangle and make meaning of what Tarantino is doing with the conventions from different genres and whether, ultimately, he's expanded the rules of the slasher film. Tarantino takes the audience on a journey through the contemporary horror film, in particular the slasher heritage initiated by Alfred Hitchcock in *Psycho* (1960) and shaped into its modern incarnation by John Carpenter in *Halloween* (1978). Mixing it up with allusions to rape revenge and car-chase films, what's presented through this grindhouse palimpsest of allusions and revisions is the reclaiming of girl power.

The slasher film's plot is one of the most consistently formulaic of sub-genres. Early examples include *Texas Chainsaw Massacre* (Tobe Hooper, 1974), *Halloween* (John Carpenter, 1978), *Friday the 13th* (Sean S. Cunningham, 1980), *Happy Birthday to Me* (J. Lee Thompson, 1981), and *The Funhouse* (Tobe Hooper, 1981), with later variations to the subgenre including *Nightmare on Elm Street* (Wes Craven, 1984), *Scream* (Wes Craven, 1996), *I Know What you Did Last Summer* (Jim Gillespie, 1997) and their sequels. Both Vera Dika and Carol Clover have written about the stalker/slasher film: Clover's analysis is more open, while Dika's is specifically focused on the period of 1978–81. Even so, there is agreement about the basic plot and character structure of these films. Usually beginning in the past, the killer's first act of violence and his (or, at times, her) making is presented. Jumping to the future, the audience is introduced to a group of young people, most being marked as future victims of the killer due to their sexual promiscuity or character flaws. One member of the group — most often a female but sometimes, as in the case of Ash from *Evil Dead*, male — is set aside as different to the rest (usually through her independence, lack of promiscuity, levelheadedness, etc.), and is also seen as different by the psycho-killer who saves her as the final victim to be hunted. Arming himself with phallic weapons (knives, chainsaws, hatchets, cleavers), he hunts and savagely murders everyone in the social group, until the final female survivor (who Clover calls the "final girl") remains. She battles

Figure 19: Friends (Sydney Poitier, Michael Bacall, Jordan Ladd, Eli Roth, Omar Doom and Vanessa Ferlito) enjoy drinks hours before the girls face death at the hands of Stuntman Mike. *Death Proof* (Dimension Films, 2007).

the psycho-killer and finally defeats him (most often by adopting phallic objects as weapons), even though the killer often survives to reappear in the sequel.

Death Proof is separated into two parts, and the narratives of both focus on a group of female protagonists. In the first part, the friends Arlene, Shanna, and "Jungle" Julia (a famous local DJ) (fig. 19), go out for a night on the town to celebrate Jungle Julia's birthday but this, we're told, is to be followed by a trip to a lake house somewhere in the woods. During the night they meet up with Stuntman Mike, an ex-film and television stuntman who's abnormally attached to his "death proof" stunt car, a 1970 Chevy Nova, and who clearly has ulterior motives in what he plans to do with the girls. Stuntman Mike is motivated by the same rage that fuels most of the slasher-film's killers, a rage — as Clover puts it — "propelled by psychosexual fury."[51] The action is set and generic expectation rings many bells associated with the slasher film: a group of girlfriends talk a great deal about their sexual exploits, but one (Arlene) is marked off as different and not as sexually "out there"; most of the men who accompany them are filthy and sex-crazed; and like the final girl survivor of so many slasher films, it's Arlene who first notices Stuntman Mike stalking them, but this psycho-killer wields no knife, chainsaw or axe — his car is his weapon of choice. Tarantino teases the audience with the possibility that they're watching a "straight" slasher film. But like Marion, the female victim in *Psycho* (Alfred Hitchcock, 1960) — the film often acknowledged as influencing the subgenre — the women in the first part of the film all suffer violent deaths at the hands of Stuntman Mike. Even Arlene, who appeared to be final-girl material, dies in the gruesome head-on collision that rips her face from her body. Her fate is sealed by a scene that occurs prior to the deaths: taking up a challenge broadcast on the radio by Jungle Julia, Stuntman Mike approaches Arlene and, as directed by Jungle Julia, calls her "Butterfly" before reciting the Robert Frost Poem "Stopping by Woods on a Snowy Evening" (whose title further echoes their planned trip to the lake house).

Arlene goes into the bar with Mike to perform that sultry lap dance that reeks of promiscuity and which was promised by Julia as a reward, the viewer knows that she and the others don't have "miles to go before they sleep." So where is the final girl?

Generic Payback: The Slasher Film — Tarantino Style

The final girl becomes four final girls in the second half of the film, which works in dialogue with the first part and which is where Tarantino presents a major revision of the slasher film and final-girl tradition. True to the slasher film, the women in the first part of the film are victims in more ways than one: they're victims of a tradition of filmmaking that frames them as objects of display rather than characters who control the narrative action. Despite the fact that they're opinionated and strong individuals, they surround themselves with men who are losers upon whom they nevertheless rely (consider Jungle Julia's disappointment when the mysterious Chris, fails to show up to the Texas Chilli Parlor after being texted). And despite her suspicions of Stuntman Mike, Arlene ignores her instinct, falling victim to his plans and, like her friends, she rides to her death, oblivious to her fate while listening to the toe-tapping rhythms of "Hold Tight!" by Dave Dee, Dozy, Beaky, Mick & Tich. And so they sleep. The link to a specific filmic representation of "passive" women is further highlighted at an earlier point in the film when the main character, Jungle Julia, is shown languishing on a couch, her outstretched limbs and evocative pose mirroring a poster of Brigitte Bardot from

Figure 20: Jungle Julia (Sydney Poitier) in *Death Proof* (Dimension Films, 2007) mirrors Brigitte Bardot's pose from the film *The Night Heaven Fell (Les Bijoutiers du claire de lune)* (Roger Vadim, 1958), which is seen in the poster that decorates the wall above her (Kobal Collection).

Figure 21: The final girl survivors (left to right: Mary Elizabeth Winstead, Rosario Dawson, Zöe Bell and Tracie Thoms) from *Death Proof* (Dimension Films, 2007).

the film *The Night Heaven Fell (Les Bijoutiers du claire de lune)* (Roger Vadim, 1958) that decorates the wall of her living room (fig. 20). Of course, there's a double meaning intended here: where Roger Vadim had his Bardot, Tarantino has his multiple Bardots!

The second half of the film, however, is a whole new ballgame. Here Tarantino mixes up the slasher film by inserting intertextual references to and formulaic rules from other exploitation genres, in particular, the car-chase film, the rape-revenge film and the girl-gang film. And the story elements, character types and iconography of each shake up the slasher-film conventions to their very core. Following the past/present convention of the stalker film, the film has jumped to 14 months later, the transition marked by the film switching to black and white. We meet three of the four protagonists (fig.21) at a convenience store in Lebanon, Tennessee: Lee (an actress), Kim (a stuntwoman) and Abernathy (a make-up artist) are on a break from a film shoot, and parked next to them is Stuntman Mike — complete with his new 1969 Dodge Charger, a car that references the iconic star mobile in the car-chase film *Dirty Mary, Crazy Larry* (John Hough, 1974). The film reverts back to color as they leave the convenience store and — with the latest issue of Italian *Vogue* in hand — they set off to pick up the fourth woman in the group, Zoe (another stuntwoman) from the airport. As they catch up in a diner, the 360-degree tracking shot that circles them places them firmly in the domain of Tarantino's earlier male-action films, in this case *Reservoir Dogs*. Zoe informs the ladies that she's located a 1970 Dodge Challenger, a car that, as Zoe and Kim make clear, was the muscle car in another carsploitation cult film, *Vanishing Point* (Richard C. Sarafian, 1971). They take the car out for a test drive and Zoe and Kim decide that not only will they try to relive the glory days of *Vanishing Point* and other cult car-chase films, but they'll also play "Ship's Mast," a game that has Zoe strap her arms with belts onto the car doors while she rides the car with her back flat down on the hood! It's at this point that Stuntman Mike makes his first appearance, seated on the hood of his car with the bulky duck ornament pushing against his genitals as he watches the girls' stunt performance. The first time they know of his presence is when he's in hot pursuit, ramming into them from all directions at dangerously high speeds, eventually sending Zoe launching off the hood of the car and off the side of the road. At one point during the chase, Stuntman Mike's phallic association with his car is made clear when he tells Kim, who's driving, "You wanna get hot? Suck on this for a while bitch!" at which point he forces them off the road. Pulling up, he gets out of his car and yells out, "Hey ladies, that was fun! Well, adios!" at which point Kim shoots him in the arm and Mike drives off, sniveling like a baby. After Zoe emerges safe and sound from the bushes the following exchange occurs, and the hunted become the hunters:

Zoe: You wanna go get him?
Kim: Oh, hell yeah!
Abernathy: Fuck, yeah! Let's kill the bastard.

However, unlike the traditional final girl, these girls don't switch from passive victim to active killer while trying to defend themselves from their attacker. They become the attackers and are in active pursuit of a Stuntman Mike who has switched over to passive victim trying to escape. Cornering him soon after, Zoe, armed with a lead pipe she's picked up along the way, jumps out of the car and dashes to the driver side of the car, pounding it across Mike's body as he screams, "Oh, why? Oh no!" before driving off. After a lengthy chase, the final girls smash into Stuntman Mike's car and send it toppling off the road. As he crawls out screaming and crying like a baby, they approach, raise him to his feet and repeatedly punch him while the slapstick combination of slow motion/freeze techniques mimics similar scenes in spaghetti Western spoofs (further grindhouse fare) like *My Name Is Trinity/Lo chiamavano Trinità* (Enzo Barboni aka E.B. Clucher, 1970) and *My Name Is Nobody/Il mio nome è Nessuno* (Tonino Valeri, 1973). As Zoe lands a kick on the pathetic figure of Mike and he hits the ground, there's a cut to "The End" titles, which disappear almost as soon as they've appeared and the action returns to the final scene and comes to a close with Abernathy ramming her foot into Stuntman Mike's head. And watching this bit of poetry, *this* lady was hooting like an owl in heat! It's payback time, and payback's a bitch!

As mentioned above, by mixing the slasher tradition up with other exploitation genres, the outcomes of the second part of the story are radically different to that of the first part. In the first part, while one girl is coded as a possible final girl, she too succumbs to the psycho-killer and they all die; in the second part of the film, they're all survivors who have inverted the rules of the slasher film by actively seeking vengeance and hunting down their tormentor. And this inversion has occurred as a result of a type of generic mixing that places each genre in dialogue with one another, the final result being the transformation of the slasher "rules." In his analysis of the *Kill Bill* films, Aleksei Semenko explains how "the concept of genre and perception are directly connected, because genre is seen as a *code* shared by the writer (creator of the text or a group of texts) and the reader (receiver of such texts)."[52] For all genre, and for Tarantino's films in particular, intertextuality is at the core of how genre operates; and while Tarantino may say that he "never do[es] proper genre movies,"[53] his films are, nevertheless, critical studies about genre movies and about how genre movies produce their meaning and the audience's understanding of that meaning. Genre is perceived as a fluid, ever-changing process. In what can be read as a Bakhtinian understanding of genre as carnivalesque, the languages of particular genres are introduced so they may interact with one another and, along the way, rewrite the rules.

By making the car-chase theme an important thread that weaves its way through both parts of the film, Tarantino invites the audience to access their cineliterate library and make sense of how this inclusion has shifted the dynamics of slasher-film language. Stuntman Mike may be a character-type familiar to the slasher film, but the requisite phallic weapon is no longer held in his hand — he drives it. We know from jibes he receives and discussions he has in part one ("I wonder if B.J. brought the bear with him?" and "Back in the *Vanishing Point, Dirty Mary, Crazy Larry, White Line Fever* days...") that his car also places Mike in the carsploitation genre. The latter is further stressed in part two of the film when two other petrol-heads — Kim and Zoe — enter the picture, also expressing their love of the heyday of 1970s car-chase movies. This fact also connects these two characters with that genre and therefore makes them different to the conventional final-girl types. However, having two stuntwomen actively embrace and act out the characterizations and actions typical of a genre that was male-dominated also gives a different spin to the carsploitation genre; this genre usually had the men driving both the narrative action and their cars (or, trucks), while the women were docile accompaniments that provided a love interest. Kim and Zoe are no docile accompaniments! With the exception of Lee, who's left behind as collateral so that the other three can go on their test drive of the white Dodge Challenger, Abernathy, Kim and Zoe's characters are further altered by being injected with traits from infamous girl-gang films like *Faster, Pussycat! Kill! Kill!* (Russ Meyer, 1965), *She-Devils on Wheels* (Herschell Gordon Lewis, 1968 — "We don't owe nobody nuthin', and we don't make no deals, we're swingin' chicks on motors, and we're man-eaters on wheels!") and *Truck Stop Women* (Mark L. Lester, 1974), which usually center on tough, badass and buxom "broads," violence, car or motorbike racing and lots of action mayhem.

Perhaps the most interesting way that Tarantino's cinephilic vision goes into overdrive is the way he merges the slasher conventions with those of the rape-revenge film. The plot of rape-revenge exploitation films like the cult classics *The Last House on the Left* (Wes Craven, 1972), *I Spit on Your Grave* (Meir Zarchi, 1978) and *Fair Game* (Mario Andreacchio, 1986) focuses on a female character who's savagely raped but who recovers to seek graphic and violent revenge against her rapists (in the case of *The Last House on the Left*, the vengeance is taken by the victim's parents). Whereas in the slasher film the psycho-killer's perverted and sexually charged attacks with a myriad of phallic symbols are displaced and expressed through violence and murder — operating as symbolic rapes — in the rape-revenge film the rape is graphically real. By bringing both exploitation subgenres in dialogue with one another,

Tarantino brings the sexual perversion of the killer to the fore, placing it out in the open so it may be dissected by the film and by the viewer. Discussing the rape-revenge connections in *Death Proof*, in her book *Rape-Revenge Film: A Critical Study*, Alexandra Heller-Nicholas makes the following observations about the influence of *Fair Game*, particularly the scene in which the rape victim Cassandra Delaney is strapped naked to the hood of a car:

> Considering *Death Proof* does not include scenes of rape or attempted rape as such, it is therefore perhaps surprising how explicitly it references rape-revenge traditions. *Death Proof* is unambiguous in its linkage of sexual violence with vehicular homicide (both attempted and otherwise).... Tarantino has openly acknowledged the influence of Clover's writing about the "final girl" in the slasher film on the film's first half in particular, but its specific reference to rape-revenge stems from its reconstruction of the memorable scene from the Australian rape-revenge film, *Fair Game*.... In the Australian film, the woman is strapped to the front of the car as an act of sexual violence, symbolizing her complete powerlessness in the face of male aggression, power and misogyny. But in *Death Proof*, Zoe not only asserts her power over the car and finds pleasure in doing so, but ultimately therefore *rejects* the notion of the car as being an inherently "masculine" object at all. She chooses to play "ship's mast" voluntarily, and Stuntman Mike's intrusion seeks to control the activities that she may find pleasurable. The relationship between Stuntman Mike and these female protagonists is therefore more than a case of the latter seeking revenge for thinly disguised metaphorical sexual violence. It is about them reconfiguring the entire symbolic language of gender in relation to car culture, so commonly ascribed as a masculine domain.[54]

As Heller-Nicholas perceptively notes, "Sharing a monster-car-as-male-sexuality metaphor, *Death Proof* reconfigures *Fair Game*'s gender relations," particularly in reversing the film's "vision of the relationship between women, cars and violence."[55] Tarantino's game is one about generic language and altering the signification of a genre's assumed norms. About this scene, Tarantino has said the following:

> If you like outrageous cinema, you live ... and breathe to wait for those weird moments that happen every once in a while in genre cinema where you can't believe you are seeing what you're seeing. *Fair Game* has one of those moments, man, and that's where after fucking the girl over like crazy, they strip her nude, tie her to the front of their monster truck, and then they just proceed to drive down the road at a hundred miles an hour with her tied naked to the front of the truck.... She's a human hood ornament. Who in *the fuck* thought of that?[56]

While Zoe "asserts her power over the car" by performing her own variation on the hood ornament motif, and responding to the earlier film through allusion and revision, a double play is also in operation because Stuntman Mike watches the scene (which places great emphasis on Zoe's outspread limbs)

5. Payback's a Bitch!   139

Figure 22: Zoe (Zoë Bell), the stuntwoman, plays "ship's mast" on the hood of a 1970 Dodge Challenger in *Death Proof* (Dimension Films, 2007).

from a distance, with his own oversized, penis-like duck hood ornament pressed against and metaphorically replacing his family jewels. From Stuntman Mike's perspective, the chase that begins is about turning back the hands of time to a rape-revenge film gone by, one that aims to deny Zoe pleasure. This last part of the film is, in a very real sense, a past and present struggle about the nature of rape-revenge conventions. And Mike may win round one by causing Zoe to be violently thrown off the hood of the car, but round two brings us back to the present and the women again gain the control they initially had when starting the ship's mast game (fig. 22). The sexually loaded language Kim uses when she and the final girls pursue Stuntman Mike after the "ship's mast" incident further flips the rules on *Fair Game* by metaphorically raping Mike with their own muscle car. As she continues to ram him from behind, Kim yells:

> Oh, you gonna wriggle your ass at me? Oh, you don't like it up the ass, you redneck lunatic bastard? ... Oh, I'm the horniest motherfucker on the road! ... Oh, you know I can't let you go without tapping that ass one more time. Booyah!

According to Clover, in the final scene, when the final girl "stops screaming, faces the killer, and reaches for the knife (sledge hammer, scalpel, gun, machete, hanger, knitting needle, chain saw), she addresses the monster on his own terms."[57] She may do this, but she does so in self-defense. *Death Proof*'s final girls aren't defending themselves, they're out for revenge and this final car chase is nothing less than a metaphoric rape, *Deliverance* style! The final girls wreak vengeance using the same signifier (a sexed-up car), but in doing so they alter the signification of the signifier.

While the enforced generic hybridity reconfigures and gives new meaning to both carsploitation and rape-revenge films, *Death Proof* also reconstructs the conventions of the slasher film and the gender relations performed therein. In interviews, Tarantino has made it clear that his films are about filmic reality. Discussing *Kill Bill*, his "big grindhouse movie," he explains how this "movie doesn't take place in the real world. It takes place in this special universe. It's very much a movie universe. It has its own rules and own mythology and a lot of these rules can be found in some of the genre films I'm dealing with in this film."[58] In the case of *Kill Bill*, he was concerned primarily with the Western, martial arts or wuxia and samurai genres and the action aesthetics they shared. Again, the film was concerned with exploring the relationship between gender and genre. The *Kill Bill* films begin in a contemporary generic context that's exposed audiences to the presence of women in action genres. As action women from samurai, wuxia, and Western traditions converge and merge with male characters who also hail from those traditions, the main character, the Bride (Uma Thurman), also follows a path back in time to John Ford's *The Searchers* (1956), which frames the opening of *Kill Bill vol. 1* and end of *Kill Bill vol. 2*. The action woman who's framed within the doorway at the beginning of *Kill Bill vol. 1* in what is a clear allusion to the opening sequence of *The Searchers* is more like a female version of John Wayne's character Ethan, but a female version who's also been influenced by the conventions of other action cinema conventions that followed in the wake of Westerns like *The Searchers*. Inverting the convention that placed women on the inside of the door and the home (which is the place of Martha in *The Searchers*), the Bride travels a journey through a movie universe that creates a dialogue between action genres across time and across nations until, finally, she reunites with her daughter and claims the role of Martha in *The Searchers* by returning to the space of the home. As is the case with the *Kill Bill* films, the director, film universe and audience of *Death Proof* interact with the rules and mythology of the horror film and other exploitation genres, and those rules are shaken up so thoroughly that a new mythology emerges around the "meaning" of the slasher film.

In her analysis of the slasher film, Clover explores Yuri Lotman's analysis of character functions in myth, and she arrives at a similar conclusion: the character functions of the victim and hero are gendered.[59] As is the case with myth, slasher films reveal only two character functions: society codes mobile, heroic functions as masculine, and immobile, victim functions as feminine.[60] Arguing that the slasher film reflects an older tradition that saw the sexes not in terms of differences but in terms of sameness — the one-sex model — she argues that the final girl is a modern remnant of that belief system. Containing both sexes (and their accompanying functions) in the one body, that's why so many final girls of the early slasher tradition have "masculine interests"[61] and boyish rather than overtly feminized qualities, including androgynous name like "Stretch, Stevie, Marti, Will, Terry, Laurie, and Ripley."[62] The convention of the final girl serves a specific function for the male spectator (even though Clover acknowledges that women also watch horror films).

> It is also the case that gender displacement can provide a kind of identificatory buffer, an emotional remove that permits the majority audience to explore taboo subjects in the relative safety of vicariousness.... The Final Girl is, on reflection, a congenial double for the adolescent male. She is feminine enough to act out in a gratifying way, a way unapproved for adult males, the terrors and masochistic pleasures of the underlying fantasy, but not so feminine as to disturb the shackles of male competence and sexuality.[63]

"Cinefantastic horror," she continues, "succeeds in incorporating its spectators as 'feminine' and then violating that body which recoils, shudders, cries out collectively in ways otherwise imaginable, for males, only in nightmare."[64] If we agree with Clover's understanding of the gendered operations at work in the slasher film and its audience, then what we're presented with in the second part of *Death Proof* is a carnivalesque inversion of these "rules." Here the final girls are both "boyish" (Kim and Zoe) and feminized (Abernathy and Lee). Yet, as Heller-Nicholas insightfully notes, Zoe and Kim reclaim the traditionally male interests in muscle cars and stunt work as integral to their sense of being women, claiming it as part of what gives these females pleasure. Again, the more "feminine" Abernathy and Lee and their proclaimed love for haute couture and Italian *Vogue* are in no way cast as victims: while Lee may be a bit surprised about being left behind with the redneck who owns the Dodge Challenger, the scene is played for laughs rather than horror; and the wonderful Abernathy is as vocal in her desire to hunt their victim ("Fuck, yeah! Let's kill the bastard!") and is the one to land the final, deadly boot-slam onto Stuntman Mike's skull. Significantly, the "abject terror," which is gendered feminine and belongs to the final girl before she becomes hero, is thrust onto the cowering, sniveling body of Stuntman Mike, who's played by Kurt Russell, one of the world's greatest action heroes! The very notion of "the femaleness of the victim"[65] is thrown out the window. In the process, Lotman's argument regarding the social coding of mobile, heroic functions as masculine, and immobile, victim functions as feminine is shattered. Times and myth, Tarantino is telling us, have changed.

Both *Planet Terror* and *Death Proof* consciously manipulate, repeat, exaggerate and radically alter style, codes, narrative conventions and iconic character types that audiences associate with the horror film. In an ultimately grotesque act, following a polemic that's akin to the cannibalizing strategy advocated by the modernist Brazilian poet Oswald de Andrade in his *Cannibalist Manifesto* of 1928, Tarantino and Rodriguez cannibalize their sources, ingest and digest them, then expel them from their old generic bodies, creating them into renewed creatures that have overthrown the previous rulers. In the words of Bakhtin:

> Finally the intentional double-voiced and internally dialogized hybrid possesses a syntactic structure utterly specific to it: in it, within the boundaries of a single utterance, two potential utterances are fused, two responses are, as it were, harnessed in a dialogue.[66]

In the next chapter I turn to another articulation of intertextual universes, one delivered by the *Doom* video games, which were popular trailblazers in cementing the tradition of horror video games and the First Person Shooter (FPS). Here, the intertwined sensory/intellectual dynamic finds both shared and different forms of articulation to *Grindhouse,* one informed by the technological difference of the video-game medium.

6

Hail to the King! Techno-Intertexts, Video Game Horror and *Doom 3*

"Nothing will come from nothing": Revisiting the Past

It was back in 1993 that the horror was unleashed in the form of the *Doom: Evil Unleashed*. Developed by the Texas-based company id Software, this computer game was to introduce radical innovations not only to the First Person Shooter (FPS) genre, but also to the soft- and hardware technology that drove gaming. In 1994, the sequel *Doom II: Hell on Earth* was to push the envelope further still. Drawing on the science fiction and horror conventions of cinematic examples like *Alien* (Ridley Scott, 1979), *Aliens* (James Cameron, 1986) and *Evil Dead II* (Sam Raimi, 1987), both *Doom* games upped the ante in game culture by transferring experiences familiar to the horror and science fiction film spectator over to game culture. Discussing *Doom*'s influences, Jay Wilbur, the then–chief executive officer of id, stated that id "wanted to make an *Alien*-like game that captured the fast-paced action, brutality and fear of those movies," while also amplifying the action and horror with *Evil Dead II*, whose "chainsaws and shotguns are an unbeatable combination!"[1] These two games are up there with the most popular, innovative and influential games in game history. Significantly, one of the concerns of the games' creators — John Carmack and John Romero — was to transfer the dread, suspense and horror that was familiar to film audiences into the game environment.

Fast forward to 2004: a new breed of game horror was born again in the form of the PC-game *Doom 3*, which was later also released on other platforms. Like its addictive predecessors, *Doom 3* introduced an even greater "filmic" quality to its game space and, yet again, a new standard of gaming aesthetics and technology was created. Todd Hollenshead, head of id Software, stated, "*Doom* 3 is a video game experience unlike any before it…. From the cinema quality visuals and the incredible 5.1 sound, to the terrifying atmosphere and hyper-realistic environments, the whole game screams 'interactive horror film.'"[2] In particular, the *Doom* games typify a strong tendency among game developers towards fetishizing the film object, and what's perceived as the cinema's convincing illusion of "realism." But the cinema is by no means the only media form that's impacted on games. Through an analysis of *Doom* 3 and its heritage, this chapter will address the question of games and their history, arguing that their reliance on past sources does not detract from their uniqueness. The creators of games like *Doom* 3 deliberately place their creations within a rich, diverse tapestry of media history not in an admission of their lack of originality, but rather so they can flag their innovation. As will be argued below, the ways in which John Carmack (lead programmer of the *Doom* trilogy) and the rest of the production team at id Software arranged and reshaped their influences has a story to tell us about how these games situate themselves within the arena of competing entertainment media. What the id games remind us of is the fact that the technology that makes possible the game experience is integral to the way the player's sensorium snaps to attention. Game technology is the means to the creation of the dark, atmospheric spaces that are typical of horror; it can ensure the success or failure of our willingness to embrace the stories and characters that we meet on our journey; and it's crucial to how convincingly the horror aesthetic lures the player into its seductive clutches.

Focusing primarily on the *Doom* games and, in particular, *Doom 3*, in this chapter I explore the reflexive dimension of contemporary horror games and focus on the ways they engage players in playful and inventive perceptual puzzles that are about the process of meaning construction in horror — meaning that radiates both around stimulation of the senses and an arousal of the intellect. In his analysis of horror video games, Christian McCrea recognizes that

> alongside horror's hot breath on our necks, there is also that subtle intellectual tickle — a play with genre, form, or media history. Disbelief is not so much "suspended" as "bound up tightly"; the navigation of both physical and intellectual registers has to dovetail, one folding over the other, in order to affect us fully…. Games have taken up their place in the hall of media mirrors, looking for ways to make sense of themselves through known media forms. That layered media history is increasingly becoming a literal part of the arsenal players equip against the wicked foulness lurking in the bleak surrounds of their castles, mansions, and abandoned towns.[3]

As I've argued elsewhere,[4] the *Doom* games place themselves within the context of their media history and, in doing so, take us on a journey that's about the history of genre and generic process. As McCrea explains, and as explored in the previous chapter, an impulse that's integral to contemporary media is a pervasive intertextuality that's expressed through a level of media literacy that requires the active engagement of the player beyond the level of story or game action. Indeed, in horror it often becomes a pleasure in and of itself. This chapter focuses on such cerebral pleasures, looking both at intertextual play but also at the process of techno-textuality, a form of intertextuality whose pleasure is located around the technological advances and transformations that have been mastered by the game creators. Relying heavily on game literacy, players find themselves engaged not only in *the* game, but also in *a* game about techno-textuality, which offers its own intellectual and emotional indulgences.

In his study on the nature and function of emotions in gameplay, Bernard Perron stresses that we "must not forget that emotions involve many elements, from bodily changes to perceptions and thoughts," to experiences of them and reactions to them.[5] Drawing on cognitive film theory,[6] he initially outlines two types of emotions: fiction emotions, which can be also called "witness emotions" because, despite having the capacity to impact on the viewer or gamer emotionally, this occurs at a distance from the fictional world. As he explains, "Fiction emotions have above all to be defined as witness emotions because they are elicited by a controlled and invisible observer's position" and because the situations the protagonists find themselves in "can't be acted upon.... Fiction emotions are principally empathetic." The second type is "artefact emotions," which come into play "as soon as the viewer or gamer is aware of artistry and manipulation"; when this occurs, "The object of the emotion is not the fictional world anymore, but film or the game as a manmade artifact."[7] As Perron explains, game history is "peppered with technological innovations" and, probably more than the technological milestones that impacted on film and television, due to the breakneck speed with which computer technology advances, the role played by technological innovation in games has an even greater role to play when compared to other media, including film and television. Perron also introduces a third type — gameplay emotions:

> Without doubt fiction and artefact emotions play a role in story-driven games. But they are certainly not the main part of the experience. Needless to say, we are playing for *gameplay emotions* or *G emotions*, the emotions arising from our actions in the game — mostly in the game-world in the case of narrative games — and the consequent reactions of the game(-world).[8]

Gameplay emotions, therefore, adapt the first two to the specific processes at work in the relationship between the game space and the game player, a relationship that requires action on the part of the player. Perron continues:

> Gameplay emotions arise from the interactions of the gamer with the game(-world). This brings us back to the questions of action readiness and action tendency. If interest is the only real action tendency in film, it is not the case in video game where many controls can lead to action.... But inasmuch as you *can* make your avatar act, you *have to* make him take action. If not, there will be no game. Otherwise, as I've often stressed with regards survival horror games, it is certainly not the avatar that is meant to be scared or have emotions, but rather the gamer. The avatar, incidentally, generally stays expressionless, whatever the situation. We saw that emotions depend on the gamer's appraisal of a given game situation. This individual appraisal will consequently produce subjective emotional reactions.[9]

While following a different path to the cognitive one followed by Perron, for the rest of this chapter I'm interested in exploring different articulations of these three types of emotions.

In their own remediation of other media, the *Doom* games reveal the complex relationships that currently exist across the entertainment industry. This crossover, in turn, tests the clear separation between distinct media forms, and the overlap has ramifications for game analysis. While many game theorists and critics are still resistant to the idea that this new entertainment form, which is driven by quick turnarounds in developments of new computer technology, can efficiently be understood in terms of other media influences (and their accompanying critical discourses), the reality is, to quote from William Shakespeare's *King Lear,* "Nothing will come from nothing." Like films, games don't emerge from a vacuum; they possess a media history that includes an array of sources — films, comic books, painting, books, television, sports, music, board games — in addition to examples from within their own medium. Video games, like other entertainment forms, are reliant on a rampant hybridity and self-reflexivity. *Resident Evil* (Capcom, 1996–2004) games engage consciously with tropes from the George Romero "living dead" films, the Italian zombie films, as well as first- and third-person action, role-playing games and survival horror. *Max Payne 2: The Fall of Max Payne* (Remedy, 2003) also draws heavily on the cinema as a point of reference. In addition to film's stylistic properties (simulated camera movements, point-of-view shots, edits, and the bullet-time effect popularized in the *Matrix* films [Wachowski Brothers, 1999–2003]) the game is heavily steeped in the conventions of the detective and film noir genres. And *Batman: Arkham Asylym* (Rocksteady Studios, 2009) quotes and transforms a range of Batman media representations borrowed from comics, animation and film as well as drawing heavily on horror film stylistics.

Media hybridization is the product of and is crucial to the larger cross-over market that currently exists as a result of the conglomeration of the entertainment industry. It's a reality of commerce that thrives on competition and diversification.

The Medal of Honor series, for example, was influenced by the Steven Spielberg–directed film *Saving Private Ryan* (1998). The film was jointly produced by Amblin Entertainment (the company established by Spielberg), DreamWorks SKG (Spielberg's partner company with Jeffrey Katzenberg and David Geffen), and Paramount Pictures Corporation. Owning partial rights to this franchise, DreamWorks developed *Medal of Honor: Frontline* for PS2, and commissioned the game company Electronic Arts to publish the game. In such an exchange, the logic assumes that viewers of the film may then be interested in the game, while gamers may be drawn to the film. As Justin Wyatt has so convincingly argued, the "relationship between economics and aesthetics" has become crucial to the formal properties of entertainment media, but beyond that, economics gives rise to new aesthetics."[10] This relationship suggests that the boundaries of our critical models must expand to consider cross-media hybrids. While the digital technology that drives games (and the responses it demands of its user) may be different to other media forms, it makes games no less susceptible to outside influences. Bolter and Grusin observe:

> No medium today, and certainly no single media event, seems to do its cultural work in isolation from other media, any more than it works in isolation from other social and economic forces. What is new about new media comes from the particular ways in which they refashion older media and the ways in which older media refashion themselves to answer the challenges of new media.[11]

Significantly, it's in the process of highlighting the range of their external sources — their process of remediation — that games like *Max Payne* 2 and *Doom 3* also insist on their difference or, rather, their uniqueness. The assertion of their originality remains paramount. In accumulating past references, styles or allusions, these games are both acquiring their history but also placing themselves reflexively within the context of that history. In adapting forms of the past and present, games often attempt to convince the player that they're transforming their sources into a more "authentic" experience. A playful discourse with the player results, one that requires that the player remains aware of the origins of the borrowings. The active and reflexive engagement of game players involves a critical understanding of the process of meaning production that's almost as integral as the gameplay. This can in itself become a source of intense pleasure — for this player, at least.

Max Payne 2, for example, begins its introduction by adapting the form of the graphic novel into its structure — complete with comic-book frames and voice bubbles (fig. 23). But this source is also altered through the addition of the sounds of narration. The game then progresses into film language that includes mimicking camera movements, edits, genres, character types from the cinema — so the addition of motion and 3D is also introduced to the pre-

Figure 23: An example from the video game *Max Payne 2* (Remedy Entertainment, 2003) showing its remediation of the comic book format.

viously static image. Then comes the third transition: to gameplay. The moving image, sound and narrative that we've just witnessed (and which we associate with the cinema) is suddenly made richer with the introduction of the player's ability to affect the actions seen on the screen. In addition, not only does *Max Payne 2* remediate the history of other media, it also refashions its predecessor *Max Payne* (Remedy, 2001), replacing the more stony-faced Max (fig. 24) with a digitally improved version that has more realistic surface texture and a wider range of facial expressions. Above all, such remediation demands attention from the player, attention that cries out, "Hey, look at me! I'm the new and improved version."

To turn the clock back to 1994 and the "interactive movie" *Under a Killing Moon* (Access Software), again, the player is presented with an introduction that's sheer exhibitionism, one that claims CD-Rom gaming technology as superior to that which produced film classics. Game introductions have, especially since the mid–1990s, functioned as showcases of advances in game technology. In keeping with this tradition, the introduction of *Under a Killing Moon* presents a pure performance of digital spectacle. The cut-scene is used to exhibit the state of game technology in a highly exhibitionistic way. It knows its player is sitting in front of the computer screen, marveling at the illusions it conjures up. The introduction runs through a mini-history of classics of film history: the two-spirit voices set against the backdrop of outer-

Figure 24: The stony-faced Max Payne from the original *Max Payne* video game (Remedy Entertainment, 2001).

space allude to the voices of the angels who discuss the fate of the main character, George Bailey, in the 1946 Frank Capra film *It's a Wonderful Life*; and the documentary footage dealing with Hitler's involvement in the dark arts is stylistically presented as an homage to the "News on the March" scene in Orson Welles's *Citizen Kane* (1941); the shift to the future sequence and the introduction of the detective — Tex Murphy — is an overt homage to Ridley Scott's 1982 science fiction classic *Blade Runner*. *Under a Killing Moon* asks its player to acknowledge the influences that these paragons of the cinema have had on its game form, but it does this so that we may then recognize the then-new CD-Rom format (which was capable of more memory storage than previous PC games) as the future of entertainment — the cinema's new competitor, the "interactive movie." This message is made loud and clear once the player shifts from the passive viewing required of the film-inspired introduction to the game itself, which shifts the role of the viewer to that of player. As in the example of *Max Payne 2*, through allusion, *Under a Killing Moon* also posits a journey about technological evolution.

Discussing the rampant intertextuality that's typical of contemporary entertainment, Jim Collins observes that the result of such a complex web of intertextual references is that narration is not simply limited to completing the plot, or to becoming involved in the "syntagmatic axis of the narrative."[12] Instead, the "layering of intertexts that occurs simultaneously informs those same topoi along a paradigmatic axis of antecedent representations."[13] Therefore, story and action sequences that unravel during gameplay are not the only drive of these examples; allusions to and the recognition of other media that have impacted on games are just as integral to the player's involvement and interpretation. Beyond the gameplay, another game takes place: citation engages the player in a game that's about an homage to and renegotiation of the past. The filmmaker Jean-Luc Godard is renowned for making cinema about the cinema. While their ultimate intent may differ, these games engage in a similar kind of logic: they are games about games. This "hyperconsciousness" permits participants to become engrossed in the gameplay in a more conventional sense, with the story and themes unraveling along syntagmatic lines; but players are also encouraged to participate with the game on the paradigmatic level via the multi-layered, intertextual references.[14] It's on this level that intertextual and technological virtuosity comes into play.

Game Horror and Dynamic Worlds

Video games and, in particular, games that introduce new technological and gameplay experiences into game culture, often engage in what film scholar Tom Gunning has called an "aesthetics of astonishment."[15] New optical entertainment technologies like the cinema at the turn of the last century and other visual devices of the 19th century (including the phantasmagoria, the zoetrope, and the photographic camera) often engaged in a game that was about technological virtuosity, staking a claim for their significance within their own medium and, by extension, making a statement about their medium's superiority over competing media. It comes as no surprise that this aesthetic tends to dominate during periods of more intense media competition. At the center of the aesthetics of astonishment is a concern with exhibitionism, virtuosity, spectacle, and active audience engagement; the emphasis is on display, performance, spectacle and intertextuality. Intertextuality is key as a mode of engagement that lays out before the viewer/player a smorgasbord of media history, which is both alluded to and outperformed by the performance of technological spectacle. *Doom 3, Under a Killing Moon* and *Max Payne 2* all engage the player in what Perron calls "artifact emotions," which are also intimately tied into Perron's third category of gameplay emotions.

The *Doom* games remain emblematic of this exhibitionist tendency in game culture. *Doom 3* delights in opening up spaces that invite the player to marvel at the games' illusionistic methods of construction. The game of virtuosity flaunts the ability of games to cannibalize older and more established media rules (genres, narrative conventions, formal properties, etc.) and transform them into new formal and technological rules that bring with them new challenges to the sensorium. Like its predecessors, *Doom 3* is heavily steeped in the intertextual web of media history: media history external to the video game medium but also from within it. What is especially striking about *Doom 3* is that it continues a game of virtuosity that's been typical of id Software productions since the early 1990s. As a reboot of *Doom, Doom 3* presents its story: the player adopts the role of a marine who reports for duty at a research installation on Mars. Soon after the marine's arrival, he meets the scientist he has been assigned to locate. True to the mad-scientist tradition of science fiction-horror cinema, the scientist's unsanctioned experiments result in the opening of a portal to a hell dimension that launches a demon invasion on Mars. Hell itself is unleashed and the base's personnel are slowly transformed into zombie stalkers. The marine and player's mission is to close the portal and destroy all demons along the way — and there are loads of them!

The visual references and themes of all three *Doom* games oscillate across a variety of genres and media. The chainsaw weapon that the player has access to is an homage to the Ash character from the cult classic *Evil Dead II* (who, in the film, maniacally chops off one of his appendages, replacing it with a chainsaw). The player is thrust into science-fiction environments that consist of moon bases, technological gadgets and teleporters as well as an oppressive atmosphere that recalls the ghoulish backdrops that dominate science fiction-horror films like *Alien* and *Aliens*. The specters, imps, "cacodemons," "Hell knights," and "Cyberdemons" not only allude to science fiction and horror film conventions, but the games also self-consciously rework the literary Lovecraftian Cthulhu Mythos, which has itself inspired an immense intertextual web of media examples.[16] The creatures of Cthulu mythology, who once inhabited and ruled the Earth, are "imprisoned or sleeping in various parts of the Earth and the galaxy, waiting for the time 'when the stars are right' and they can reclaim their rule."[17] Like their demon cousins in the *Doom* games, they can gain access to our world through portals that teleport them to various locations. In fact, Sandy Petersen, who created the hugely successful "Call of Cthulhu" role-playing game, also worked with id software on the *Doom* games, and the equally successful id-produced *Quake* series, which included a creature taken directly from Cthulhu mythology — the Shub-Niggurath.

It's not due to a lack of creativity that *Doom 3* relies on these and other sources. Likewise, it's not a lack of creativity that underlies the return to the first *Doom* (fig. 25). In returning to *Doom, Doom 3* writes over its history, further layering the palimpsest that is *Doom* culture. Taking a leaf out of the George Lucas book-of-*Star Wars*-production history, id Software's Todd Hol-

Figure 25: A screenshot from *Doom: Evil Unleashed* (id Software, 1993), the horror video game that introduced new 3D imaging to the First Person Shooter.

lenshead has stated that, in the production of *Doom 3*, "We pretend that *Doom* and *Doom 2* didn't happen. Those games were massively successful in their own right so we had this great creative universe to draw upon, but really only the surface of it had been scratched because of the technological limitations of the time."[18] Rather than wiping out history, which is an impossible task because *Doom* and *Doom 2* are so deeply embedded in the psyche of gamer culture, what *Doom 3* does is to create a new layer over *Doom* history. Like ruins and fragments, these entertainment forms evoke the existence of a past in the present while simultaneously transforming the ruin into a restored, majestic structure that still contains its past in the foundations beneath it. The intensified self-consciousness that is typical of games like *Doom 3* is driven by virtuosity, the primary concern being to outperform predecessors and contemporaries and to stamp its own identity across game history. According to Sypher, a distinction needs to be made between style and stylization or technique. Style "is based on the technique it transcends"[19] and in this sense, *Doom 3* is brimming over with "style." Media conventions and past techniques are synthesized in order to transcend or perfect those techniques. Additionally, stylistic coherence is the result of the reorganization of past signs and stylizations into new combinations so that a discourse emerges between past and present.

However, it's not only external media that are assimilated and "transcended." Like its precursors *Doom* and *Doom 2*, *Doom 3* revisits game history as well as the history of the *Doom* series with the intention of outperforming its predecessors' technological and gameplay prowess. While the gameplay is a straightforward FPS, it does introduce innovations to the thorny problem of story presentation within game space. The delivery of story to the player without awkward and prolonged interruptions of play (for example, in the form of cut scenes) has greatly improved in *Doom 3*. With the use of a personal PDA as well as those of discarded PDAs of dead prior owners, the plot slowly builds. Emails, personal notes, audio logs, video clips all add to the sense of mystery of and mastery over the story that unravels. In addition, the implementation of scripted triggers introduces the player not only to a series of surprise attacks from the monstrous baddies, but to other NPCs (Non-Player Characters) who present further information that's crucial to the mayhem that surround the marine. All this aside, it's on the level of effects that the innovations of this game emerge.

In its day (which may not be that long ago timewise, but is eons away

Figure 26: Some of the enemy from *Doom 3* (id Software , 2004), the game that upped the ante in game realism by introducing an even greater "filmic" quality compared to its predecessors.

in terms of digital advances in technology) *Doom 3* was without doubt one of the most realistic and visually astounding games ever produced. The graphics approached the quality of a pre-rendered computer graphic movie (fig. 26), with the result that the atmosphere of this game left *Doom 2* of 1994, and many groundbreaking games that followed — *Halo* (Gearbox, 2003), *Half-Life* (Sierra, 1998), and the *Tomb Raider* (Core Design, 1996–2003) and *Grand Theft Auto* (Rockstar Games, 1998–2004) series — miles behind in terms of the quality of audio-visual effects. With its release, *Doom 3* set a new standard for the look of 3D games. John Carmack of id Software not only created a graphics engine from scratch but a sound engine was also implemented in the production of *Doom 3*. In addition to introducing Dolby 5.1, six-channel surround-sound into its space, which not only adds to the drama but creates an off-screen space that directs players to the placement of enemies, Carmack has also created real-time dynamic lighting and shadow effects that, when experienced in gameplay, can generate some very serious scare effects. Objects not only cast shadows, but those shadows shift and change according to the light that the player directs towards them.

The technological construction of game spaces is crucial to how we perceive them. Drawing on the work of psychologist James Gibson, Paul Rodaway makes the important point that not only are perception and the senses interconnected, but that the "the structure and texture of the environment itself is a necessary determinant of what is perceived."[20] Rodaway explains how "Gibson abandoned the traditional sensation/perception distinction and transcended the behaviour/cognition debate and presents a theory which attends specifically to spatial perception and the active observer moving in a dynamic world."[21] Game spaces and, in particular, game spaces that depend on a realist aesthetic rely heavily on this spatial perception and as active players who move through "dynamic worlds," our senses are continually changing and responding to triggers that confront them. One sense can set off another while also generating shifts in our perception of the world around us. I have a memory that vividly reveals this in action. A couple of years ago I remember making my way to Orange Grove Avenue in Los Angeles. My intention? To visit the houses that were the backdrop to Michael Myers's psychotic explosion in *Halloween* (John Carpenter, 1978). I was excited. Moving along the street and taking in the façades and details of the houses, I turned to focus on Laurie's house, and as I slowly walked towards it I experienced the most bizarre sense of *déjà vu*. It was, indeed, as if I'd been here before. The sensation of building horror took me over before any rational explanation did: I had been here before, but I'd been here thanks to the mediation of a camera, which had filmed the action. But this was no simple camera viewpoint, I realized, suddenly understanding the reason for the fear that had overcome me; this camera stood in for the viewpoint of Michael Myers, whose place I'd now mimicked in my movement along Orange Grove Avenue. For a second or so I'd merged the sense of who I was with my experience and memory of watching Michael Myers so many times move through this exact same space. In the real place that was Orange Grove Avenue, I had also become the viewpoint of Michael Myers and, for a split second that had scared the bejesus out of me! In my mind, I'd entered the virtual space of *Halloween* and adopted Michael Myers as my avatar. Relying on a different form of technological mediation — video games, and horror games in particular — present a similar experience of spatial encounter where the senses and perception merge fluidly with one another, shifting and changing at every turn.

When playing *Doom 3*, once Hell was unleashed, the lights in the military base went haywire. In some rooms and along corridors the lights strobed on and off intermittently, creating pockets of eerie darkness that generated intense levels of suspense and horror. Armed with a flashlight (one of the new additions to the *Doom 3* marine's supplies), I began navigating the labyrinthine spaces, aiming my torch into areas of darkness: this very action of attempted control over the chaotic space, however, also evoked dread in that it carried with it the possibility of illuminating what lay in the shadows in wait for the

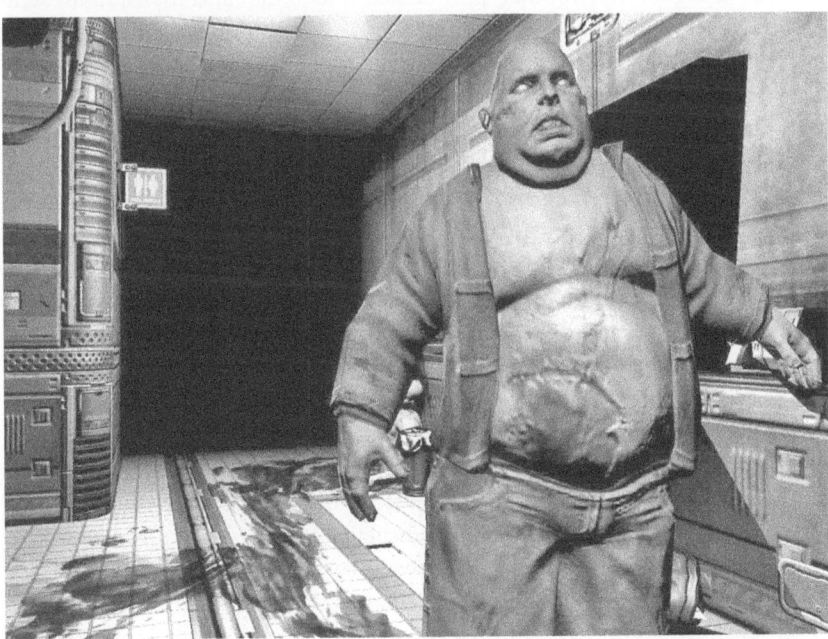

Figure 27: One of the zombies from *Doom 3* (id Software, 2004), the game that introduced graphics that approached the quality of a pre-rendered computer graphic movie.

living. And what *did* lie in the shadows? Many of the alien-demons found in the first two games — imps, Pinky Demons, Hell Knights, Cacodemons, and Revenant — but now they'd undergone some serious cosmetic surgery (fig. 27). The level of detail in each creature was a technological feat: all of the creatures present an array of skins and features, as well as some pretty creepy and distinctive screams, moans, and cries.

A description of the feeling of sensory immersion experienced while playing this game couldn't do it justice, but let me try anyway. With my surround sound system blaring around me, as my marine alter-ego and I crept through the shadows of a corridor early on in the game, exploring the spooky shadows with the flashlight (and ready to switch over to one of the very cool weapons) I could hear screams and whispers coming from all around me. The cries of victims, and the taunting voices of demons murmuring, "Over here" or "your soul is mine" — and sometimes it felt as if they were whispering in my ear. Imagine my state when, after completing a 90-degree sweep of a corridor with the flashlight, I turned to find myself virtual face to virtual face with one ugly, horrifying and mean-looking jawless zombie. He lunged at me and I walloped him over the head with the torch while hysterically telling another part of my brain (the bit that deals with rational functions) to arm myself with the shotgun. The rational part kicked into action and my shotgun sent his body every which way, splattering bits of flesh into a multitude of gory, yucky pieces. Yes, he scared the living daylights out of me, but it was worth it! His destruction sent a blast of adrenaline rushing through me that could have juiced me up for a serious run around the block.

To share yet another embarrassing story, I was reminded of the time I visited the live action *Alien Wars* (based on the films and comics), which used to operate underneath Leicester Square in London. While not experiencing space through an avatar, the sensation of experiencing "dynamic worlds" was similar. Entering an underground labyrinth, marines commandeered participants around a scientific installation that was experimenting with the DNA properties of aliens, while also breeding them. Of course, a third of the way into the "experience," alarms went off and my fellow tourist-adventurers and I were informed that the aliens had escaped. No sooner are we told this than the first "chase-through-the-corridors" by people in alien suits begins. Aided by the dark environment, flashing lights, smoke, and sound effects, it was very easy to shift over to the realm of disbelief and become immersed in the event. At one stage, my friend and I were cornered by an alien and as she cowered in the corner like the coward she was, I stood my ground while my mind screamed, "Oh, my God, it's going to spray acid on my face!" only to then placate myself with the thought, "This is pretend. Calm down." It wasn't the voice of reason that won, however. My intention was to save my friend and escape (meanwhile, I soon discovered that she'd already made a run for it!), so I grabbed the alien by its outstretched arms, noting the strange feel of rubber rather than the scaly flesh I'd imagined, and slammed its body against a wall with all my might. And, yes, I was screaming the whole way through, which made the experience both horrifying and exhilarating. To this day I think back on this action with shame: that poor guy in the alien suit would have been nursing some serious bruises for days afterwards. On the plus side, it proved to me that, if there were a real alien attack, I'd certainly adopt the role of hero. Like my experience at *Alien Wars*—and the one at Orange Grove Avenue—playing *Doom 3* evoked a similar kind of response. I knew that the events I saw before me weren't real, and yet my body and mind responded to them as if they were. What games like *Doom 3* can do so well is immerse the player into their representational spaces while also encouraging the player to recall *Doom* and *Doom 2*'s prior attempts in creating a similar aesthetic experience. For the player, there's no comparison. *Doom 3* has outdone its predecessors. In the sensorial assault that ensued, the player was invited to believe that the illusion they witnessed was perceptually real. As Tom Gunning observes in relation to the pre-cinematic technologies: "Optical entertainments exemplify the state of suspended disbelief that [French psychoanalyst] Octave Mannoni describes as 'I know very well, and all the same.'"[22]

An assumption often made by critics who focus on what is perceived as the "problem" of game design's "cinema envy" is that it's not the cinema as such that's being emulated or envied: it's the realist effect that the cinema can produce—and ironically nowadays, this realist effect is increasingly being created with digital effects in the cinema. Stephen Prince has made an important point, however, in relation to the use of digital effects in the cinema—and this is equally applicable to games. Theory fails to account for the paradox that, while images may be *perceptually* realistic, they are *referentially* unreal.[23] In this case, representational reality does not seek to create a world of resemblance. As Tuve has explained in a different context, "imitation" is not necessarily about the relationship between art and reality; the issue of representation is not significant in the sense of its capacity to reproduce material reality.[24] Rather, imitation and representation evoke alternate "realities" that reflect the ability of the effects to trigger emotional and sensory responses and almost instinctive reactions from the player. Existing reality is devalued in favor of an effects space that incites the senses into active awareness. To "represent" does not mean to "stand for the reality or concept behind it"; its ultimate concern is with the abstract nature of the senses. The senses are playfully deceived. The virtuosity for a game like *Doom 3* comes from flaunting its capacity to audio-visually present constructions that have no parallel basis in the real world, yet which temporarily confront the player with the possibility that zombies and the Mancubus may really do us major bodily harm. It is the means to the deception (the technology) that's important. Like *Doom 2*, *Doom 3* responds to the game's historical context, specifically, its relationship to the first two games and to other id Software productions, including the famous Quake series. The story *Doom 3* has to tell us is one that critically engages with issues of originality, "creative process" and technological advancement in gaming culture.

id Software and Technological Milestones

In the 1960s Marshall McLuhan extended his famous statement "the medium is the message" by proclaiming in the book of the same title, "All media are extensions of some human faculty — psychic or physical"[25] and, as such, they "massage" and have an immediate effect on the sensorium. McLuhan may not have been referring to *Doom 3* and game culture when he wrote this, but games reflect the extent to which media have become integrated into human experience. In the case of the Doom games and other milestone games like *Heavy Rain* (Quantic Dream, 2010), *Batman: Arkham Asylum* (Rocksteady Studios, 2009) or *Bioshock* (Irrational Games, 2007) which have been released since then, the technology that generates the effect of the medium quite literally is an important part of the message, that then allows the medium to be the massage of the player's sensorium. Consider the dramatic transformations that video games technology has sped through over the years: the range of platforms that speedily supersede one another; controllers that mediate the player's interaction with the game world—from gamepads, to joysticks, to steering wheels, to guns, to touch screens; the new screens, large and tiny, that are introducing 3D and augmented reality into the gamer world; and the rise in technologies that amplify the haptic and auditory sensations when playing. The effects and experiences produced by games like *Doom 3* don't only display virtuosity with regard to the way they tap into and reframe media history, they also tell a crucial story about the technological history of game development. This objective is nothing new to the games produced by id Software. But tied into this is a story about the affective potential of technology.

The games of this company display a self-reflexive attitude to the creative process that's reliant upon the relationship between past and present. In addition to placing themselves within the context of media history, on a formal level, id Software has always been obsessed with telling players a "paradigmatic" story about its place within the history of game technology. Each of the games released by id Software has set new benchmarks for game developers and the computer systems that gamers use to play their games. Not only have gamers continued to marvel at the amazing graphics and engines of id games, but often the technological demands of most id games have resulted in technological shifts: the high-end requirements of computer hardware have literally encouraged the consumer's shift to more advanced PC systems. The penchant id Software possesses for pushing the boundaries and striving towards extending the game market and experience was evident in *Wolfenstein 3D* (1992), which transformed the two-dimensional platform game into a separate genre known as the First Person Shooter (FPS). Rather than moving characters across a series of platforms that ran parallel to the screen, the player maneuvered them through a series of corridors that stressed movement into the simulated depth of the computer screen space. John Carmack and John Romero included texture mapping, which made possible more realistic textures to surfaces. In turn, *Wolfenstein 3D*'s advanced graphics engine and memory requirements became important in showcasing Intel's next generation Pentium chip.

Doom (1993) extended *Wolfenstein 3D*'s advances further still: one year after its release, the previously realistic 3D space of *Wolfenstein 3D* suddenly became a cartoonish, two-dimensional articulation of a three-dimensional space. In light of *Doom*'s (and, in 1994, *Doom 2*'s) more detailed and colorful environments and characters, *Wolfenstein 3D* seemed to offer a monotonous environment. With the introduction of more advanced texture mapping and the addition of diminished lighting, *Doom* provided hue variations that aided the illusion of shadows and recession into space. Not only did *Doom* make possible a more convincing and atmospheric immersion into the game space, but it was pivotal in broadening the conventions and expectations of the FPS genre. As outlined in the previous chapter, *Doom* became the form to which all FPSs would aspire. Carmack and Romero designed *Doom* with VGA (Video Graphics Adapter) cards in mind. Hitting the market in 1987, the VGA cards had greater graphics capabilities and superseded the EGA (Enchanced Graphics Adapter) cards, which were first released in 1984. In much the same way, in 1990, id had insisted on working with the most current graphics advances: they designed *Commander Keen* as a game best played on the new EGA cards, rather than the CGA (Computer Graphics Adapter) which was, by 1990, old technology. In privileging the most current developments in graphics card capabilities and hardware, Carmack ensured that id's games would represent the technological cutting edge. Discussing *Doom*, one game reviewer explained that the release of this game actually encouraged individuals to replace their computers with the "shiny new 486SX/DX just to play the game." Being far more capable of handling the memory requirements of *Doom*, the earlier 286 and 386 PC models were abandoned for the 486, which had a more powerful microprocessor. Again, in favoring the technological cutting edge, id software also supported a shift in the computer industry's hardware advances.[26] *Doom 2* then developed on this further still.

Quake (1996), another FPS, expanded the boundaries of the genre by incorporating new features, adding an even greater realism and more intensive form of gameplay by shifting a significant role of the graphics from the central processing unit (CPU) to the graphics card. In freeing up the CPU, which is the part of the computer that carries out the commands of software (such as games), the game could not only run more smoothly, but its effects could be even more impressive compared to those of the Doom duo. In addition, graphics and sound effects became high resolution and even more detailed, and the character movement included greater mobility: aside from walking, running and turning, heroes could now also look up and down, jump, swim and crouch. As Kushner explains, video games have driven the evolution of video cards, and *Quake* was integral to the next stage in the evolution. Its primary innovation centered on light mapping and the production of real-time light sources, which more effectively created the illusion of three-dimensionality and perspective. However, in order to play *Quake* effectively, previously cutting-edge computer technology was relegated to history: the 486s that had run *Doom* and *Doom 2* could no longer do *Quake*'s graphics justice. New history was being made and the new Pentium chips became the technology to have. To quote a reviewer, "*Quake* soon became the de facto benchmark for the consumer graphics card industry."[27] With each game id released, the company also sought to produce the technological cutting edge, in the process creating a dialogue with history. Developing on the popularity of the *Doom* game death matches, *Quake* advanced on this through network gaming — its revolutionary effects are still felt today in multiplayer gaming. In addition, developing on the modification possibilities introduced by the first two *Doom* games, John Carmack's programming code was made available to players in the game itself, with the result that gamers and developers could modify the *Quake* engine: the environment, NPCs, objects could be changed to suit their own requirements. Since the licensing of the Quake source code in 1999, and "improvements" that followed with the release of *Quake III Arena* (1999), the *Quake* engine became the programming foundation for many games, including *Return to the Castle Wolfenstein* (id Software, 2003), American *McGee's Alice* (Electronic Arts, 2000), *Jedi Knight II: Jedi Outcast* (Raven Software, 2000), *Star Trek Voyager Elite Force* (Raven Software, 2000) and *Medal of Honor: Allied Assault* (2015, Inc., 2002). The possibility of game modification introduced with the *Quake* engine has also been instrumental in advancing the Machinima phenomenon that allows the production of videos made in game engines — one of the most successful of these without doubt being the *Red vs*

Blue series (www.redvsblue.com) that's based on the *Halo* games (which, influenced by the premise of the *Quake* engine, produced the *Halo* engine).

Then *Doom 3* was released. A separate sound code was written which, as discussed above, introduced a layered complexity that was convincingly realistic, especially in the context of the surround sound system that was intended to support it. Above all, the sound produced a spatial realism that hadn't been experienced before in game design. The new rendering engine, written by Carmack, included the innovation of bump-maps, which, as their name implies, created greater texture on surfaces and related lighting effects: steel surfaces have the sleek texture of steel; skin has the texture we associate with flesh (from healthy to rotting flesh); the smoke that erupts from pipes in the base has the ephemeral consistency of smoke; and so on. Drawing on the animation skills of Fred Nilsson (animator of the 2001 DreamWorks box-office hit *Shrek*), and thanks to the advanced 3D engine created for the game, 3D modeling software like Maya was used more effectively to create impressive cinematic animation effects. Add to this the real-time lighting and shadow effects, and it wasn't difficult to imagine why PC gamers ran out to their local computer shops by the millions to upgrade their systems or to replace their PCs with new systems that could do justice to the game.

In May 2003, before the release of *Doom 3*, Kyle Bennett of the online gaming service HardOCP benchmarked *Doom 3* using the most recent ATI and NVIDIA graphics cards. NVIDIA's GeForceFX 5900 outran the main competition offered by the company ATI. Significantly, Bennett made a crucial point about the way game software technologies (such as that of *Doom 3*) can drive the future direction of computer companies and the hardware technologies that they develop. He explained that *Doom 3* "is likely to have more impact on the gaming and hardware industries overall than any other game to come in the next decade, as it is surely one of those quantum leaps in technology that are becoming so rare. NVIDIA is obviously aware of this and doing everything they can to be *the Doom 3 video card*."[28] Not only do individual games like *Doom 3* and game companies like id Software engage in a game about virtuosity, but computer companies can't resist the exhibitionist showcasing of their technology. In the case of NVIDIA, *Doom 3* becomes the vehicle of the corporation's technological virtuosity: the game displays NVIDIA's superiority and mastery over the products of competing companies like ATI.

In short, by pushing the envelope in terms of game effects and therefore altering game history and opening up the way to producing new horror-game aesthetics, companies like id Software also encouraged the invention and implementation of new hardware technology within the computer industry. They created both game and game technology's future. In turn, this technological innovation relegates older technology into its place in history. In this case, a further meta-text is introduced into Collins's example of the function on the paradigmatic axis: this story is one about the realities of commerce, industry and their history. Entertainment forms like video games have increasingly displayed a concern for engulfing and engaging the spectator actively in games that are concerned with their own remediated and media-specific sensory and playful experiences. The main focus of such spectacle is to conjure wondrous and sensorially invasive illusions that both immerse us in their representational spaces, a process that Bolter and Grusin label *immediacy*, and also expose the processes of the technological mediation, which Bolter and Grusin call *hypermediacy*— or, in Perron's terms, fictive and artifact emotions. Perhaps more than other entertainment forms, video games perform and compete with inter- and intra-media effects traditions, continually attempting to technically outperform these effects technologies — and the perceptions of reality that these technologies delivered. In their efforts to remediate themselves, video games often display a virtuosity and theatricality that cannot resist exposing the technology that drives them. Framing itself within its own media history, therefore, games like *Doom 3* and others produced by companies like id Software invade the player's space in deceptively real and immediately experiential ways. This spectacle is, however, also displayed in order that the player may admire it as a multi-technological feat of game technology. The experiences that games articulate, flaunt their capacity for making a reality out of an illusion — or, rather, for making the fantastic enter our world in such immediate and sensorially invasive ways. Who can say what new feat the technology that drives these game worlds will produce in the future? For the time being, to paraphrase Ash from the third *Evil Dead* film, *Army of Darkness* (Sam Raimi, 1993), "All, hail to the King!"

7

Transmedia and the Sensorium: From *Blair Witch* to *True Blood*

Viral Marketing and Transmedia Storytelling

One of the creepiest horror scenes I've experienced takes place in the Japanese horror film *Ringu* (Hideo Nakata, 1998) when the ghost of the vengeful Sadako appears on television and then slowly, almost painfully, forces her body through the screen. Limbs and joints contort and eyes roll back in her head, occasionally peeking through the layers of long black hair, as Sadako climbs her way out of the screen and crawls towards her target. In a strategy that layered the diegetic action, as the onscreen victim squirmed in fear at the prospect of fiction becoming reality, I, too, squirmed at the possibility of that fear coming to life. Sure, I knew it couldn't *really* happen, but that didn't stop the feeling that it *might*. The horror genre, more than any other genre, has relied on the powerful relationship that's forged between spectator, game player or reader and the fictional worlds it weaves for their consumption. One of the most powerful effects that horror has is to be able to affect the sensorium in such a way that it perceptually collapses the boundaries between reality and fiction. To this day, and despite the number of times I've seen it, *The Exorcist* (William Friedkin, 1973) manages to leave its mark on my mind and body: the film's evocative style, its atmosphere of evil, the themes it deals with, and the images of horror it portrays — all work in unison to make me feel less than secure in the actual space I occupy both while I'm watching the film and in the aftermath. In a sense, I take the essence of the film's horror with me after its end credits have rolled and that essence follows me for minutes, hours, days — the memory of it still lingering and eerily invading my everyday reality.

Like so many of the examples discussed in other chapters — the zombie attack in *Zombi 2*, the assault of *los ganados* in *Resident Evil 4*, the gaping mouth of the mummy in The Mummy ride, the sexual adventures in paranormal romances — horror can assault the senses with an immediacy that impacts directly on our very being, making us feel the sensory encounters that occur onscreen (and, sometimes off) in very real ways. But also in very different ways depending on the context of the horror and the medium in which it's presented. Great horror can even extend its power and, as is the case with my relationship to *The Exorcist*, can continue to replay itself in our lives through a presence that persists through memory: the memory of a scene, an image, a sound, or a mood. This chapter explores the interplay between reality and horror fiction but it does so by focusing on a more recent phenomenon introduced by the entertainment industry: viral marketing as a new form of extended storytelling. Viral marketing finds its starting point in advertising and marketing. The term is often attributed to the venture capitalist Tim Draper who, along with his company Draper Fisher Jurvetson, was instrumental in devising the viral campaigns that launched Hotmail and Yahoo! Mail. Viral marketing relies on techniques that use pre-existing social networks like websites and YouTube in order to increase franchise or brand awareness, the idea being that buzz will spread about the product by word of (digital) mouth much like a virus. As Jurvetson and Draper explain:

> A lot of the energy behind the Internet is the ability for everyone to be a publisher. Consequently, we are in a land grab for precious spectrum — people's attention. Attention is finite. Rising above the noise of a thousand voices requires creativity. Shouting is not very creative. Just hanging up a web shingle and hoping for visitors is not very creative. Rather, new companies can structure their businesses in a way that allows them to grow like a virus and lock out the existing bricks and mortar competitors through innovative pricing and exploitation of these competitors' legacy distribution channel conflict.[1]

In recent years, the entertainment industry has tapped into the potential of this strategy and, in the process, some highly inventive viral marketing campaigns have accompanied the release of films, television series and video games; and the campaign usually takes the form of transmedia story extensions — a media franchise. The examples of transmedia, however, are no longer necessarily connected to traditional media technologies (for example, the story of a film extending into a television series or game). In fact, frequently the stories spill into the spaces that fans inhabit. Some of the most inventive and successful transmedia events are associated with examples of genres that lean more towards the fantastic: science fiction, the supernatural and horror — genres perceived as least likely to find a real parallel in everyday reality and most likely to be embraced as cult objects. In fact, horror cinema is one of the most prolific in terms of adopting viral marketing strategies, which isn't surprising given that the most effective campaigns have played on the blurring of boundaries between reality and fiction — a key tactic favored by horror.

However, in the fictional expansion that occurs across media the sensorium turns its attention to an intensive cognitive and sensorial immersion into fictions that are dispersed across multiple media environments, which also include the "spectator's" actual geographic landscape. As will be discussed in this chapter, new forms of transmedia have radically transformed how participants engage with fictional universes. Transmedia events such as those that accompanied the television series *Lost* (ABC, 2004–10) and *True Blood* (HBO, 2008–), the blockbuster films *A.I. Artificial Intelligence* (Steven Spielberg, 2001) and *The Dark Knight* (Christopher Nolan, 2008), and the video game *Halo 2* (Microsoft Game Studios, 2004) introduced the idea of the endlessly expanding mediascape. In such a mediascape, we're no longer just a spectator or game player; instead (if choosing to participate), we become embroiled in a collective experience that not only requires us to communicate with other media fans, but which also places us in fictional scenarios that present themselves as "realities." This chapter focuses on examples of viral marketing campaigns and transmedia events that have accompanied the release of the films *The Blair Witch Project* (Daniel Myrick, 1999), *The Dark Knight*, *Cloverfield* (Matt Reeves, 2008) and *The Crazies* (Breck Eisner, 2010) and the television series *Lost* and *True Blood*. In doing so, my interest is in exploring the ways these examples address the fiction/reality interplay by migrating their stories more invasively into the social sphere. Developing strategies familiar to alternate reality games, they produce a networked environment; characters often escape their media-delivery systems and enter the world that we inhabit, demanding that we interact with their reality while they occupy our reality. When faced with such fictions, the demands on our sensorium are different to how we interact with screen or text media because often (as is the case with theme parks) we're required to physically navigate our city spaces in search of fictional fragments that have escaped their media screens. Sensory correspondences are no longer required because in this, our reality, we smell, taste, touch, hear, see and move our way towards our beloved media object. Such transmedia events create spaces that both perform *for* the audience and which are for performing *within*.

The transmedia examples discussed in this chapter, and their function as viral "campaigns," are driven by today's "Experience Economy," a new form of late 20th early 21st-century consumer experience that's closely affiliated with the entertainment industry, digital media, and conglomeration. The strategies integral to this economy are heavily dependent on multimedia environments that create networked links across geographic space: their ultimate aim is to engage the senses and demand sensory play. Economists and business strategists Joseph Pine and James Gilmore have provided in-depth studies on how the Experience Economy has affected consumption and marketing strategies over the last decade.[2] Arguing that businesses must orchestrate memorable events for their customers, they also stress that memory itself becomes the product: it's the experience and the memory that's purchased. In order to create a memorable experience (whether in a museum, a retail store, a cinema event, a theme park visit, a viral-transmedia fiction) the company responsible must address the "consumer" as an actor who's part of a performance. The primary strategy used to fully immerse the "actor-consumer" in their performance as gallery visitor, retail shopper, film viewer and, I'd add, transmedia participant, is to directly activate as many of the senses as possible.[3] In an experience-based economy, goods and services are no longer enough, Pine and Gilmore proclaim. The new demand is for experiences that appeal to visceral interests. Brian Lonsway expands on how the Experience Economy has been heavily influenced by the immersive encounters that are typical of theme parks:

> It is literally an economy of branded emotion, where the spatio-temporal production of sites of experience correlates to brand affiliation and repeat consumerism. Its experiences are staged, performed, and executed according to script, yet are meant to be participant in the unpredictable arenas of everyday life.[4]

Transmedia storytelling as a form of viral marketing exemplifies the qualities required of Experience Economy strategies. As our favorite fictions enter our everyday world, and as we become embroiled in adventures they throw our way with combined intellectual and sensory intensity, we forget that they're a marketing strategy devised to sell a product. What we do remember is the memory of the experience and how it seduces our sensorium.

Puppet Masters, Rabbit Holes and Operational Aesthetics

In the 1950s, the famous (and infamous) horror filmmaker William Castle devised some inventive and sometimes not-so-inventive gimmicks and illusions that played on the fiction/reality divide that's at the center of the horror experience. In what were effectively publicity stunts, his intention was to create the perception that the horror had escaped the screen and entered the space of the auditorium. For example, publicized as being filmed in "Emergo," during the screening of *House on Haunted Hill* (1959), a glow-in-the-dark skeleton attached to a wire appeared over the audience, as if emerging from within the screen; in *The Tingler* (1959), which was filmed in "Percepto," one of the creatures (that attaches itself to the human spine) escaped the film and entered the space of the theater, whose seats were fitted with buzzers that shocked select audience members who were also encouraged to scream for their lives; and in *Homicidal* (1961) a voiceover interrupted the film to let the audience know how much time they had to leave the cinema (in case they were too scared to watch the rest of the film) and still receive a refund.[5] Castle's publicity stunts, however, were most often contained within the confines of the viewing experience itself. More recently, these kinds of marketing strategies that display horror exiting the safety of the media screen have reached new limits. In addition to the popularity of real fusion and 3D cinema and television (new media experiences that the horror genre has adopted with ease), other media — including computers and mobile phones — have further adapted to new forms of storytelling that actively involve the audience in the process of meaning construction. In light of these shifts, the nature of storytelling itself needs to be reassessed in order to take into account the intense emphasis on transmediality.

In the chapter titled "Searching for the Origami Unicorn: *The Matrix* and Transmedia Storytelling" and on his blog, Henry Jenkins provides a neat summation of some of the key features of transmedia storytelling.

> Transmedia storytelling represents a process where integral elements of a fiction get dispersed systematically across multiple delivery channels for the purpose of creating a unified and coordinated entertainment experience.... There is no one single source or ur-text where one can turn to gain all of the information needed to comprehend the ... [fictional] universe.... Most often, transmedia stories are based not on individual characters or specific plots but rather complex fictional worlds which can sustain multiple interrelated characters and their stories. This process of world-building encourages an encyclopedic impulse in both readers and writers. We are drawn to master what can be known about a world which always expands beyond our grasp.[6]

So when did this encyclopedic world building across multiple delivery channels begin? In 2001, Elan Lee, Sean Stewart and Jordan Weisman formulated an alternate reality game (ARG) called "The Beast" which would precede, provide publicity for, and market the release of the science fiction film *A.I. Artificial Intelligence*. Financed by Microsoft (for whom Lee and Weisman worked), the online game focused on blurring the line between game and reality. Having previously created games on Xbox, Lee explains how

> we thought, what if we built a game that didn't actually live on any platform, it just sorta lived everywhere. And characters could call you, and characters could send you email, and the characters that you saw in one game could hop out of that game into the real world for a while, and you'd play along with them. And then they'd hop into the next game, and that's episode two. Episode three

they're gonna hop back out into the real world, play with you, and then episode four they jump into the next Xbox game. So we built that, and we called it The Beast, because we didn't know what else to call it and we thought it would be cool.[7]

This new form of seriality was orchestrated by the "puppet masters" (game creators) who set this real-time game in the year 2142, 50 years after the events in *A.I.* A series of rabbit holes (entries into the game) triggered a complex chain of events in the gameplay involving emails, trailers, posters, phone calls, and interviews with characters about Jeanine Salla, a sentient machine therapist. A murder mystery ensued and the "player" followed a series of clues over a period of three months, which unraveled as games to be solved, and which included a plot involving an Anti-Robot Militia and a Coalition for Robot Freedom.[8] Relying on the collaborative effort of players, online puzzles were solved and other activities emerged, which included phoning a security guard and trying to convince him to save someone being tortured, and attending anti-robot protest rallies held in at "real" locations in New York, Los Angeles, and Chicago. As Adrian Hon explains,

> By the time the game ended in July, it had attracted an audience of over a million and gained international media attention from CNN, ABC, BBC, the New York Times, USA Today and any number of websites. "The Beast" ... had been a resounding success in promoting *A.I.* and is acknowledged to be the first ever alternate reality game; it had created a consistent reality, expressed through the Internet and other media, that told a rich and interactive story to a million people around the world.[9]

Considered to be the first transmedia ARG to be used for viral marketing purposes, the success of the campaign was such that Lee and Weisman co-founded their own company — 42 Entertainment — in 2003. And with that move, a new transmedia-entertainment industry was born.

The next project for 42 Entertainment was "I Love Bees," an ARG-development to promote the release of the Xbox game *Halo 2*. "I Love Bees" went "live" in 2003, at which point "some half a million players engaged in a kind of informational scavenger hunt, sometimes working in smaller teams, sometimes working together as a mass problem-solving community."[10] Some of the online action and puzzles directed them to actual geographical locations, including payphone locations across the U.S. where players had to answer questions posed to them by actors. Produced on a limited budget, "I Love Bees" became a cost-effective way to create interest about the game before its release "and demonstrated perfectly how the viral nature of ARGs allows them to attract large audiences ... and just as importantly, create a rich and compelling 'alternate reality' storyline."[11] Yet, as Henry Jenkins stresses, these ARGs moved beyond only being considered as a means to a marketing end; not only do they teach players to "navigate complex information environments" but they rely on what cyber theorist Pierre Levy calls "collective intelligence" in order to solve the puzzles and questions the games pose.[12]

> Pierre Levy coined the term, collective intelligence, to refer to new social structures that enable the production and circulation of knowledge within a networked society. Participants pool information and tap each others expertise as they work together to solve problems. Levy argues that art in an age of collective intelligence functions as a cultural attractor, drawing together like-minded individuals to form new knowledge communities.... Consumers become hunters and gatherers moving back across the various narratives trying to stitch together a coherent picture from the dispersed information.[13]

Linking information collected through mobile technologies, players/fans collectively pooled information in order to find solutions to problems presented by the ARG; and, in doing so, they contributed to and advanced the story of "I Love Bees." Consumer as "hunters and gatherers" become embroiled in what Jason Mittell calls an "operational aesthetic." While Mittell is analyzing changes that have occurred in television viewing practices in light of DVD technology, his argument is also pertinent to transmedia events:

> Having control of when and how you watch also helps deepen one of the major pleasures afforded by complex narratives: the operational aesthetic. Deriving from Neil Harris's analysis of P.T. Barnum's public entertainments, the operational aesthetic takes pleasure in marveling at how a cleverly crafted bit of entertainment is put together, highlighting a meta-appreciation of a hoax or contraption. I extend this concept to the act of watching narrative television, as viewers simultaneously immerse themselves in a fictional world and step back to consider how the story is constructed — in essence, it is taking pleasure in both a story and its telling.[14]

Transmedia events offer similar kinds of operational aesthetics. Part of the pleasure comes from choosing to participate in the unraveling of increasingly complex narratives that both reflect back on a media fiction that may be a film or game, but which also open up their own distinctive forms of pleasure. As will be explained below, the sensory assault of horror experienced in films, for example, now takes a back seat to make way for new kinds of cognitive and sensory pleasures.

In transmedia-horror events, rather than seeking out the thrill of the scare, we instead extract cerebral and sensory pleasure by participating in and contributing to a highly crafted fictional world that's in the process of unveiling itself. Much like the buzz a media-literate spectator or player gets from recognizing how a text constructs an intertextual game, the thrill of transmedia fictions comes from a "meta-appreciation" of the fiction: this meta-appreciation is the result of the active role we play both as participants who make the narrative unfold and make sense, and as observers who delight in the unveiling of deciphered clues, which, in turn, exposes the mastery of the puppet masters who built these complex, networked worlds. These pervasive games require a reconsideration of storytelling practices in that they rely on active player interaction and immersion — sometimes individually, sometimes collectively — across media and in physical reality.

The Blair Witch Project and the Arrival of Viral Horror

Elan Lee is keenly aware of the power inherent in digital technology as a new delivery system for such extended ARG stories. The home page to Fourth Wall Studios, Lee's new company, states the following:

> The fourth wall is the imaginary barrier between the audience and the stage. We create compelling worlds that live on the other side of that wall. These are stories you can visit with your browser, hear on your cell phone, or see out of your window. Beyond the fourth wall ... beyond the book covers, beyond the frame of a television set, beyond the boundaries of a game console ... is where the stories of the 21st century want to live.[15]

Yet, the collapse of the fourth wall has a long history across a variety of media. I'm reminded especially of that infamous performance that occurred on October 30, 1938, when Orson Welles and the Mercury Theater actors presented a live broadcast of H.G. Wells's *The War of the Worlds* on the CBS radio network. The Halloween performance of this radio drama has gone down in history for causing panic among some listeners who believed that Martians had actually landed on planet Earth. Updating the Wells story by presenting it as a series of live news bulletins, for this one-hour production Welles strategically relied on a realist aesthetic that dramatically impacted the listeners' perception of the audience/stage divide. The extent of the mayhem can be gleaned from the headlines that appeared the next day in newspapers across the U.S.A. The Chicago *Herald-Examiner* proclaimed, "Radio Fake Scares Nation," the *New York Daily News* announced, "Fake Radio 'War' Stirs Terror Through US," while *The New York Times*' headline read, "Radio Listeners in Panic, Taking War Drama as Fact."[16] For listeners who were oblivious to the fact that they were listening to an updated version of the Wells classic, there was no barrier: the staged events were real and occupied the space of the audience. The result was that real horror had entered their space, threatening their lives and human society at large.

This blurring of boundaries between reality and fiction — all in the name of horror — would happen again at the end of the 20th century heralded by the publicity that preceded the release of *The Blair Witch Project* in 1999. But this time there was a new media kid on the block that would facilitate the illusion of the collapse of the fourth wall: the internet. The film is about a group of film students who, in 1994, decide to make a documentary about the "real" Blair Witch. Trekking to Burkittsville, Maryland, and armed with cameras, they interview locals about the legendary witch and then trek to the woods in search of her presence. One by one they disappear and all that's left in the end is the footage they filmed on their final journey. This fact, however, is not one that was first unveiled during the film; instead it was a "fact" that became the buzz generator leading up to the film's release. The first screening of the film occurred on the January 29, 1999, at the Sundance Film Festival, and this was soon followed by Artisan Entertainment buying the film for distribution. For the next six months prior to the film's U.S. release on July 14, Artisan and the team at Haxan Films — the independent company that produced *The Blair Witch Project*— transformed the film's website www.blairwitch.com into an innovative marketing tool that bargained on the film's status as "real." The website became a repository in which found footage left behind by the victims was released in segments along with posters about the missing students (which had also been distributed at festival screenings), creating a sense of urgency about the soon-to-be released "documentary." In addition, limited screenings of the film were held on university campuses and a special "investigative" show called *The Curse of the Blair Witch* was aired on the Sci-Fi channel.[17] The television show unveiled the back-story and revealed the objects that were discovered by students from the University of Maryland's Anthropology Department in the Black Hills of Maryland on October 16, 1995 — a year after the film students supposedly disappeared — which included "film cans, DAT tapes, video-cassettes, a Hi-8 video camera, Heather's journal and a CP-16 film camera buried under the foundation of a 100 year-old cabin." The "crime scene" discoveries, we were told, were eventually released by the Frederick County Sheriff's office.[18] As Tim Carvell observes, "These low-key responses helped foster the belief amongst audience members that they'd discovered the film for themselves, a belief that, in turn, fed traffic to the site."[19] On the opening weekend, the full-page ad for the film in *Variety* didn't plug the film but instead proclaimed, "Blairwitch.com. 21,222,589 hits to date,"[20] generating even greater interest in the film as an event not to be missed.

The innovation of *The Blair Witch Project* lay in its external relationship to the web publicity and the television exposé. For someone unaware of the hoax, the information delivered on the web served to heighten the horror in anticipation of the viewing of the film. Remediating a horror tradition that bargained on the old "based on real events" ploy (for example, *Psycho* and *Texas Chainsaw Massacre*), the producers of *The Blair Witch Project* fabricated the "real events." The horror had, future spectators were told, originated in the real-world environment of Burkittsville, Maryland, and here was all the proof! As Gregg Hale, one of the film's producers, explains, "We allow people the illusion it's all real." In Australia, however, the film was released on December 9, 1999 — over four months after the publicity blitz — by which time the proverbial cat was out of the bag. Did this make the film a flop? No. In fact, it attracted a huge audience because of the sheer virtuosity of the marketing hoax. Sure, the eventual experience of *The Blair Witch Project* was a different one in that not many viewers were creeped out by the "based on real events" hoax, but the pleasure now circulated around both film and extratextual information being about a game of horror. It was a game about participating in the production of horror.

In her fine analysis of *The Blair Witch Project* and the extratextual experiences associated with it, Jane Roscoe explains that even in the U.S. not all viewers were duped by the publicity stunt; in fact, many were aware of the "this is real horror" hoax. But, as she notes, this made possible a dual experience of the film both as horror and as a critical discourse about immersing ourselves in *The Blair Witch Project* as a horror film.[21] Part of the pleasure, therefore, came from a critical game; the participant was invited to untangle the story events online and onscreen as puzzles to be deciphered, and this made *The Blair Witch Project* a radically different experience to the radio broadcast of *The War of the Worlds*. In both instances, a realist aesthetic was evoked; however, *The Blair Witch Project*[22] also extended its story across media, therefore prompting the audience's active engagement with the storytelling process. In doing so, however, aside from scaring some people who believed in the deception, *The Blair Witch Project* is emblematic of most transmedia horror ARGs: rather than duplicating the cinematic (or televisual) experience of horror, in horror ARGs it's more about participating in the game and its puzzles and in untangling the pieces in an expanding narrative web.

Since the release of *The Blair Witch Project*, entertainment media have undergone dramatic transformations that amplify the performative potential of multiple modes of media reception that center on the same narrative premise. The emphasis on playing on the illusion that the media fiction is real is central to the performance. The key words in this instance are "play" and "performance:" the participant is invited to literally play and become part of a performance *as if it's real*. Roscoe's preference for the term "extratextual," however, no longer fully encapsulates the nature of viral-media extensions. "Transmedia," a term coined by the interactive narrative designer and writer Stephen Dinehart, best reflects the new era of viral marketing ARGs. Whereas "extratextual" implies something outside the main text, and "crossmedia" involves diversification of one media franchise across multiple media, in the case of transmedia storytelling, "content becomes invasive and permeates fully the audience's lifestyle."[23] Transmediality doesn't necessarily prioritize a single text; instead, multiple media fragments extend from the primary franchise (for example, *Lost, True Blood, Cloverfield, The Crazies*) and the new center becomes the viewer/user/player (VUP).[24] According to Dinehart,

> In a transmedial work the viewer/user/player transforms the story via his or her own natural cognitive psychological abilities, and enables the Artwork to surpass [the] medium. It is in transmedial play that the ultimate story agency, and decentralized authorship can be realized. Thus the VUP becomes the true producer of the Artwork. The Artist authored transmedia elements act as story guide for the inherently narratological nature of the human mind ... to become thought, both conscious and subconscious, in the imagination of the VUP.[25]

The television show *Lost*, for example, has played a significant, even groundbreaking, role in using viral marketing to create transmedia stories that permeated the fictional space of its TV universe to enter the media worlds of mobile phones, podcasts, comic books, novels and the internet. In doing so, the television viewer became Dinehart's VUP, actively generating and unraveling the *Lost* story as they engaged with each transmedia development. Embracing the era of viral marketing (and the social networking upon which it relies to sell its products) head on, *Lost* also encouraged the transformation of the cityscape itself into a theatrical space; the performance that is the television show filtered through and beyond the boundaries of the television medium.

Lost, and "The *Lost* Experience" alternative reality game/viral marketing experience that developed from it, drives home the fact that meaning and coherence of the text in media culture of the last decade is reliant on an audience that's capable of embracing multiple-media "texts" in order to extract more complex layers of meaning from the experience that is the main franchise. "The *Lost* Experience" ran alongside the second season of *Lost*. Labeled a "game" and influenced by one of the earliest forays into viral marketing as extended storytelling, it is that and so much more. By adapting the "rules" of viral marketing, the *Lost* team aimed for the viewer/user/player to actively participate in the experience and bring the narrative information extracted from that experience back with them to inform their understanding of "TV— *Lost*." While not an example of "straight" horror, part of the puzzle to be solved in *Lost* centered on its generic hybridity. Was the source of the numerous mysteries encountered by characters in *Lost* the result of horror, science, religion or the supernatural?

The "Experience" involved the audience becoming integrated into extended *Lost* stories; some unraveled on the web, some on television and some in the player's "real" space. For example, Hanso Foundation advertisements were aired during the commercial breaks for the *Lost* TV series and included a number to call for information about the Hanso Foundation website. Here, players then discovered that the Hanso Foundation, through its funding of the Dharma Initiative (the secret science project apparently funded by the Hanso Foundation in the 1970s) was involved in the construction of facilities on the island that were depicted in *Lost*. Significantly, nearly all information that viewers had at that stage about the Hanso Foundation was drawn from its fictional website, TheHansoFoundation.org and other sites that were part of the *Lost Experience*, rather than narrative events occurring in the television series.

Identifying the Holes

Dinehart outlines the key strategy involved in this type of transmedia-narrative development, explaining how it's important to "identify the holes" in the main franchise:

> The story will have holes, it's inevitable; sometimes BIG holes, ones you can't cover up. That is, things will be unanswered for the audience, and some questions will beg to be answered. By no means are you required to address these holes, heck you might want to ignore them altogether, but you need to ask yourself and your team which ones are important to expanding the franchise and compelling it forward? ... Just how is a player going to experience your story? Or how will they create their own? Looking at narrative delivery in the previous installments and entry points to the franchise can help you identify key systems for development. This is true for any medium your transmedia franchise is covering.... Identifying the parts which deliver your narrative allows you to design the "narremes," or story elements within a particular media, to fit just right within your transmedia sphere. A transmedia sphere is a collection of the media types you are using to execute the transmedia property.[26]

In *Lost*, the holes included information about the Hanso Foundation, the Dharma Initiative, Oceanic Airlines, Apollo Candy and the Bad Twin script — all "holes" that were deliberately left unfilled by the scriptwriters during the first few seasons. To feed the interest in filling some of these holes a fictional Oceanic Airlines website was established that posted announcements about flight cancellations, and players could check for the victims of flight 815. The site ApolloCandy.com appeared and promoted a chocolate bar named Apollo (which characters had been seen eating in the TV series) and it was later revealed that the Apollo Candy Company was bought by Alvar Hanso, the founder of the Hanso Foundation.[27] And on the television show characters were seen reading a manuscript titled "Bad Twin," which was written by Gary Troup, who died in the crash of Oceanic Flight 815; those participating in "The *Lost* Experience," however, would discover that the manuscript had been delivered to the publisher and the book was, in fact, available for purchase from Amazon.com.[28]

One of the most dramatic strategies involved the character Rachel Blake (also known as Persephone), who was introduced to guide players through "The *Lost* Experience" and to also encourage belief in a real-world conspiracy orchestrated by the Hanso Foundation — the idea being that the secret experiments taking place on the island were also taking place in our reality. At an event that took place at the San Diego Comic Con in 2006, in a room full of thousands of fans, the "real" Rachel Blake stood up and confronted the *Lost* writers, stars, and producers on the *Lost* panel, demanding they tell the truth about the real-life conspiracy that they were covering up. As the panel insisted that the show was only fictional, and accompanied by the cheers and applause of fans in the crowd, Rachel Blake was carried off by Comic Con security.[29] All of these interconnected transmedia activities and experiences generated and heightened the *Lost* mythology and, in the process, aimed at playfully blurring the boundaries between illusion and reality.[30] In doing so, *Lost*'s transmedia strategy created a cult experience around the consumption of the text.

Horror, science fiction and fantasy genres have, historically, been more susceptible to the wiles of cult and transmediality. Yet, as Gwenllian-Jones and Pearson explain, cult films belong "to a 'paracinematic culture' that seeks to promote an alternative vision of cinema," one that questions "the legitimacy of reigning aesthetic discourses" which favor linear, self-contained stories that aspire to narrative resolution and closure.[31] That which distinguishes cult film from cult television is "a characteristic shared with the many other American television dramas": the serial form. According to Gwenllian-Jones and Pearson:

> Interconnected story lines, both realized and implied, extend far beyond any single episode to become a metatext that structures production, diegesis, and reception. Cult television's imaginary universes support an inexhaustible range of narrative possibilities, inviting, supporting, and rewarding close textual analysis, interpretation, and inventive reformulations.[32]

The cult experience can become dramatically amplified by the serial logic of television and, in the process, attract audiences that "inspire significant interpretive fan cultures" that frequently diverge from the meanings "intended" by the television show producers. The very nature of these series is to be participatory and to become immersed in an emergent mythological universe that rewards an understanding of its content. The recent addition of transmedia storytelling has transferred this intense seriality to a number of other media, including film and video games, but has added to a more intense form of activity. When considering the transmedia ARGs, the extreme serialization and dispersal of the fiction across a range of media and into the lived environment of the participant requires a sensorium that's always on the alert. *Lost* was a series that bargained on the fluid and slippery nature of its generic status — was it science fiction, was it horror, or was it supernatural? The audience really never found out and yet while watching, through generic expectation we were called upon to adjust our cognitive and sensory responses accordingly, depending on how a scene or storyline was playing out. The shift into "The *Lost* Experience" offers a different experience.

As Dinehart explains, our cognitive ability "enables the Artwork to surpass [the] medium." The dispersal of the text that is the television show across media and geographic spaces requires the VUP to become involved in an active cognitive role that not only deciphers bits of information, but also constructs a narrative that's the product of their own orchestration: the "Artist authored transmedia elements act as story guide for the inherently narratological nature of the human mind," which actively expands the *Lost* mythology as it unravels in time and space. However, our participation alternates from meta-appreciation of the narrative events and how they're delivered (for example, the Rachel Blake stunt at the Comic Con), to an emotional and sensory immersion in that very narrative — a desire to, in a sense, believe in it as if it is a reality. The latter is attested to by the audience response at the Comic Con: as the writers and actors of the show denied that the Hanso Corporation existed in our real world, the audience went wild, only too willing to support Rachel in her quest to expose the conspiracy. Part of the pleasure derived from participating in the transmedia ARGs is because of the dualistic interplay between the metatextual awareness and appreciation of the text's artistry, and the desire to lose oneself in that artistry and perform in it as if it's a reality.

While *Lost* and its transmedia venture didn't bargain heavily on its horror status, the HBO series *True Blood* did. The series upped the ante on its viral blitz, consciously tapping into the show's mainstream-cult potential. In *True Blood,* the existence of "Tru Blood," the synthetic blood invented by scientists, was the trigger that influenced the vampire race to "come out" to the humans. But this iconic product consumed by so many vamps in the fictional world of Bon Temps would soon also become available to humans in the real world: consume the television series that is *True Blood*? Now you can consume the fictional product that was the impetus for the show's narrative premise. But this Tru Blood comes not in Types A, B and O-positive; instead it's a soda drink in the flavor of blood-orange that comes with the tag-lines "All Flavor. No Bite" and "Suck on this" (TruBeverage.com) (fig. 28).[33] And while you can follow the vampire lead by heating up your Tru Blood to 98.6 degrees to match human body temperature, it just doesn't have the same kick to it as the cooled-down version. The Tru Blood soda was advertised on giant billboards across the world, including Russia (fig. 29), the U.S., France (fig. 30) and China (fig. 31). Other ads were included in magazines and on the internet, adding strength to the sensation that *True Blood*'s fictional world and its characters where actually part of our own world. In New Zealand, a billboard was inserted onto a building site that warned, "On Hold. Vampire Lair Discovered. Sorry for the Inconvenience," while other posters read "In case of Vampire ... snap here" and included wooden stakes below that could be snapped off in case of vampire emergency. For convenience, the poster even included an icon of a vampire outline with a hand plunging a stake into the area of the heart![34]

In the lead up to the beginning of Season One, the marketing company Campfire (which had also worked on the viral campaign for *The Blair Witch Project*) created buzz about the series by releasing a faux vampire dating site, a blog, fake vampire websites, a mockumentary presented in news format about the coming out of vampires in our reality. A series of videos released (on bloodcopy.com and on You Tube) showed previously undercover vampires coming out to the world, while others showed normal humans freaking out

Figure 28: Tru Blood, the fictional product that was the impetus for the narrative premise of *True Blood* (HBO) (*True Blood*, HBO).

Figure 29: The Tru Blood soda was advertised on giant billboards across the world, including in Russia (*True Blood*, HBO).

about this revelation. Gregg Hale, from Campfire, announced: "We built this on solid storytelling and the idea of immersing people in this world.... We never tried to fool anybody; we wanted to give them an entertaining experience and a way down the rabbit hole."[35] Digital Kitchen, the company that produced the show's riveting opening-title sequence, also contributed to the viral campaign across all seasons, targeting actual companies which, in turn, also plugged their own products. The advertisements targeted vampire consumers as if they actually existed in the real world and included: giant billboard campaigns for the BMW Mini whose tagline read, "Feel the Wind in Your Fangs" (fig. 32); Harley-Davidson ("Outrun the sun"); Monster.com ("Vampires unique physiology qualifies them for jobs too dangerous for humans"); Gillette ("Dead Sexy. Vampires prefer the fusion shave," fig. 33); Geico ("The money you could save if you were immortal. Even vampires save 15%"); and the fragrance Marc Ecko ("Attract a human").[36] Advertising spots for full-page ads were also bought in *US Weekly, USA Today, Financial Times*, and the *New York Observer*.[37] The Fellowship of the Sun, the show's anti-vampire Christian organization that featured heavily in Season Two, has its own fully functional (and hysterically funny) website, which includes information about living a better, sanctified, vampire-free life.[38] The Fellowship was also responsible for the numerous giant posters that appeared plastered on walls around the world, one showing a cute little boy with text that read, "To them he's

Figure 30: The Tru Blood soda drink billboard displayed in France (*True Blood*, HBO).

just a midnight snack" (fig. 34). On the flip side, the American Vampire League (americanvampireleague.com) posted their own posters, advocating equality for all citizens and asking for support for the vampire rights amendment act, stating that "vampires were people too," but anti-vampire sympathizers then graffitied the faces of politicians advocating these rights, drawing vampire fangs on them and scribbling "Killers" across the ad (fig. 35).

Figure 31: The Tru Blood soda drink billboard displayed in China (*True Blood*, HBO).

Figure 32: Part of the HBO viral marketing campaign for *True Blood* included "real" advertisements that targeted vampire consumers as if they actually existed in the real world. In this billboard was for the BMW Mini the tagline read, "Feel the Wind in Your Fangs" (*True Blood*, HBO).

Figure 33: The *True Blood* Gillette billboard claimed the following: "Dead Sexy. Vampires prefer the fusion shave" (*True Blood*, HBO).

There's a crucial difference, however, in terms of how the sensorium responds to these emerging fictions as compare to the television show. In Chapter Four I discussed the way *True Blood* explores the darker, more sinister dimensions of sexuality and eroticism. Scenes like the one between Bill and Lorena having violent, vampiric sex not only have the capacity to play out their horrifying actions across the body of the spectator, but they also reveal a kind of sensory intelligence — what Korsmeyer calls an "aesthetic of disgust"— that, through disgust and horror forces us to deliberate on the narrative actions onscreen. The series is like the dark double of *Twilight:* where *Twilight* avoids graphic displays of splatter, gore, horror and sex, *True Blood* basks in it (remember Season 3, when Russell Edgington, the Vampire King of Mississippi, insisted on carrying the decimated, gluggy remains of his dead vampire lover in a jar?). Yet, in the shift to transmedia expansions that pretend that vampires are indeed part of our everyday reality, a new experience is offered. Here, *True Blood* participates in a performance that's about meta-horror — we take delight in the playful fiction that insists that, like the series, vampires are part of our community. But unlike the series, which can trigger sensory responses of disgust, horror, shock and laughter, the transmedia fictions invite responses of amusement and cognitive play. The sensory reactions in this instance have as much to do with the day-to-day negotiation of our bodies, for example, as we drive down a busy street then happen to see a billboard ad for Gillette shavers for vampires. Or, as we sit in front of computer watching the online vampire variety show *The Perspective* hosted by Victoria Davis (which is part of the transmedia experience) when we happen across celebrity chef Tom Colicchio (from *Top Chef*) appearing in one of the cooking segments.[39] Admittedly, watching Colicchio create recipes for those awkward situations when your vampire friends have been invited to dinner but can't eat human food had me guffawing no end. But while I felt a thrill of pleasure

Figure 34: Fellowship of the Sun, the fictional anti-vampire Christian group from *True Blood*, spread their warnings about the evil of vampires across the real world. (*True Blood*, HBO).

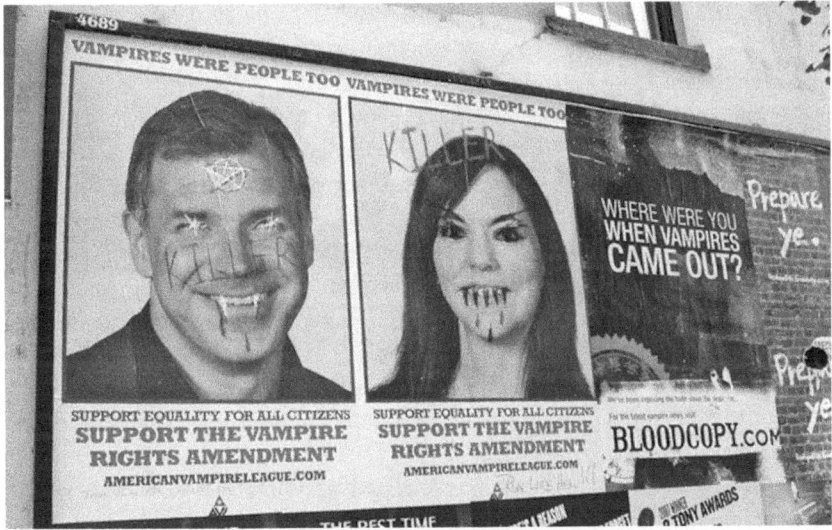

Figure 35: The American Vampire League advocated equality for all citizens and support for the vampire rights amendment act, but anti-vampire sympathizers graffitied the faces of the supporters, defacing them with vampire fangs (*True Blood*, HBO).

run through my body, this sensory response was more the result of the metatextual reflexivity than a response akin to "Oh, my god! Vampires exist and Colicchio's in on it!" The sensation of horror takes a back seat in these transmedia fictions, and is replaced by a cognitive and sensory satisfaction that relishes in the performativity and playfulness of the text.

The films *Cloverfield* and *The Crazies* released similar transmedia assaults on the eager horror, science fiction and fantasy fan community. The blurring of reality and fiction was a strategy adopted by *The Crazies*, a remake of the 1973 film by the same name directed by George Romero. In the film, the locals of the town of Odgen Marsh, infected by a toxic secret military virus, become crazy psycho-killers. That's the premise of the horror and the viral campaign aimed at spilling this into the social sphere by setting up sites like SaveOgdenMarsh.com, which is the blog of real-but-fictional character Kim Jonson. Kim uploaded her activist beliefs and video blogs in an effort to expose the Dakon/Prendrill Chemicals, a local plant that's the cause of the horror in the film. But the site merged reality and fiction: while following information about Dakon/Prendrill Chemicals and watching the unraveling threat to Kim that viewers witnessed through her video blogs, other blogs included: exposés about real environmental threats posed by actual companies; posts about President Obama's support of the U.S. subsidiaries of two French companies agreeing to install new pollution controlling technologies in 28 plants; and plugs and links to Greenpeace.

The Crazies' ARG campaign didn't achieve the desired success — for the ARG or for the film. The same can't be said for the teaser viral campaign that accompanied the pre-release of *Cloverfield*. It all began with a mysterious trailer that hit the screens before the screening of *Transformers* (Michael Bay, 2007). It showed a party scene that was videoed by a shaky camcorder; the partying ceased as soon as noises were heard and the group, including the camcorder holder, ran for the apartment rooftop to see what was happening. Views of New York revealed explosions and people running in the streets. The chaos was soon followed by a giant object that smashed down on the pavement, soon revealed to be the head of the Statue of Liberty. "'It's alive! It's huge,' someone screams, and soon the screen goes black. There's no hint of a title. Just a release date of 1-18-08."[40] Word spread like wildfire and the clip was soon released on YouTube. The rabbit hole was opened and fans dove in, searching for new clues. The trailer was followed by the site www.1-18-08.com, which initially included a single photo and then was followed by others that depicted scenes of destruction and glimpses of gigantic, mangled corpses of strange-looking creatures. On another site, www.slusho.jp, information was released about the drink Slusho:

> In the history section of the Slusho website, you can read the outlandish story of renown beverage-maker Noriko "Smallest Whale" Yoshida, who perished on a deep-sea search for a secret drink ingredient. Noriko's beverage-making enterprise was later revived by her son, Ganu, a scientist who was inspired to return to the family business after discovering an incredible "deep sea ingredient" that is the key to Slusho's flavor and lauded health benefits. Might this secret ingredient, as silly as it sounds, have some connection to the origins of the *Cloverfield* monster? After all, we learn that it was "discovered on the deep ocean floor, under amazing pressure and in the most extreme cold."[41]

Godzilla fans rejoice! As was the case with *Lost* and *The Lost Experience* (which J.J. Abrams also produced), story details were provided to the participant that existed outside what would be the main film franchise. As the transmedia event continued, it was revealed that Ganu Yoshida was also the CEO of the company Tagruato, a Japanese company whose activities involved deep-sea drilling (www.tagruato.jp), and an interactive on the Tagruato website revealed that one of their drilling sites — the Chuai Station — was on the East Coast of the U.S., right near New York City. Press releases, news reports from around the world, and new websites that provided exposés of Tagruato followed,[42] all arming the future viewers with narrative fragments that would help them fill in gaps (we realized in retrospect) in the upcoming film, which was primarily about the horror of the monster attack and personal dilemmas rather than explanations about where the monster came from. In this case, Dinehart's narrative "holes" were effectively used before the film was released, providing the participant with vital information about the narrative events that they'd eventually experience on the big screen.

Conglomeration and digital technologies have resulted in a convergence culture that connects and makes possible interaction between producers and consumers around media products.[43] The result is a complex set of viewing environments and modes of interaction that nurture the cult experience, fan culture and the worship of the text. Jenkins argues:

> The encyclopedic ambitions of transmedia texts often results in what might be seen as gaps or excesses in the unfolding of the story: that is, they introduce potential plots which can not be fully told or extra details which hint at more than can be revealed. Readers, thus, have a strong incentive to continue to elaborate on these story elements, working them over through their speculations, until they take on a life of their own. Fan fiction can be seen as an unauthorized expansion of these media franchises into new directions which reflect the reader's desire to "fill in the gaps" they have discovered in the commercially produced material.[44]

Transmedia experiences have extended the sensorium trope into the realm of participatory culture in ways that move beyond traditional practices of unauthorized fan culture. Fans usually fill the story "gaps" or "holes" with their own fan fiction or other forms of creative output. Entertainment companies have adapted participatory culture experiences so that it's now the authorized entertainment company that sprinkles the holes with fragments of information that need to be deciphered collectively in order that the narrative is fleshed out. But as Jenkins explains, "A transmedia text does not simply disperse information: it provides a set of roles and goals which readers can assume as they enact aspects of the story through their everyday life."[45] As is the case with video games, but requiring greater interaction across a media network, if fans don't adopt a performative role by decoding the clues and actively participating in the actions required of them, then the fiction won't unfold to completion. The VUP's participation requires intellectual and physical engagement, and the pleasure gained from performing the story across the cityscape is more thrilling than the completion or revelation of the story itself. In short, these new forms of transmedia storytelling require the VUPs to take an active role in creating their own horror media sensorium.

Gotham City as Playground: Transmediality and Dramatic Play

A rigorously holistic approach is the strategy used to target followers of the series. Ensuring that there are multiple ways to access the franchise, the worlds of *Lost*, *True Blood*, *Cloverfield* and *The Crazies* infiltrated the viewer/user/player's everyday environment in intense and immediate ways. To some extent paralleling experiences found in video games, as Dinehart points out, transmedia ARGs aim at "dramatic play" and, in so doing, impact the sensorium with great directness and from multiple media perspectives. This form of dramatic play requires that the participant switch between media and the variety of sensory experiences and intellectual modes of engagement each has to offer. In addition to alternating from television, computer or mobile phone, dramatic play can also involve participants in a drama that extends to the city space itself. Such a move engages the senses more directly when compared to film spectatorship, for example, which relies more on sensory correspondences and memory. And, as will become clear below, the cognition needed to decipher the narrative labyrinths of transmedia ARGs often requires physical motion and a literal kineticism that's foreign both to films and video games.

For example, the massive and innovative viral-marketing campaign — which was called whysoserious.com? — launched over a year before and leading up to the release of *The Dark Knight* in 2008 generated a theatre around a text that hadn't yet been realized but which had been obsessively worshipped (via other Batman stories). While technically a superhero story, the universe of Batman draws upon a variety of generic forms, including horror (consider Batman's iconic association with vampires, a source often consciously alluded to in the comics, and how many of the supervillains often cross the line to become the crazed psycho killers familiar to horror — the Joker being the prime example) and it set the bar for many future horror viral campaigns. A huge viral-blitz campaign, the likes of which hadn't been seen before, relied on a variety of transmedia experiences that also infiltrated the urban sphere. A website supporting the political campaign of the apparently "real" Harvey Dent appeared online (fig. 36) and his image on one of the sites was (over months of increased word-of-mouth viewer access) slowly defaced with graffitied Joker-eyes and the Joker's red-rimmed diabolical smile; in other words, the collective participant access to the site was responsible for defacing the good-guy lawyer and, therefore, mirroring his soon-to-be anticipated fate (in the film) as the defaced supervillain Two-Face.[46] Numerous sites online presented Gotham City as if it were a real city, but more than this, the serial buildup to *The Dark Knight* film addressed fans as actual citizens of "an entire working fake city"[47]; there were real websites for Gotham City cab companies (www.gothamcab.com), the Gotham City newspaper (www.gothamtimes.com), a cable company (www.gothamcablenews.com), the subway (www.gothamcityrail.com), the police (www.gothampolice.com), a pizzeria (www.gothamcitypizerria.com), the Gotham National Bank (www.gothamnationalbank.com), and many others. Inviting participants to side with the Joker, Har-

Figure 36: The viral marketing campaign for *The Dark Knight* (Warner Bros., 2008) included a website supporting the political campaign of the apparently "real" Harvey Dent.

vey Dent or Bruce Wayne/Batman, real-cities-as-Gotham-City were set up as a huge performance spaces in which the transmedia story could play itself out. I remember signing up online in support of Harvey Dent (www.ibelieveinharveydent.com) and Batman (www.citizensforbatman.com) and soon afterwards Commissioner Gordon himself sent me an email thanking me for my support of the Gotham police force and the fight against crime.

Online, the Joker provided clues to be decoded by participants and, in many instances, the solution required going to actual locations in cities in the U.S. in order to find further information that would unlock the next stage of the story. For example, on December 3, 2007, the site whysoserious.com appeared and included numerous images of stuffed toys (fig.37). Each bear included an address located in cities across the U.S. Arriving at the location (a bakery in all instances), and after saying that your name was "Robin Banks," the player received a cake with a phone number written on it and an evidence bag pilfered from Gotham City Police that contained a mobile phone, a charger, a Joker playing card and a note with instructions that provided a number to call. After calling the number, a woman answered from Rent-a-Clown thanking the caller, and soon after a text message was received on the discovered mobile phone: "Good work, clown! Keep this phone charged and with you at all times. Don't call me. I will call you ... eventually." The impli-

Figure 37: On the site whysoserious.com the Joker posted a series of stuffed toys that sent *The Dark Knight* (Warner Bros., 2008) viral participants to various locations across the U.S.

cation was, of course, that the Joker occupied the space of the participant, plotting his crimes against Gotham citizens and the Batman.[48]

Other events involved the Joker asking participants to congregate around famous monuments in their city on a set date dressed as their fearless leader. Then the "clowns" were asked to take photos of themselves and send them to the Joker by uploading them onto the site http://www.rorysdeathkiss.com/. The social dimension of *The Dark Knight* viral campaign reached new heights with the Harvey Dent political rally, which was announced via a phone call in early March 2007 to those who had subscribed as followers of Harvey Dent. The phone call went as follows:

> Hello, I'm Harvey Dent, Assistant District Attorney of Gotham, and I'm calling to ask for your support. We all know what's wrong with Gotham. Crime is out of control. And instead of protecting our streets, too many cops have become criminals themselves. This is why my mission has been to stamp out police corruption, and this is why I'm considering a run for district attorney. But I can't do it alone. I need to know if you, the people of Gotham, want change. Do you want a Gotham free from the grip of criminals and the corrupt? Are you ready to join a crusade to take back our city? If this is a change you desire, if you are fed up with living in fear, go to ibelieveinharveydent.com and see how you can join the struggle to take back our city. I'm ready to fight for Gotham, if you are ready to fight too.

The website announced the touring campaign of the Dentmobile across 34 cities in the U.S. and followers were asked to show their support as Gotham City citizens by attending the rally and voicing their support for Harvey Dent as district attorney. People showed up in the thousands receiving rewards that included Harvey Dent support badges, posters, a Gotham City newspaper and other paraphernalia, and they were also encouraged to plaster Dent posters before (via downloads) and after the event across the walls of their cities. Cognition and the senses united in order to participate in and unveil the secrets of *The Dark Knight*.

On their website, the designers of *The Dark Knight* viral marketing ARG — 42 Entertainment — explain the rationale behind the series of web and live sites they created:

> Why so serious? gave comic book fans and mainstream movie goers the chance to live in the world of the Dark Knight. Playing out the events of Gotham City in real time, the ARG provided the opportunity to explore the strong characters, themes and backdrop of the world while punctuating the experience with activities that "eventized" the web — like ringing cakes with baked-in cell phones, clearing Harvey Dent of vicious campaign attacks or helping the Joker to steal a District 22 school bus to rob Gotham National Bank.[49]

Considering this "eventizing" from the perspective of Giuliano Bruno's concepts of "site-seeing" and "haptic visuality," the participant interaction with *The Dark Knight* viral event and eventual film-viewing experience involved shifting understandings of these concepts. The event entailed a journey into the film that fired up the sensorium through memories that triggered corresponding sensory and synaesthetic encounters; our experience and movement into the film's architectural spaces was enhanced by the canny use of IMAX screens that expanded in width and height to amplify the illusion of movement into the fictional screen world; and our cognitive abilities deciphered the plot, character developments and themes. The internet sites engaged similar experiences, but the haptic also became quite literal because of the required action of the touch of our keyboard and mouse, or the glide of a finger across an iPad screen, and the different cognitive skills necessary to decipher the puzzles and clues that continued to be updated online. The adventures across city locales were actual journeys through city spaces; and integral to these adventures were the accompanying sensations of body movement, sights, smells, sounds, touch and taste. Consider the task required to decode the Joker's cake clue: the cake had to be taken apart by probing hands in order that the evidence contained inside was discovered. The impact of this intense bombardment of the sensorium in transmedia experiences produces the feeling that players are participating in an emerging narrative that isn't fixed or pre-staged but which they perform a key role in unraveling. The participants play with the transmedia narratives as much as the narratives play with them, and this play is written in very real and immediate ways across the body of the viewer/ user/player.

The Total Work of Art and the Return of Baroque Theatricality

Discussing video games and new forms of transmedia-interactive narratives, Dinehart states that it's "at the intersections of interactive media, games, and drama that dramatic play exists." Inspired by the work and theories of the 19th century German composer Richard Wagner, Dinehart encourages the return of the "Gesamtkunstwerk," or

> "the total artwork," the embodiment of all the arts into one fusion in which the fourth wall (screen) is dissolved and the spectator becomes actor-player. Drawing from an adapted definition of his *Total Artwork*, the *Gesamtkunstwerk*, is described as the art work of the future, a work that transplants the player into a dramatic space by all means of his visual and aural faculties, making one forget the confines of reality; to live and breathe in the drama which seems to the player as life itself, and on in the work where seems the wide expanse of a whole world [Wagner 1859]. The key to this dramatic play is the craft of Interactive Narrative Design.[50]

The total work of art desired by Dinehart and Wagner, in fact, has an earlier historical predecessor: the baroque and the concept and strategy of the *bel composto* or, the "beautiful unity of the arts." The intention of *bel composto* was to seamlessly bleed one media form into another, the aim being to produce a total work of art that not only seduces the viewer into its working through "visual and aural faculties" but also entwines them in its narrative action as combined viewer/player/participant. In the baroque unity of the arts, the world succumbed to highly theatrical rules that collapsed the boundaries between fiction and reality; and in collapsing the fourth wall, the world itself became part of the transmedia experience of the baroque: to quote Shakespeare, "All the world's a stage." The viral marketing that generates the production of transmedia narratives aims to promote itself as a microcosmic universe that weaves its way into the VUP's world and which encourages participation with it. From a marketing perspective, the transmedia event becomes emblematic of the media conglomerate that brought it into existence in the first place. Yet, while the media conglomerate may have a marketing directive in mind, the target of that market is the consumer of the text who, as Dinehart stresses, becomes the center of dramatic play during the era of transmediality. The total work of transmedia art makes "one forget the confines of reality; to live and breathe in the drama which seems to the player as life itself."[51]

Transmedia ARGs present modern articulations of the baroque concept of "theatre of the world." Here, the multiplicity that Dinehart discusses is integral to the viewing experience and requires active participation on the part of the VUP in order that sense may be made of object of cult play. Relying on a unity of media arts, *The Blair Witch Project, Lost, True Blood* and *The Dark Knight* take the seriality of television to new limits by extending the medium boundary of the franchise into the everyday environment. In the process, the VUP becomes yet another part of transmedia theater and performance. Returning to the example of *The Dark Knight,* in the ARG involving the Dent rally, participants were also invited to leave a mark of the Batman mythology on their real environment by doing the following:

> Get a video of your school's cheerleading team yelling out chants for Harvey Dent
> Try to cover every square inch of someone's cubicle area with Harvey Dent posters
> Write and perform a "Take Back Gotham" song
> Make up a "Dent Dance" routine
> See if you can get up a Harvey Dent sign in every single window of your dorm building
> Turn your own car into a "Dentmobile"
> Arrange a Dent parade down Main Street
> Make a human pyramid with other Harvey Dent supporters[52]

Harvey Dent's presence became visible as a reality in cities across the U.S., and VUPs were encouraged to enforce the presence of the fiction in reality, in the process leaving innocent bystanders oblivious to the performance of this fictional fragment that was part of the Batman legend, and wondering about who this Dent guy was! In another virtuoso performance, the Dent rallies consisted of combinations of actors pretending to be real citizens supporting Dent for District Attorney and actual citizens pretending to be "real" citizens of Gotham City. The rally turnouts were filmed by Gotham City Cable News and many of the Gotham citizens were interviewed by (fake) journalists about their support for Dent; they played their roles as Dent supporters to the max and their responses were then uploaded onto the Gotham Cable News site and presented as "real" news updates covering the event. Fiction had entered reality, and reality had entered fiction. The cityscape and the networked media environment upon which it relies had become a playground for extending the fictional world of film (and comics) into its spaces; and the real world, in turn, filtered back into the transmedia fictions.

Ultimately, the *Lost, True Blood,* and *The Dark Knight* viral-marketing campaigns bargain on their placement within our reality for their status as "real." Invoking a 21st-century neo-baroque[53] articulation of the "unity of the arts," diverse media — television, films, video games, YouTube, websites, mobile phones, DVDs, podcasts, bowling alleys, bakeries, street corners, parking lots — combine in a harmonious whole and, in the process "surpass their own limits, transcending one into another."[54] Careri argues that the effect of the *bel composto* on the baroque viewer is one that creates a "montage consisting of a series of progressions or leaps from one component of the composto to another"[55]; furthermore, it "is an aesthetic operation in which the heterogeneous multiplicity of the ensemble is taken apart and recomposed by the viewer himself."[56] While he discusses the work of Bernini, the same principle of *bel composto* holds for encounters with transmedia ARGs. Reflecting the logic of operational aesthetics, each media fragment combines cumulatively to give the VUP a more cerebral, participatory and heightened sensorial experience of the primary franchise. The VUP is rewarded by contributing to the fiction — by recomposing the ensemble of networked bits of information distributed across media and across the urban landscape — and therefore making possible a richer, more comprehensive, more corporeal manifestation of the fictional world.

The conglomeration of the media industry that facilitates transmediality is tied in with what's come to be known as the Experience Economy, which has become a new strategy for addressing consumers since the 1990s. The strategies of the Experience Economy involve greater emphasis on theatricality and performativity within the public sphere. The Experience Economy aims to seduce the senses by drawing participants into a theatrical experience that places consumerism at its center. The spatio-temporal production of sites of experience correlates to brand (corporate) affiliation and repeat consumerism. To return to the passage quoted from Lonsway above, the Experience Economy's "experiences are staged, performed, and executed according to script, yet are meant to be participant in the unpredictable arenas of everyday life."[57] As a product of the Experience Economy, transmedia events direct themselves to "the multi-sensory and cognitive dimensions of a staged experience"[58] that place the VUP at the center of a happening that aims to jolt the sensorium into action. In her evaluation of the ARG transmedia craze, Jenka Gurfinkel draws a parallel between the viral ARGs and

> the concept of a secret "code" embedded in clothes — of hidden meanings conveyed in the way people dressed — it all made perfect sense to me. This was already a game all of us in the modern world were playing. It was called Lifestyle.... Whereas in a deliberately produced ARG the key elements of the game's narrative are painstakingly planned out and scripted, the narrative of any Lifestyle ARG becomes the evolving story that its own culture tells about itself.... Whether it's a certain type of music, a fashion aesthetic, an ethos or set of values, specific kinds of community-reinforcing events and experiences, or a particular cultural mythology, these all become indelible components of any Lifestyle ARG "narrative."[59]

Like the clothes you wear, music you listen to, and social networking sites to which you subscribe, transmedia ARGs are another brand that becomes an expression of who you are. Just like many of the other media experiences of horror discussed in this book — the horror films, horror video games, paranormal romances — have their own discrete ways of engaging the sensorium, the transmedia ARGs shift the focus towards sensory experiences that rely on multiple media and spatial encounters that are associated with a "lived experience," a lifestyle. The transmedia performances and their demanding theatricality become intimately intertwined with our bodies, which are integral to the articulation of their media fictions. We have become part of the media sensorium.

Chapter Notes

Introduction

1. Giuliana Bruno, *Atlas of Emotion: Journeys in Art, Architecture and Film* (London: Verso, 2002), 4.
2. Ibid., 9.
3. Ibid., 6.
4. Ibid., 219.
5. Ibid.
6. Ibid., 260.
7. Vivian Sobchack, *Carnal Thoughts: Embodiment and Moving Image Culture* (Berkeley: California University Press, 2004), 67.
8. Ibid., 68–9.
9. Brigitte Peucker, *The Material Image: Art and the Real in Film* (Stanford: Stanford University Press, 2007), 159.
10. Bruno, 256.
11. Ibid., 15.
12. Lisa G. Propst, "Bloody Chambers and Labyrinths of Desire: Sexual Violence in Marina Warner's Fairy Tales and Myths," *Marvels & Tales* 22, no. 1 (2008): 130.
13. Jody Messler Davies, "The Times We Sizzle, and the Times We Sigh: The Multiple Erotics of Arousal, Anticipation, and Release," *Psychoanalytic Dialogues* 16, no. 6 (2006): 674.
14. Sobchack from *The Address of the Eye*, quoted in Linda Williams, *Screening Sex* (Durham: Duke University Press, 2008), 20.
15. Williams, 16.
16. Roland Barthes, *S/Z: an Essay* (London: Hill and Wang, 1970) and *Image-Music-Text* (London: Hill and Wang, 1977).

Chapter 1

1. Susan Buck-Morss, "Aesthetic and Anaesthetic: Walter Benjamin's Artwork Essay Reconsidered," *October* 62 (Autumn 1992): 6.
2. See, for example, Richard Abel and Rick Altman, eds., *The Sounds of Early Cinema* (Bloomington: Indiana University Press, 2001).
3. Giuliana Bruno, *Atlas of Emotion: Journeys in Art, Architecture and Film* (London: Verso, 2002), 254.
4. Ibid., 277.
5. Axelle Carolyn, *It Lives Again! Horror Movies in the New Millennium* (Tolsworth: Telos, 2008), 129.
6. Bishop, Kyle, "Dead Man Still Walking: Explaining the Zombie Renaissance," *Journal of Popular Film & Television* 37:1 (2009), 17.
7. Ibid., 20.
8. Brian Lowry, "Political Anger Finds 'Homecoming' on TV," *Daily Variety* 289:42 (November 30, 2005): 4.
9. Dennis Lim, "Dante's Inferno: A Horror Movie Brings Out the Zombie Vote to Protest Bush's War," *Village Voice* (November 22, 2005): n.p. Also see Cyril Pearl, "Zombie Politics," *Video Business* 26:25 (June 19, 2006): 16.
10. Bishop, 17.
11. Carolyn, 17.
12. Laura U. Marks, *Touch: Sensuous Theory and Multisensory Media* (Minneapolis: Minnesota University Press, 2002), 3. See also Jennifer M. Barker, *The Tactile Eye: Touch and the Cinematic Experience* (Berkeley: University of California Press, 2009).
13. Like many of the originals upon which

the New Horror remakes are based, the 1977 version of *The Hills Have Eyes* was independently produced on a low budget of approximately $250,000 and belongs to an exploitation tradition of filmmaking. *Hills* 2006, on the other hand, was produced for $15 million and released by Fox Searchlight Pictures (see Carolyn, 11); *Hills* 1977 was produced by the independent Blood Relations Company, and found theatrical distribution through New Line Cinema and United Artists Films. As such it belongs to the semi-independent rather than mainstream model of production and distribution. Finding funding from independent sources, Wes Craven then found support from within mainstream for distribution of the film. Commenting on the interest among film critics of the 1980s on "[exploitation horror] films, which situated themselves on the margins of the industry," D.N. Rodowick (among others) has claimed that this is because "the low-budget horror film is often considered as presenting an ideological alternative to mainstream film practice." ("The Enemy Within: The Economy of Violence in *The Hills Have Eyes*," in *The Planks of Reason: Essays on the Horror Film*, ed. Barry K. Grant and Christopher Sharrett (Lanham: Scarecrow Press, 1984), 321.

14. Carolyn, 118.

15. Craven's inspiration for the desert family was the infamous story of Sawney Bean, the 15th-century murderer who set up a family based on incest and interbreeding in the caves of Bannane head in Scotland, surviving on the corpses of the victims who invaded the area — or so the story goes.

16. Robin Wood, "Return of the Repressed," *Film Comment* 14:4 (1978): 27.

17. Christopher Sharrett, "The Idea of Apocalypse in *The Texas Chainsaw Massacre*," in *The Planks of Reason: Essays on the Horror Film*, ed. Barry K. Grant and Christopher Sharrett (Lanham, Scarecrow Press, 1984), 142.

18. This propagation of the nuclear family is parodied ruthlessly in both versions of *Texas Chainsaw Massacre*, where three generations are again represented but this time in the monstrous, cannibal family: Leatherface (who also performs the role of mother), his brother, father, grandfather and the mummified grandmother of the 1974 *Texas*, and the barely alive granny of the 2003 version.

19. Sharrett, 272.

20. Ibid., 298.

21. Julian Hanich, *Cinematic Emotion in Horror Films and Thrillers: The Aesthetic Paradox of Pleasurable Fear* (London: Routledge, 2010), 4.

22. Noel Carroll, *The Philosophy of Horror, or Paradox of the Heart* (New York: Routledge, 1990), 28.

23. Hanich, 8.

24. Carroll, 35.

25. Ibid., 53.

26. Hanich, 5.

27. Vivian Sobchack, *Carnal Thoughts: Embodiment and Moving Image Culture* (Berkeley: California University Press, 2004), 54.

28. Ibid., 54–5.

29. Ibid., 58–9.

30. Paul Rodaway, *Sensuous Geographies: Body Sense, and Place* (London: Routledge, 1994), 3.

31. Ibid., 4

32. Brigitte Peucker, *The Material Image: Art and the Real in Film* (Stanford: Stanford University Press, 2007), 159.

33. Sobchack, 67.

34. Peucker, 159.

35. Ibid., 161.

36. The film is also known as *Zombi, Zombie Flesh Eaters, Gli ultimi zombie*, and *Island of the Living Dead*.

37. Peucker, 164.

38. Of course, during the 1980s there was a lively exchange of conventions between Italian and horror and American horror, and it's difficult to untangle who influenced whom first. It should also be mentioned that, while the Italian horror film of the 1970s and '80s developed its own distinctive brand of splatter and gore (which came from a merger of both Italian and U.S. traditions), this tradition also has precedents in U.S. film culture. Filmmaker Herschell Gordon Lewis, for example, is known as the "Father of Splatter." His films *Blood Feast* (1963) and *Two Thousand Maniacs!* (1964) introduced explicit gore and a new brand of visceral effect into the cinema that would give expression to exploitation cinema.

39. Crétien van Campen, *The Hidden Sense Synesthesia in Art and Science* (Cambridge: MIT Press, 2008), 32.

40. Melinda Szalosky, "Sounding Images in Silent Film: Visual Acoustics in Murnau's *Sunrise*," *Cinema Journal* 41:2 (Winter 2002): 113.

41. Peucker, 159.

42. Aurel Kolnai, *On Disgust*, ed. Barry Smith and Carolyn Korsmeyer (Chicago: Open Court, 2004), 39.

43. Barry Smith and Carolyn Korsmeyer in Kolnai, 1–2.
44. Kolnai, 53.
45. Ibid., 18.
46. Marina Warner, *Phantasmagoria: Spirit Visions, Metaphors, and Media into the Twenty-First Century* (Oxford: Oxford University Press, 2006), 357.
47. Ibid. 357.
48. William Arens, *The Man-Eating Myth: Anthropology and Anthropophagy* (New York: Oxford University Press, 1980), 17.
49. Ibid., 18.
50. Miller, Susan, *Disgust: The Gatekeeper Emotion* (London: Routledge, 2004), 174.
51. Antonius C. G. M. Robben, "Death and Anthropology: An Introduction," in *Death, Mourning, and Burial: A Cross-Cultural Reader*, ed. Antonius C. G. M. Robben (Malden: Wiley-Blackwell, 2004), 9.
52. Phoebe Fletcher, "'Fucking Americans': Postmodern Nationalism and the Contemporary Splatter Film," *Colloquy* 18 (December 2009): 77.
53. Ibid., 81.
54. Bruno, 219.

Chapter 2

1. See John Funge, *Artificial Intelligence for Computer Games: An Introduction* (Wellesley: A K Peters, 2004).
2. The Resident Evil games are as follows: *Resident Evil* (1996), *Resident Evil 2* (1998), *Resident Evil 3: Nemesis* (1999), *Resident Evil Code: Veronica* (2000), *Resident Evil Zero* (2002), *Resident Evil 4* (2005), *Resident Evil 5* (2009). In addition, they include the spin-off "Survivor" and "Outbreak" series. The Survivor series consisted of *Resident Evil: Survivor* (2000), *Resident Evil: Survivor 2 Code: Veronica* (2001), *Resident Evil: Dead Aim* (2003), *Resident Evil: The Umbrella Chronicles* (2007), *Resident Evil: The Darkside Chronicles* (2009), and the Outbreak series of *Resident Evil Outbreak* (2003) and *Resident Evil Outbreak File #2* (2004). The series was also adapted to portable game systems and mobile phones.
3. Bernard Perron, "A Cognitive Psychological Approach to Gameplay Emotions," (paper presented at the 2009 Conference, "Breaking New Ground: Innovation in Games, Play, Practice and Theory," Brunel University, London, United Kingdom, September 1–4, 2009).
4. Tanya Krzywinska, "Hands-On Horror," in *ScreenPlay: Cinema/Videogames/Interfaces*, ed. Geoff King and Tanya Krzywinska (London: Wallflower Press, 2002): 206–223, 208.
5. Peter Brooks, *The Melodramatic Imagination: Balzac, Henry James, Melodrama, and the Mode of Excess* (New Haven: Yale University Press, 1995), ix.
6. Bruno, 15.
7. Marks, 2.
8. Diane Carr, "Play Dead Genre and Affect in *Silent Hill* and *Planetscape Torment*," *Game Studies* 3:1 (May 2003), n.p.
9. Lois Rostow Kuznets, *When Toys Come Alive: Narratives of Animation, Metamorphosis, and Development* (New Haven: Yale University Press, 1994), 7.
10. Kuznets, 180.
11. Matthew Potteiger and Jamie Purinton, *Landscape Narrative: Design Practices for Telling Stories* (New York: John Wiley & Sons, 1998), 3.
12. Henry Jenkins, "Game Design as Narrative Architecture," *First Person: New Media as Story, Performance, Game*, ed. Noah Wardrip-Fruin and Pat Harrigan (Cambridge: MIT Press: 2004).
13. Bruno, 64.
14. Graeme Kirkpatrick "Controller, Hand, Screen: Aesthetic Form in the Computer Game," *Games and Culture* 4:2 (April 2009): 130.
15. Rodaway, 12.
16. Campen, 98.
17. Maurice Merleau-Ponty, *Phenomenology of Perception*, trans. Colin Smith (London: Routledge and Kegan Paul, 1962), 144.
18. See also Markus Waltl, Christian Timmerer, Benjamin Rainer, and Hermann Hellwagner, "Sensory Effects for Ambient Experiences in the World Wide Web," Institute of Information Technology Alpen-Adria-University Klagenfurt, Technical Report No TR/ITEC/11/1.13 (July 2011); and Aaron M. Levisohn, "The Body as a Medium: Reassessing the Role of Kinesthetic Awareness in Interactive Applications," (Multimedia '07 Proceedings of the 15th international conference on Multimedia New York, ACM, 2007).
19. Fiona Macpherson, "Taxonomising the Senses," *Philosophical Studies* 153 (2011): 125. Macpherson elaborates on current studies dealing with an expanded range of sensory modalities: "Candidates for yet more human senses include distinctive pain, temperature and pressure senses instead of one amalga-

mated sense of touch. Scientists have found that there are distinctive receptors that detect temperature, pressure, and painful stimuli and that there are separate spots in the skin receptive to pressure, warmth, cold, and painful stimuli. This has been the main reason that has persuaded some people that there are several senses here. However, in addition to this, some people have thought that the experiences of pressure, temperature, and pain are fairly distinctive; that is, they have rather different phenomenal characters."

20. Levisohn, 485.

21. Potteiger and Purinton, 213.

22. Barbara Maria Stafford, *Artful Science: Enlightenment Entertainment and the Eclipse of Visual Education* (Cambridge: MIT Press, 1994), 121.

23. Stafford, 121.

24. Horst Bredekamp, *The Lure of Antiquity and the Cult of the Machine, the Kunstkammer and the Evolution of Nature, Art and Technology* (Princeton: Markus Wiener, 1995), 2.

25. Bredekamp, 2.

26. Ibid., 4.

27. Ibid., 39.

28. Ibid., 36–9.

29. Steve Grand, *Growing Up with Lucy: How to Build an Android in Twenty Easy Steps* (London: Weidenfeld & Nicolson, 2004).

30. Hugh Everett III, "The Theory of the Universal Wavefunction" in *The Many-Worlds Interpretation of Quantum Mechanics*, ed. Bryce DeWitt and R. Neill Graham (Princeton: Princeton University Press, 1973), 3–140.

31. Anthony Saville, *Leibniz and the Monadology* (London: Routledge, 2000), 121.

32. Gilles Deleuze, *The Fold: Leibniz and the Baroque*, trans. Tom Conley (Minneapolis: University of Minnesota Press, 1993), 51.

Chapter 3

1. The Revenge of the Mummy ride site is available at http://www.revengeofthemummy.com/.

2. Noel Carroll, *The Philosophy of Horror, or Paradox of the Heart* (New York: Routledge, 1990), 19.

3. Like much of the original Coney Island, many of these locations have since met their demise in blazing fires. For information about horror attractions past and present, see *The Haunted Attraction Magazine*, available online at http://www.hauntedattraction.com/. For a detailed listing of all the Coney Island rides and attractions, see the Coney Island Project at http://naid.sppsr.ucla.edu/coneyisland/index.html.

4. See, for example, Wolfgang Schivelbusch, *The Railway Journey: The Industrialization and Perception of Time and Space* (Berkeley: University of California Press, 1986) and *Disenchanted Night: The Industrialization of Light in the Nineteenth Century* (Berkeley: University of California Press, 1988); Tom Gunning, "The Cinema of Attractions—Early Film, Its Spectator and the Avant-Garde" in *Early Cinema—Space, Frame, Narrative*, ed. Thomas Elsaesser with Adam Barker (London: British Film Institute, 1990): 56–62; and Leo Charney and Vanessa R. Schwartz, *Cinema and the Invention of Modern Life* (Berkeley: University of California Press, 1995).

5. See Rob MacRea, "The Boo Business," *Haunted Attraction Magazine* 39 (2005); and Hal B. Rappaport, "The Legend of Castle Dracula," *Haunted Attraction Magazine* 29.

6. William Paul, *Laughing, Screaming: Modern Hollywood Horror and Comedy* (New York: Columbia University Press, 1994).

7. The Sally Corporation site is accessible at http://www.sallycorp.com/. Other theme-park ride companies include International Theme Park Services Inc., http://www.interthemepark.com/; Rhythm & Hues, http://www.rhythm.com; and one of the most successful, the Landmark Entertainment Group, http://landmarkusa.com/.

8. Written by Marv Wolfman, the release date was May 9, 2001. Chaos Comics' website is available at http://www.chaoscomics.com/.

9. The Inkworks website is http://www.inkworks.com.

10. The ride has itself generated its own crossover market, as evidenced by the toys, T-shirts, hats, action figures and other merchandise, as well as a multi-million dollar deal with Coca-Cola and Burger King for advertising tie-in promotions.

11. For further information about the mergers, see Comcast Corporation and General Electric Company (January 29, 2011), "Comcast and GE Complete Transaction to Form NBC Universal, LLC," press release, http://www.comcast.com/About/PressRelease/PressReleaseDetail.ashx?PRID=1038; and "NBC and Vivendi Universal Entertainment Unite to Create NBC Universal," CNBC (May 12, 2004), http://www.vivendi.com/vivendi/NBC-and-Vivendi-Universal.

12. Universal Interactive and Sierra Entertainment are now merged with Activision and trade under the name Activision Blizzard, http://www.activision.com/index.html.

13. Justin Wyatt, *High Concept: Movies and Marketing in Hollywood* (Austin: Texas University Press, 1994), 160.

14. For more information about the economic structure of the classical studio as compared to the contemporary Hollywood system, see Wyatt, chapter 3.

15. In the 1940s and 1950s, for example, comic books that featured famous movie stars were extremely popular. For example, John Wayne, Alan Ladd, Buster Crabbe, Dorothy Lamour and Dick Powell all had comic book series named after them. See Denis Gifford, *The International Book of Comics* (London: Hamlyn, 1984), 224–225. Other cross-media merchandise was also available, including the popular Shirley Temple dolls, http://www.shirleytempledolls.com/dolls.html.

16. I thank Ian Conrich for pointing out that pre-1940s horror films were predominantly stage adaptations. The film *Dracula* (1931), for example, was based on the popular Broadway play of the same title, which was, in turn, based on Bram Stoker's novel. Starring in the play was Bela Lugosi, who would also portray Dracula on the silver screen. Similarly, the film *Frankenstein* (1931) was adapted from the 1927 play written by Peggy Webling—*Frankenstein: An Adventure into the Macabre*. See Joseph Maddrey, *Nightmares in Red, White and Blue: The Evolution of the American Horror Film* (Jefferson, NC: McFarland, 2004), 12–13.

17. Jay David Bolter and Richard Grusin, *Remediation: Understanding New Media* (Cambridge: Cambridge University Press, 1999).

18. For a detailed account of the hybrid media structure of *The Amazing Adventures of Spiderman*, see Angela Ndalianis, *Neo-Baroque Aesthetics and Contemporary Entertainment* (Cambridge: MIT Press, 2004), chapter 5.

19. John Calhoun, "Mummy Dearest," *Live Design* (August 1, 2004).

20. Even before films were presented to a mass audience, George Hale anticipated the dark rides of the 20th century by devising his "Hale's Tours and Scenes of the World." Constructing a theater whose interior looked like a railway car, the audience would enter and participate in a ride that took them to filmed locations from all over the world. Showing Hale's Tours for the first time at the St. Louis World's Fair of 1903, these film "rides" proved to be so successful that Hale began syndication, and his Hale's Tours became the concept behind and content of Adolph Zukor's first motion picture theater. See Forsher, 11–12.

21. This extremely popular ride would have drawn inspiration from the classic science fiction novel *From the Earth to the Moon* (1865) by Jules Verne. Interestingly, in the same year that the ride *A Trip to the Moon* appeared at the Exposition, H. G. Wells also published his *First Men in the Moon* (1901). A year later, Georges Méliès would release his film of the same title. Given its popularity, it seems likely that Méliès would have at least heard of the Thompson and Dundy for the Pan-American Exposition in Buffalo, New York, in 1901. For a detailed account of the rides at Coney Island in the early 20th century, see Edo McCullough, *Good Old Coney Island: A Sentimental Journey Into the Past* (New York: Fordham University Press, 2000; originally published in 1957) and the Coney Island Project at http://naid.sppsr.ucla.edu/coneyisland/index.html.

22. The Orlando, Florida, version opened in 1971; the one in EuroDisney (which is called the Phantom Manor) opened in 1992. For a detailed analysis and overview of the Haunted Mansion ride, its influences and its various locations, see the exhaustive website at http://www.Doombuggies.com.

23. J. A. Secord, "Portraits of Science: Quick and Magical Shaper of Science," *Science Magazine* 297:5587 (September 6, 2002): 1648–49.

24. Terry Castle, "Phantasmagoria: Spectral Technology and the Metaphorics of Modern Reverie," *Critical Inquiry* 15 (Fall 1988): 26–61.30. For more information on the magic lantern, see also McGrath, 13–23.

25. General Electric sponsored the Carousel of Progress. This ride and It's a Small World were to enter the Disney parks after the fair came to an end. For both rides, the Disney Imagineers devised a hi-tech variation of the mobile seating that had been a part of amusement parks for decades. For information on Disney's involvement with the New York World's Fair of 1964 and the impact this had on rides like the Haunted Mansion, see Karal Ann Marling, *Designing Disney's Theme Parks: The Architecture of Reassurance* (New York: Flammarion, 1998), 114–32.

26. Brandon Kwiatek, "An Age-Old Ter-

ror: The Spirit of the Dark Ride Has Been Around for Centuries," *Skew* 11 (October 1995): n.p.

27. Ronald C. Simons, *Boo!: Culture, Experience, and the Startle Reflex* (Oxford: Oxford University Press, 1996), 82.

28. Ibid.

29. Kawin, 103.

30. Ron Tamborini, "A Model of Empathy and Emotional reactions to Horror," in *Horror Films Current Research on Audience Preferences and Reactions*, ed. James B. Weaver III and Ron Tamborini (New Jersey: Lawrence Erlbaum Associates, 1996), 107–10.

31. For further information on the expanded, non–Aristotelian view of the senses see Macpherson, Levisohn, Waltl, et al., and David Vender, *Three Mistakes About the Senses* (Ph.D. thesis, University of Tasmania, 2010), http://eprints.utas.edu.au/10779/.

32. For addition information about the Spiderman ride, see Ndalianis, chapter 5.

33. Carroll, 18.

34. Ibid., 22.

35. Steffen Hantke, "Shudder As We Think: Reflections on Horror and/or Criticism," *Paradoxa: Studies in World Literary Genres* 17 (Fall 2002): 2.

36. Jennifer M. Barker, *The Tactile Eye: Touch and the Cinematic Experience* (Berkeley: University of California Press, 2009), 2.

37. Ibid., 3.

Chapter 4

1. Laurell K. Hamilton, *Blue Moon* (New York: Jove, 2002), 175–6.

2. Ibid., 4.

3. The film *Buffy the Vampire Slayer*, which was written by Joss Whedon, the creator of the television show, was released earlier in 1992.

4. For an analysis of both book series and their television versions, see Kathleen Miller, "A Little Extra Bite: Dis/Ability and Romance in Tanya Huff and Charlaine Harris's Vampire Fiction," *Journal of Popular Romance Studies* 1, no. 1 (2010), http://jprstudies.org/2010/08/a-little-extra-bite-disability-and-romance-in-tanya-huff-and-charlaine-harris-vampire-fiction-by-kathleen-miller/.

5. See Silver Anna Silver, "Twilight is Not Good for Maidens: Gender, Sexuality, and the Family in Stephenie Meyer's Twilight Series," *Studies in the Novel* 42, no. 1 & 2 (Spring-Summer 2010): 121–138.

6. Linda Williams, *Screening Sex* (Durham: Duke University Press, 2008), 1.

7. Ibid., 6.

8. Jody Messler Davies, "The Times We Sizzle, and the Times We Sigh: The Multiple Erotics of Arousal, Anticipation, and Release," *Psychoanalytic Dialogues* 16, no. 6 (2006): 666.

9. Ibid., 667.

10. Linda Williams "Film Bodies: Gender, Genre, and Excess." *Film Quarterly* 44, no. 4 (Summer 1991): 3.

11. Ibid.

12. Ibid., 4.

13. Ibid.

14. Ibid, 4–5.

15. Davies, 668.

16. Contemporary romance is set after World War II; historical romance combines historical fiction and romance; Regency romance is set between the years 1811–20, during the time of Prince Regent, who later became George IV; suspense romance reveals links with the 18th- and 19th-century gothic novel. See http://www.rwa.org/cs/the_romance_genre.

17. Laura Bell Wright, *The Appeal of Vampire Romance: Why Do Readers Like These Stories?* (A Master's in Library Services, School of Information and Library Science, University of North Carolina at Chapel Hill, 2003), www.ils.unc.edu/MSpapers/2890.pdf. According to Pamela Regis, who adapts Northrop Frye's romance plot, there are eight narrative events in the romance, which follow a movement that begins with an encumbered heroine and ends with one who is free: "In one or more scenes, romance novels always depict the following: the initial state of society in which heroine and hero must court, the meeting between heroine and hero, the barrier to the union of heroine and hero, the attraction between the heroine and hero, the declaration of love between heroine and hero, the point of ritual death, the recognition by heroine and hero of the means to overcome the barrier, and the betrothal." Pamela Regis, *A Natural History of the Romance Novel* (Philadelphia: University of Pennsylvania Press, 2003), 30.

18. See Neal Wyatt, Georgine Olson, et al., "Core Collections in Genre Studies," *Romance Fiction 101*," *Reference & User Services Quarterly* 47, no. 2 (2008): 124; Linda J. Lee, "Guilty Pleasures: Reading Romance Novels as Reworked Fairy Tales," *Marvels & Tales* 22, no. 1 (2008): 53.

19. See http://www.paranormalromancewriters.com/topics.cfm.
20. See http://www.rwa.org/cs/the_romance_genre.
21. Wyatt, 124.
22. See Regis, 22; Frantz, n.p.; and Deborah Lutz, *The Dangerous Lover: Gothic Villains, Byronism, and the Nineteenth-Century Seduction Narrative* (Columbus: Ohio State University Press, 2006).
23. Jane Austen and Seth Grahame-Smith, *Pride and Prejudice and Zombies* (Philadelphia: Quirk Books, 2009), 6.
24. Ibid., 317.
25. Eric Murphy Selinger, "Rereading the Romance," *Contemporary Literature* 48, no. 2 (Summer 2007), 321. Bailey also points to the influence of American Gothic and Southern Gothic on paranormal romances, as evidenced in Anne Rice's *Vampire Chronicles* and Charlaine Harris's Southern Vampire series. The emphasis in both is on "the workings of obsession and monomania, and the naïveté or outright falsehood of foundational tenets of American society." Peggy Dunn Bailey, "Female Gothic Fiction, Grotesque Realities, and Bastard Out of Carolina: Dorothy Allison Revises the Southern Gothic," *Mississippi Quarterly* (Winter-Spring 2010).
26. Lutz in Selinger, 321–2.
27. Frantz, n.p.
28. Selinger, 322; Lutz, 95.
29. Alison Milbank, 156.
30. Kathleen Ann Miller, "Haunted Heroines: The Gothic Imagination and the Female *Bildungsromane* of Jane Austen, Charlotte Brontë, and L. M. Montgomery," *The Lion and the Unicorn* 34 (2010): 125–47, 129.
31. Ibid., 128.
32. Davis, 667.
33. Christine Feehan, *Dark Gold* (New York: Avon Books), 272–3.
34. Alphonso F. Lingis, "Sense and Non-Sense in the Sexed Body" *Philosophy Social Criticism* 4 (1977): 358.
35. Helen T. Bailie, "Blood Ties: The Vampire Lover in the Popular Romance," *The Journal of American Culture* 34, no. 2 (June 2011):141.
36. Ibid., 145.
37. Tarja Laine, "Cinema as Second Skin," *New Review of Film and Television Studies* 4:2 (2006), 99–100. Laine cites Jean Paul Sartre's *The Emotions: Outline of a Theory* (New York: Kensington, 1993).
38. Ibid., 34.
39. Jeana Jorgensen, "Innocent Initiations: Female Agency in Eroticized Fairy Tales," *Marvels & Tales* 22, no. 1 (2008): 28.
40. Ibid., 35.
41. Lohmann, "'Beauty and the Beast' Themes in Romance Novels" (Master's paper, University of North Carolina, 2006), 9.
42. Jorgensen, 29. Jorgensen focuses on the fairy tales for the following collections: *Once Upon a Time: Erotic Fairy Tales for Women*, ed. Michael Ford; *Erotic Fairy Tales: A Romp through the Classics*, by Mitzi Szereto; *The Empress's New Lingerie and Other Erotic Fairy Tales*, by Hillary Rollins; and *Naughty Fairy Tales from A to Z*, ed. Alison Tyler.
43. Lisa G. Propst, "Bloody Chambers and Labyrinths of Desire: Sexual Violence in Marina Warner's Fairy Tales and Myths," *Marvels & Tales* 22, no. 1 (2008): 126.
44. Marina Warner, *From the Beast to the Blonde: On Fairy Tales and Their Tellers* (London: Vintage, 1995), xii.
45. Propst, 12.
46. Ibid., 130.
47. Bacchilega, in Jorgensen, 28.
48. Lee, 57.
49. Ibid., 59.
50. Ibid., 60–1.
51. Jonathan Allan A., "Theorising the Monstrous and the Virginal in Popular Romance Novels" (International Association for the Study of Popular Romance, New York Conference, June 26–28, 2011), http://iaspr.org/conferences/previous-conferences/belgium/speaker-biographies-and-workshop-summaries/.
52. Davies, 674.
53. Ibid.
54. Georges Bataille, *Erotism: Death and Sensuality* (San Francisco: First City Lights, 1986), 12.
55. Ibid.
56. Laurell K. Hamilton, *Narcissus in Chains* (New York: Jove, 2002), 33.
57. Williams, *Screening Sex*, 15.
58. Bataille, 17–18.
59. Ibid., 19.
60. Bailie, 146.
61. Sarah Sceats, "Oral Sex: Vampiric Transgression and the Writing of Angela Carter," *Tulsa Studies in Women's Literature* 20, no. 1 (Spring 2001): 107.
62. Ibid.
63. Carolyn Korsmeyer, *Savoring Disgust: The Foul and the Air in Aesthetics* (Oxford: Oxford University Press, 2011), 5.
64. Ibid., 30
65. Ibid., 35.

66. Night Wolf Publications, http://nightwolfpress.yolasite.com/submissions.php.
67. Bataille, 11.
68. Ibid., 59.
69. Laurell K. Hamilton, *Bloody Bones* (New York: Jove, 2008), 234.
70. Bataille, 94.
71. Ibid., 59.
72. Ibid., 57.
73. Ibid., 59.
74. Korsmeyer, 3.
75. Jeanne Deslandes, "A Philosophy of Emoting," *Journal of Narrative Theory* 34, no. 3, (Fall 2004): 335.
76. Ibid., 339.
77. Ibid., 343.
78. Miriam Bratu Hansen, "The Mass Production of the Senses: Classical Cinema as Vernacular Modernism," *Modernism/Modernity* 6, no. 2 (1999): 71.
79. Williams, *Screening Sex*, 15.
80. Sobchack, in Williams, 20.
81. Williams, 16.
82. Riley, n.p.
83. Ibid.
84. Korsmeyer, 4.
85. Ibid., 8.
86. Ibid., 57.
87. Ibid.
88. Korsmeyer states (on p. 88): "When I refer to aesthetic disgust I mean the arousal of disgust in an audience, a spectator, or a reader, under circumstances where that emotion both apprehends artistic properties and constitutes a component of appreciation."
89. Ibid., 33.
90. Ibid.
91. Lingis, 353.
92. Ibid.
93. Korsmeyer, 125.
94. Barker, 34.
95. See Marks, 3 and 12; Barker, 34–5.

Chapter 5

1. William Paul, *Laughing, Screaming: Modern Hollywood Horror and Comedy*, 4. That the film wears its gross-out heritage proudly and self-consciously is evident from the homage to the "animal comedy" *Porky's* (Bob Clark, 1982), which is visible in the sign that advertises the local barbeque joint owned by J. T.: here, a neon-lit pig sits above the Bone Shack sign, its image recalling the neon sign at the *Porky's* girlie bar.
2. Ibid., 10.
3. Ibid., 20.
4. See Julia Kristeva, *Desire in Language: A Semiotic Approach to Literature and Art* (New York: Columbia University Press, 1980), 82.
5. Paul, 22–3.
6. Robert Stam, *Subversive Pleasures: Bakhtin, Cultural Criticism, and Film* (Baltimore: Johns Hopkins University Press, 1989), 113. Stam states (on p. 111) that films like *Rocky Horror Picture Show* reveal "distorted echoes of carnival" and that "even 'slasher' films such as *Halloween* can be seen as offering inverted, dystopian versions of carnival, in which phenomena that had once been the objects of cathartic laughter undergo a kind of sickly mutation, now transformed into morbid and pathological stigmata of merely private terrors."
7. Kristeva, 5.
8. Mikhail Mikhailovich Bakhtin, *The Dialogic Imagination* (Austin: University of Texas Press, 1981), 5.
9. Jim Collins, *Architectures of Excess: Cultural Life in the Information Age* (London: Routledge, 1995), 128.
10. Ibid., 135.
11. Mikhail Bakhtin, *Rabelais and His World* (Bloomington: Indiana University Press, 1984), 5–7.
12. Ibid., 11.
13. Ibid., 66.
14. Ibid., 66–7.
15. Ibid., 77.
16. See Mike Atkinson, "Givers of the Viscera," *Sight & Sound*. 17.6 (June 2007): 19–21.
17. Schaefer explains how, by the 1920s, once vertical integration and the Hollywood studio system were established, independent distributors and producers floundered financially and value judgments were set in place. Hollywood films were associated with "an intellectual or aesthetic" appeal and "loftier purpose" when compared to the exploitation productions, which were viewed as emphasizing an "affective" appeal. See Eric Schaefer, "'You Gotta Tell 'Em to Sell 'Em': Distribution, Advertising and Exhibition of Exploitation Film." *"Bold! Daring! Shocking! True!" A History of Exploitation Films, 1919–1959* (Durham: Duke University Press, 1999), 96–103.
18. Atkinson, 20.
19. Schaefer, 103.
20. I'm indebted to Jim Collins for suggesting these valuable distinctions.
21. Rodaway, 11.

22. Paul, 4.
23. Ibid., 158–9.
24. Or consider JT's Bone Shack and the meat specialties served there: thanks to generic expectation, the audience becomes suspicious that the meat may actually have a human source.
25. Bakhtin, *Rabelais*, 36.
26. Ibid., 37.
27. Ibid., 38.
28. Ibid., 38–9.
29. Paul, 47.
30. Ibid., 65–6.
31. Ibid., 65.
32. Ibid., 67.
33. Vera Dika, *The Stalker Film, 1978–81 American Horrors* (Madison: Fairleigh Dickinson University Press, 1990), 88.
34. Ibid., 97.
35. Brenda Cromb, "Gorno: Violence, Shock and Comedy," *Cinephile: The University of British Columbia's Film Journal* 4 (Summer 2004), http://cinephile.ca/archives/volume-4-post-genre/gorno-violence-shock-and-comedy/.
36. Ibid.
37. Kristeva, 87.
38. Paul, 95.
39. Bakhtin *Rabelais*, 72.
40. See http://www.moma.org/visit/calendar/films/565.
41. Bakhtin *Dialogic*, 7.
42. Ibid., 7.
43. Ibid., 282.
44. Kristeva, 78–9.
45. Caetlin Benson-Allott, "Grindhouse: An Experiment in the Death of Cinema," *Film Quarterly* 62.1 (Fall 2008), 21–2.
46. Ibid., 21.
47. Ibid., 23.
48. Kristeva, 302.
49. James, Nick. "Tarantino Bites Back," *Sight & Sound* (February 2008), n.p., http://www.bfi.org.uk/sightandsound/feature/49432.
50. Maximilian Le Cain, "Tarantino and the Vengeful Ghosts of Cinema," *Senses of Cinema* 32 (April–June 2004), http://www.sensesofcinema.com/2004/32/tarantino/.
51. Carol J. Clover, *Men, Women, and Chain Saws: Gender in the Modern Horror Film* (Princeton: Princeton University Press, 1993), 27.
52. Aleksei Semeneko, "Quentin Tarantino's Milk Shake: On the Problem of Intertext and Genre," in *Intertextuality and Intersemiosis*, ed. Marina Grishakova and Markku Lehtimäki (Tartu: Tartu University Press, 2004), 134–50.
53. James, n.p.
54. Alexandra Heller-Nicholas, *Rape-Revenge Film: A Critical Study* (Jefferson, NC: McFarland, 2011), 158.
55. Ibid., 159.
56. Ibid., 158.
57. Clover, 48.
58. Anthony C. Ferrante, "Fu Fighter: The Quentin Tarantino interview," *Cinescape* 7 (September 2003): 50.
59. Lotman, in Clover, 12.
60. Clover, 13.
61. Ibid., 48.
62. Ibid., 51.
63. Ibid., 51.
64. Ibid., 53.
65. Ibid., 51.
66. Bakhtin, *Dialogic*, 361.

Chapter 6

1. In "Violence is Golden," *PC Gamer* 1, no. 4 (March 1994): 42.
2. In Alfred Hermida, "Long-awaited Doom 3 leaked online," BBC.co.uk (August 2, 2004), http://news.bbc.co.uk/2/hi/technology/3527332.stm.
3. Christian McCrea, "Gaming's Hauntology: Dead Media in *Dead Rising*, *Siren* and *Michigan: Report from Hell*, in *Horror Video Games: Essays on the Fusion of Fear and Play* (Jefferson, NC: McFarland, 2009), 220.
4. See Ndalianis *Neo-Baroque*, chapter 2.
5. Bernard Perron, "A Cognitive Psychological Approach to Gameplay Emotions" (2009 Conference: "Breaking New Ground: Innovation in Games, Play, Practice and Theory," September 1–4, 2009, Brunel University, London, United Kingdom).
6. He draws his schema from Ed S. Tan's *Emotion and the Structure of Narrative Film: Film as an Emotion Machine* (New Jersey: Lawrence Erlbaum, 1996).
7. Perron, 2.
8. Ibid., 3.
9. Ibid., 7.
10. Wyatt, *High Concept*, 160.
11. Bolter and Grusin, *Remediation*, 15.
12. Jim Collins, "*Batman: The Movie*, Narrative: The Hyperconscious," in *The Many Lives of the Batman: Critical Approaches to a Superhero and His Media*, ed. Roberta E. Pearson and William Uricchio (New York: Routledge, 1991), 168.
13. Ibid., 169.
14. Ibid., 172.

15. See Tom Gunning, "The Cinema of Attractions — Early Film, Its Spectator and the Avant-Garde," in *Early Cinema — Space, Frame, Narrative*, ed. Thomas Elsaesser with Adam Barker (London: British Film Institute, 1990), 56–62.

16. The characters Cthulhu, Azathoth, Dagon, Shub-Niggurath, Elder Beings, Hastur and the Night-gaunts were all creatures that initiated the Cthulhu mythology by making appearances, initially in the 1928 story "The Call of Cthulhu" (published in the pulp magazine series *Weird Tales,* which was first published in 1924), and later in other tales, including "The Temple," "Dreams of the Witch-House," "The Haunter in the Dark," "The Shadow out of Time," and "The Shadow over Innsmouth." See "Call of Cthulhu" at http://en.wikisource.org/wiki/The_Call_of_Cthulhu.

17. Erik Davis, "Calling Cthulhu: H. P. Lovecraft's Magick Realism," Levity.com. (2006), http://www.levity.com/figment/lovecraft.html (originally published as "Calling Cthulhu," *Gnosis* (Fall 1995).

18. James Bregman, 'Reaping the Profits of Doom," BBC.co.uk (August 13, 2004), http://news.bbc.co.uk/1/hi/technology/3559624.stm.

19. Wylie Sypher, *Rococo to Cubism in Art and Literature* (New York: Vintage, 1960), xxiv.

20. Rodaway, 19.

21. Ibid.

22. In Gunning, 471.

23. Stephen Prince, "True Lies: Perceptual Realism, Digital Images, and Film Theory," *Film Quarterly* 49:3 (Spring 1996): 36.

24. Rosemond Tuve, *Elizabethan and Metaphysical Imagery: Renaissance Poetic and Twentieth-Century Critics* (Chicago: University of Chicago Press, 1947), 13.

25. Marshall McLuhan and Quentin Fiore, *The Medium is the Massage: An Inventory of Effects* (New York: Gingo Press, 1967), 26.

26. See Zaldron, "Doom 3 Technology," *Doom World* (September 22, 2004), http://www.doomworld.com/lordflathead/zaldron.html; David Kushner, "The Wizardry of Id," Spectrum Online, <http://web.archive.org/web/20050325063428/http://www.spectrum.ieee.org/WEBONLY/publicfeature/aug02/id.html> and Kyle Bennett and Brent Justice; "The Official Doom 3 [H]ardware Guide," *[H]ardxOCP* (July 29, 2004), http://www.hardocp.com/article/2004/07/29/official_doom_3_hardware_guide/.

27. Zaldron, n.p.

28. Bennett, n.p.

Chapter 7

1. Steve Jurvetson and Tim Draper, "Viral Marketing," *Draper Fisher Jurvetson* (2010), http://hackvan.com/etext/viral-marketing.html (originally published in the *Netscape M-Files*, 1997; edited version published in *Business 2.0*, November 1998).

2. James H. Gilmore and B. Joseph Pine II, *The Experience Economy: Work Is Theater & Every Business a Stage* (Cambridge: Harvard Business Press, 1999).

3. Ibid. See also James H. Gilmore and B. Joseph Pine II, *Authenticity: What Consumers Really Want* (Cambridge: Harvard Business Press, 2007); Anna Klingmann, *Brandscapes: Architecture in the Experience Economy* (Cambridge: MIT Press, 2007); Brian Lonsway, *Making Leisure Work: Architecture and the Experience Economy* (New York: Routledge, 2009).

4. Lonsway, 1.

5. See William Castle, *STEP RIGHT UP! ... I'm Gonna Scare the Pants Off America* (New York: Pharos Books, 1992); and Kevin Heffernan, *Ghouls, Gimmicks, and Gold: Horror Films and the American Movie Business, 1953–1968* (Durham: Duke University Press, 2004).

6. Henry Jenkins, "Transmedia Storytelling 101, "Confessions of an ACA Fan" (March 22, 2007), http://www.henryjenkins.org/2007/03/transmedia_storytelling_101.html.

7. See Phoebe, "Elan Lee: The *Rolling Stone* Interview, Parts 1, 2 & 3." *WorkBook Project // Cultural Hacker* (July 7, 2010).

8. See Adrian Hon, "The Rise of ARGs," Gamasutra.com (May 9, 2005); Taya Fabijanic, "Down the Rabbit Hole," The Age.com.au (February 26, 2005); and Phoebe, Ibid.

9. Hon, n.p.

10. Henry Jenkins, "Chasing Bees, Without the Hive Mind," *Technology Review* (December 3, 2004), n.p.

11. Hon, n.p.

12. Jenkins, "Chasing Bees," n.p.

13. Jenkins, Transmedia 101, n.p.

14. Jason Mittell, "Serial Boxes," *Just TV* (January 20, 2010), http://justtv.wordpress.com/2010/01/20/serial-boxes/.

15. http://www.fourthwallstudios.com/.

16. Lee Ann Potter, "'Jitterbugs' and 'Crack-pots.' Letters to the FCC about the 'War of the Worlds' Broadcast," *Prologue Magazine*, 35:3 (Fall 2003), http://www.archives.gov/publications/prologue/2003/fall/war-of-worlds.html; and Caroline McCarthy, "Could the 'War of the Worlds' Scare Happen Today?" *CNET News* (October 31, 2007), http://news.cnet.com/Could-the-War-of-the-Worlds-scare-happen-today/2100-1025_3-6216098.html#ixzz12CLwo7nQ. The audio of the broadcast is available online from the West Windsor Branch of the Mercer County, New Jersey, Chamber of Commerce at www.waroftheworlds.org.

17. Tim Carvell, "How *The Blair Witch Project* Built Up So Much Buzz," *Fortune* 140.4 (August 16, 1999): 32–33; and Jane Roscoe, "*The Blair Witch Project* Mock Documentary Goes Mainstream," *Jump Cut: A Review of Contemporary Media* 43 (July 2000): 3.

18. http://www.blairwitch.com/mythology.html.

19. Carvell, 32.

20. Ibid.

21. Roscoe, 7.

22. Martin Harris makes the point that there is an older tradition of such extratextual forms of storytelling. For example, prior to the publication of Samuel Richardson's novel *Pamela, or Virtue Rewarded*, in 1740, an anonymous letter appeared in an issue of *Weekly Miscellany* that referred to Pamela as if she were real. As occurred with Richardson's novel, the creators of *The Blair Witch Project* manipulated the various media through which its narrative was presented in a manner that encouraged initial audiences to experience its fictional story as if it were non-fictional. In both cases, such "truth" claims abetted the works' commercial success while also enabling their creators to interrogate contemporary debates about a specific kind of cultural production (i.e., the novel and the horror film). Martin Harris, "The 'Witchcraft' of Media Manipulation: *Pamela* and *The Blair Witch Project*," *Journal of Popular Culture* 34.4 (Spring 2001), 76.

23. Nicoletta Iacobacci, "From Crossmedia to Transmedia: Thoughts on the Future of Entertainment," LoverOverIP (May 24, 2008), http://www.lunchoverip.com/2008/05/from-crossmedia.html. See also Henry Jenkins, "Transmedia Storytelling: Moving Characters from Books to Films to Video Games Can Make Them Stronger and More Compelling," *Technology Review* (January 15, 2003); and "Searching for the Origami Unicorn: *The Matrix* and Transmedia Storytelling," in *Convergence Culture: Where Old and New Media Collide* (New York: New York University Press, 2006), chapter 3.

24. Transmedia Franchise Development, *The Narrative Design Exploratorium: A Publication Dedicated to Exploring Interactive Storytelling* (June 28, 2009), n.p., http://narrativedesign.org/2009/06/transmedia-franchise-development/.

25. Stephen E. Dinehart, "Transmedial Play: Cognitive and Cross-platform Narrative," *The Narrative Design Exploratorium: A Publication Dedicated to Exploring Interactive Storytelling* (May 14, 2008), http://exploratorium.interactivenarrativedesign.com/2008/05/transmedial-play-cognitive-and-cross-platform-narrative/.

26. Dinehart, "Transmedia Franchise" n.p.

27. Through a series of fictitious blogs (in Australia it was the *Lost* Ninja blog) were presented as being posted by "real" people — and here it was announced that some Apollo Candy bars had "fallen off the back of a truck" and managed to make it to certain locations around the world, which meant that the avid fan/participant in the conspiracy could make their way to stores to claim their very own Apollo chocolate bar (after saying the secret password: "What did one polar bear say to the other polar bear?").

28. In "reality," ABC teamed with Hyperion Books — another Disney subsidiary — to publish the manuscript *Bad Twin*, which was written by Laurence Shames with guidance from show's writers. Gary Troup (played by an actor) also appeared in a series of online interviews on the website Book Talk, in which he was interviewed about the controversy surrounding his mysteriously out-of-print first book, *The Valenzetti Equation*.

29. To see video footage of this event, go to http://www.youtube.com/watch?v=QvVJNYZ5PuQ (accessed 21/8/10:10).

30. More recently, the viewer's desire to understand the intricacies of the series resulted in the formation of "The *Lost* University" (http://lostuniversity.org/). On September 22, 2009 (coinciding with Season 5), future students were allowed to enroll online. To enroll, each student took a 23-question test in order to gauge his or her knowledge of the *Lost* universe. The student card, which came with its own ID and PIN number, then allowed access to the *Lost* University courses

through a feature on the Season 5 Blu-ray. Basing each course around a central theme in the show, courses included: LOST 101, HIST 101: Ancient Writing on the Wall; LAN 101: Foreign Language for Beginners; LAN 201: Advanced Foreign Language; ART 101: Inspiration and Expression with Jack Bender; PHY 101: Introductory Physics for Time Travel; PHI 101: I'm Lost, Therefore I Am; PHY 201: Advanced Physics of Time Travel; PHI 201: I'm Right, You're Wrong: The Us Vs. Them Mentality; PSY 201: Self Discovery Through Family Relationships; SCI 201: Jungle Survival Basics; PHY 301: New Physics with Jeremy Davies. The *Lost* University Master's Program is also available in correlation with the Season 6 Blu-ray.

31. Sara Gwenllian-Jones and Roberta E. Pearson, "Introduction," in *Cult Television*, ed. Gwenllian-Jones, Sara and Roberta Pearson (Minneapolis: University of Minnesota Press, 2004), x–xi.

32. Ibid., xii.

33. T. L. Stanley, "HBO Markets Bloodsucker Beverage," *Brandweek* 50.29 (August 3, 2009), 21.

34. Alissa Walker, "Did HBO's 'True Blood' Campaign Achieve Immortality or Just Plain Suck?" FastCompany.Com (Monday, June 15, 2009), http://www.fastcompany.com/blog/alissa-walker/designerati/did-seasons-true-blood-campaign-achieve-immortality-or-just-plain-suc.

35. Stanley, 21; also see R. Thomas Umstead, "HBO Sinks Its Teeth into 'True Blood' Campaign," *Multichannel News* 29.29(28 July 2009): 12–13.

36. On the BMW mini campaign, see http://www.bmwblog.com/2009/05/27/bmws-mini-usa-division-launches-true-blood-campaign/. For the Digital Kitchen campaign, go to the Digital Kitchen website at http://www.d-kitchen.com/projects/True-Blood-Season-2-Campaign#; also see the site of the designer Yvonne Cheng at http://www.mindeveon.com/index/index.php?/project/hbo-true-blood/.

37. Walker, n.p.

38. See http://fellowshipofthesun.org/.

39. The scene is available at http://www.youtube.com/watch?v=oCqh3thvmJI.

40. IGN Staff, "Cloverfield: A Viral Guide: We Unearth the Mysteries of Cloverfield's Secret Tie-in Websites" (January 15, 2008), http://movies.ign.com/articles/845/845649p1.html.

41. Ibid.

42. "Tagruato: Bleeding our planet dry since 1945," www.tidowave.com.

43. Jenkins, *Convergence*, 25–8.

44. Jenkins, "Transmedia 101," n.p.

45. Ibid.

46. http://www.ibelieveinharveydent.com.

47. Alex Billington, "Why *The Dark Knight*'s Viral Marketing is Absolutely Brilliant," *FirstShowing.net* (March 28 2008), http://www.firstshowing.net/2008/03/28/why-the-dark-knights-viral-marketing-is-absolutely-brilliant/#ixzz0neXrAYwG.

48. See http://www.moviechronicles.com/batman-dark-knight/batman-promotional/.

49. http://www.alternaterealitybranding.com/tdk_sxsw/.

50. Stephen E. Dinehart, "Dramatic Play: The Near-Future of Interactive Narrative Transmedia Franchise Development," *The Narrative Design Exploratorium: A Publication Dedicated to Exploring Interactive Storytelling* (April 27, 2010), n.p.

51. Ibid.

52. http://www.moviechronicles.com/batman-dark-knight/batman-images/2007-12/step-right-up-countdown-challenge/.

53. For an in depth account of current entertainment as neo-baroque, see Ndalianis, *Neo-Baroque.*

54. Giovanni Careri, *Bernini: Flights of Love, the Art of Devotion* (Chicago: University of Chicago Press, 1995), 8.

55. Ibid., 2.

56. Careri, 5.

57. Lonsway, *Leisure*, 1.

58. Ibid., 3.

59. Jenka Gurfinkel, "Your Lifestyle Is an Alternate Reality Game," *Social Creature* (June 8, 2009), n.p., http://social-creature.com/your-lifestyle-is-an-alternate-reality-game.

Bibliography

Abel, Richard, and Rick Altman, eds. *The Sounds of Early Cinema.* Bloomington: Indiana University Press, 2001.

Aercke, Kristian. *Gods of Play: Baroque Festive Performances as Rhetorical Discourse*, Albany: State University of New York Press, 1997.

Allan, Jonathan A. "Theorising the Monstrous and the Virginal in Popular Romance Novels." *International Association for the Study of Popular Romance*, New York Conference, June 26–28, 2011, http://iaspr.org/conferences/previous-conferences/belgium/speaker-biographies-and-workshop-summaries/.

Anwar, Farrah. "Bloody and Absurd." *Monthly Film Bulletin* 57:683 (December 1990): 347–348.

Arens, William. *The Man-Eating Myth: Anthropology and Anthropophagy.* New York: Oxford University Press, 1980.

Atkinson, Mike. "Givers of the Viscera." *Sight & Sound* 17.6 (June 2007): 19–21.

Austen, Jane, and Seth Grahame-Smith. *Pride and Prejudice and Zombies.* Philadelphia: Quirk Books, 2009.

Bacchilega, Cristina. "Preface to the Special Issue on Erotic Tales." *Marvels & Tales* 22, no.1 (2008): 13–23.

Bailey, Peggy Dunn. "Female Gothic Fiction, Grotesque Realities, and Bastard Out of Carolina: Dorothy Allison Revises the Southern Gothic." *Mississippi Quarterly* (Winter-Spring 2010), http://findarticles.com/p/articles/mi_hb3524/is_1-2_63/ai_n56892606/.

Bailie, Helen T. "Blood Ties: The Vampire Lover in the Popular Romance." *The Journal of American Culture* 34, no. 2 (June 2011):141–148.

Bakhtin, Mikhail. *The Dialogic Imagination.* Austin: University of Texas Press, 1981.

_____. *Rabelais and His World.* Bloomington: Indiana University Press, 1984.

Barker, Jennifer M. *The Tactile Eye: Touch and the Cinematic Experience.* Berkeley: University of California Press, 2009.

Barthes, Roland. *Image-Music-Text.* London: Hill and Wang, 1977.

_____. *S/Z: an Essay.* London: Hill and Wang, 1970.

Bataille, Georges. *Eroticism: Death and Sensuality.* San Francisco: First City Lights, 1986.

Bennett, Kyle. "Doom 3 Benchmarks." *[H]ardxOCP* (July 24, 2004), http://www2.hardocp.com/article/2004/07/20/id_softwares_official_doom3_benchmarks.

_____, and Brent Justice. "The Official Doom 3 [H]ardware Guide." *[H]ardxOCP* (July 29, 2004), http://www.hardocp.com/article/2004/07/29/official_doom_3_hardware_guide/.

Benson, Caetlin-Allott. "Grindhouse: An Experiment in the Death of Cinema." *Film Quarterly* 62.1 (Fall 2008): 20–24.

Billington, Alex. "Harvey Dent's Campaign Tour Continues — Phone Calls, Website, and More!" *FirstShowing.net* (March 8, 2008), http://www.firstshowing.net/2008/03/08/harvey-dents-campaign-tour-continues-phone-calls-website-and-more/.

_____. "Why *The Dark Knight*'s Viral Marketing is Absolutely Brilliant." *FirstShow-*

ing.net (March 28, 2008), http://www.firstshowing.net/2008/03/28/why-the-dark-knights-viral-marketing-is-absolutely-brilliant/#ixzz0neXrAYwG.

Bishop, Kyle. "Dead Man Still Walking: Explaining the Zombie Renaissance." *Journal of Popular Film & Television* 37:1 (2009): 16–25.

Bolter, Jay David, and Richard Grusin. *Remediation: Understanding New Media*. Cambridge: Cambridge University Press, 1999.

Bredekamp, Horst. *The Lure of Antiquity and the Cult of the Machine. The Kunstkammer and The Evolution of Nature, Art and Technology*. Princeton: Markus Wiener, 1995.

Bregman, James. "Reaping the Profits of Doom." BBC.co.uk (September 26, 2010), http://news.bbc.co.uk/1/hi/technology/3559624.stm.

Brooker, Will. *Using the Force: Creativity, Community and Star Wars Fans*. London: Continuum, 2003.

Brooks, Peter. *The Melodramatic Imagination: Balzac, Henry James, Melodrama, and the Mode of Excess*. New Haven: Yale University Press, 1995.

Bruno, Giuliana. *Atlas of Emotion: Journeys in Art, Architecture and Film*. London: Verso, 2002.

Buck-Morss, Susan. "Aesthetic and Anesthetic: Walter Benjamin's Artwork Essay Reconsidered." *October* 62 (Fall 1992): 3–41.

Caldwell, John Thornton. "Industrial Reflexivity as Viral Marketing." *Production Culture: Industrial Reflexivity and Critical Practice in Film and Television*. Durham: Duke University Press, 2008.

Calhoun, John. "Mummy Dearest." *Live Design* (August 1, 2004), http://entertainmentdesignmag.com/mag/show_business_mummy_dearest/index.html.

Campen, Crétien van. *The Hidden Sense Synesthesia in Art and Science*. Cambridge: MIT Press, 2008.

Careri, Giovanni. *Bernini: Flights of Love, the Art of Devotion*. Introduction by Herbert Damish. Chicago: University of Chicago Press, 1995.

Carolyn, Axelle. *It Lives Again!: Horror Movies in the New Millennium*. Tolsworth: Telos, 2008.

Carr, Diane. "Play Dead Genre and Affect in *Silent Hill* and *Planetscape Torment*." *Game Studies* 3:1 (May 2003), http://www.gamestudies.org/0301/carr/.

_____. "Textual Analysis, Digital Games, Zombies." Proceedings of DiGRA 2009 Conference: *Breaking New Ground: Innovation in Games, Play, Practice and Theory*, http://www.digra.org/dl/db/09287.24171.pdf.

_____, David Buckingham, Andrew Burn, and Gareth Schott, eds. *Computer Games: Time, Narrative and Play*. Malden: Polity Press, 2007.

Carroll, Noel. *The Philosophy of Horror, or Paradox of the Heart*. New York: Routledge, 1990.

Carvell, Tim. "How *The Blair Witch Project* Built Up So Much Buzz." *Fortune* 140.4 (August 16, 1999): 32–33, http://proquest.umi.com/pdqweb?did=43594124&Fmt=3&clientId=208288&RQT=309&VName=PQD.

Castle, Terry. "Phantasmagoria: Spectral Technology and the Metaphorics of Modern Reverie." *Critical Inquiry* 15 (Fall 1988): 26–61.

Castle, William. *STEP RIGHT UP! ... I'm Gonna Scare the Pants Off America*. New York: Pharos, 1992.

Chapman, Glen. "Robert Rodriquez" (2010), http://www.denofgeek.com/misc/523072/music_in_the_movies_robert_rodriguez.html.

Clover, Carol J. *Men, Women, and Chain Saws: Gender in the Modern Horror Film*. Princeton: Princeton University Press, 1993.

Collins, Jim. *Architectures of Excess: Cultural Life in the Information Age*. London: Routledge, 1995.

_____. "*Batman: The Movie*, Narrative: The Hyperconscious" in *The Many Lives of the Batman: Critical Approaches to a Superhero and His Media*. Edited by Roberta E. Pearson and William Uricchio. New York: Routledge, 1991.

Comcast Corporation and General Electric Company. "Comcast and GE Complete Transaction to Form NBC Universal, LLC." Press release (January 29, 2011), http://www.comcast.com/About/PressRelease/PressReleaseDetail.ashx?PRID=1038.

Cook, Pam, ed. *The Cinema Book*. London: British Film Institute, 2007.

Cromb, Brenda. "Gorno: Violence, Shock and Comedy." *Cinephile: University of British Columbia's Film Journal* 4 (Summer 2004), http://cinephile.ca/archives/volume-4-post-genre/gorno-violence-shock-and-comedy/.

Davies, Jody Messler. "The Times We Sizzle, and the Times We Sigh: The Multiple Erotics of Arousal, Anticipation, and Release." *Psychoanalytic Dialogues* 16, no. 6 (2006): 665–686.

Davis, Erik. "Calling Cthulhu: H. P. Lovecraft's Magick Realism." Levity.com. (Originally published as "Calling Cthulhu," *Gnosis* [Fall 1995]), http://www.levity.com/figment/lovecraft.html.

Deleuze, Gilles. *The Fold: Leibniz and the Baroque*. Translated by Tom Conley. Minneapolis: University of Minneapolis Press, 1993.

Deslandes, Jeanne. "A Philosophy of Emoting." *Journal of Narrative Theory* 34, no. 3, (Fall 2004): 335–372.

Dika, Vera. *The Stalker Film, 1978–81 American Horrors*. Madison: Fairleigh Dickinson University Press, 1990.

Dinehart, Stephen E. "Dramatic Play: The Near-Future of Interactive Narrative Transmedia Franchise Development." *The Narrative Design Exploratorium: A Publication Dedicated to Exploring Interactive Storytelling* (April 27, 2010).

_____. "Transmedia Franchise Development." *The Narrative Design Exploratorium: A Publication Dedicated to Exploring Interactive Storytelling* (June 28, 2009), http://narrativedesign.org/2009/06/transmedia-franchise-development/.

_____. "Transmedial Play: Cognitive and Cross-platform Narrative." *The Narrative Design Exploratorium: A Publication Dedicated to Exploring Interactive Storytelling* (May 14, 2008), http://exploratorium.interactivenarrativedesign.com/2008/05/transmedial-play-cognitive-and-cross-platform-narrative/.

Edwards, Phil, and Alan Jones. "The Evil Dead Speak." *Starburst* 57 (1983): 24–29.

Everett, Hugh III. "The Theory of the Universal Wavefunction" in *The Many-Worlds Interpretation of Quantum Mechanics*. Edited by Bryce DeWitt and R. Neill Graham, 3–140. Princeton: Princeton University Press, 1973.

Fabijanic, Taya. "Down the Rabbit Hole." *The Age* (February 26, 2005), http://www.theage.com.au/articles/2005/02/24/1109180026375.htm.

Ferrante, Anthony C. "Fu Fighter: The Quentin Tarantino Interview." *Cinescape* 7 (September 2003): 46–51.

Fletcher, Phoebe. "'Fucking Americans': Postmodern Nationalism and the Contemporary Splatter Film." *Colloquy* 18 (December 2009), http://www.colloquy.monash.edu.au/issue018/fletcher.pdf.

Forsher, James. *The Community of Cinema: How Cinema and Spectacle Transformed the American Downtown*. Westport: Praeger, 2003.

Frantz, Sarah S. G. "Darcy's Vampiric Descendants: Austen's Perfect Romance Hero and J. R. Ward's Black Dagger Brotherhood." *Jane Austen Society of North America* 30, no.1 (Winter 2009), http://www.jasna.org/persuasions/on-line/vol30no1/frantz.html.

Funge, John. *Artificial Intelligence for Computer Games: An Introduction*. Wellesley: A K Peters, 2004.

Gray, Jonathan. *Fandom: Identities and Communities in a Mediated World*. New York: New York University Press, 2007.

Gwenllian-Jones, Sara, and Roberta E. Pearson, eds. *Cult Television*. Minneapolis: University of Minnesota Press, 2004.

Hansen, Miriam Bratu. "The Mass Production of the Senses: Classical Cinema as Vernacular Modernism." *Modernism/Modernity* 6, no. 2 (1999): 59–77.

Heller-Nicholas, Alexandra. *Rape-Revenge Film: A Critical Study*. Jefferson, NC: McFarland, 2011.

Hills, Matthew. *Fan Cultures*. London: Routledge, 2002.

Hofman-Howley, Ingrid. "Romancing the Vampire: The Lives and Loves of Two Vampire Slayers — Anita and Buffy." *Refractory: A Journal of Entertainment Media* 10, no.14 (2005), http://refractory.unimelb.edu.au/2005/10/14/romancing-the-vampire-the-lives-and-loves-of-two-vampire-slayers-anita-and-buffy-ingrid-hofman-howley/.

Hon, Adrian. "The Rise of ARGs." Gamasutra.com (May 9, 2005), http://www.gamasutra.com/features/20050509/hon_01.shtml.

James, Nick. "Tarantino Bites Back." *Sight & Sound* (February 2008), http://www.bfi.org.uk/sightandsound/feature/49432.

———. "Welcome to the Grindhouse." *Sight & Sound* (June 2007): 16–18.

Jorgensen, Jeana. "Innocent Initiations: Female Agency in Eroticized Fairy Tales." *Marvels & Tales* 22, no.1 (2008): 27–37.

Jurvetson, Steve, and Tim Draper. "Viral Marketing" *Draper Fisher Jurvetson*. (Originally published in the *Netscape M-Files*, 1997; edited version published in *Business 2.0*, November 1998), http://hackvan.com/etext/viral-marketing.html.

Gibson, James J. *The Senses Considered as Perceptual Systems*. Boston: Houghton Mifflin, 1966.

Gilmore, James H., and B. Joseph Pine II. *Authenticity: What Consumers Really Want*. Cambridge: Harvard Business Press, 2007.

———. *The Experience Economy: Work Is Theater & Every Business a Stage*. Cambridge: Harvard Business Press, 1999.

Grand, Steve. *Growing Up with Lucy: How to Build an Android in Twenty Easy Steps*. London: Weidenfeld & Nicolson, 2004.

Graser, Marc. "HBO Promo Taps a Fresh Vein." *Variety*, June 22–28, 2009: 3, 29.

Gray, Jonathan. *Show Sold Separately: Promos, Spoilers, and Other Media Paratexts*, New York: New York University Press, 2010.

Gunning, Tom. "'Animated Pictures,' Tales of Cinema's Forgotten Future." *Michigan Quarterly Review* 34:4 (1995): 465–85.

———. "The Cinema of Attractions — Early Film, Its Spectator and the Avant-Garde." *Early Cinema — Space, Frame, Narrative*. Edited by Thomas Elsaesser with Adam Barker, 56–62. London: British Film Institute, 1990.

Gurfinkel, Jenka "Your Lifestyle Is an Alternate Reality Game." *Social Creature* (June 8, 2009), http://social-creature.com/your-lifestyle-is-an-alternate-reality-game.

Hanich, Julian. *Cinematic Emotion in Horror Films and Thrillers: The Aesthetic Paradox of Pleasurable Fear*. London: Routledge, 2010.

Hantke, Steffen. "Shudder As We Think: Reflections on Horror and/or Criticism." *Paradoxa: Studies in World Literary Genres* 17 (Fall 2002): 1–9.

Harris, Martin. "The 'Witchcraft' of Media Manipulation: *Pamela* and *The Blair Witch Project*." *Journal of Popular Culture* 34.4 (Spring 2001): 75–107.

Hartley, John. *Tele-ology: Studies in Television*. London: Routledge, 1992.

Heffernan, Kevin. *Ghouls, Gimmicks, and Gold: Horror Films and the American Movie Business*. Durham: Duke University Press, 2004.

Hermida, Alfred. "Long-awaited Doom 3 leaked online." BBC.co.uk (August 2, 2004), http://news.bbc.co.uk/2/hi/technology/3527332.stm.

Hervey, Ben. *Night of the Living Dead*. London: British Film Institute, 2008.

Howard, Theresa. "'True Blood' Sucks in Brands to Produce Faux Ads Linked to Season 2." *USA Today*, May 26, 2009, Money section, 06b.

Iacobacci, Nicoletta. "From Crossmedia to Transmedia: Thoughts on the Future of Entertainment." *LoverOverIP* (May 24, 2008), http://www.lunchoverip.com/2008/05/from-crossmedia.html.

IGN Staff. "Cloverfield: A Viral Guide: We Unearth the Mysteries of Cloverfield's Secret Tie-in Websites." (January 15, 2008), http://movies.ign.com/articles/845/845649p1.html.

Jancovich, Mark. *Horror*. London: Batsford Ltd., 1992.

Jenkins, Henry. "Chasing Bees, Without the Hive Mind." *Technology Review* (December 2004), http://www.technologyreview.com/communications/13561/?a=f.

———. *Convergence Culture: Where Old and New Media Collide*. New York: New York University Press, 2006.

———. "Game Design as Narrative Architecture." *First Person: New Media as Story, Performance, Game*. Edited by Noah Wardrip-Fruin and Pat Harrigan. Cambridge: MIT Press, 2004.

———. "Transmedia Storytelling: Moving Characters from Books to Films to Video Games Can Make Them Stronger and More Compelling." *Technology Review* (January 15, 2003), http://www.technologyreview.com/biomedicine/13052/.

———. "Transmedia Storytelling 101." Confessions of an ACA Fan (March 22, 2007), http://www.henryjenkins.org/2007/03/transmedia_storytelling_101.html.

Kaler, Anne K., and Rosemary E. Johnson-Kurek, eds. *Romantic Conventions*. Bowling Green: Bowling Green State University Popular Press, 1999.

Kawin, Bruce. "Children of the Light." *Film Genre Reader*. Edited by Barry Keith Grant. Austin: University of Texas Press, 2003.

Keyser, Tonya. "Passion for the Paranormal: The Supernatural in Romance Fiction." *Skeptical Inquirer* (November-December, 2010): 51–3.

Kirkland, Ewan. "Horror Videogames and the Uncanny." Proceedings of DiGRA 2005 Conference: *Changing Views — Worlds in Play*. http://www.digra.org/dl/db/09287.25453.pdf.

———. "Resident Evil's Typewriter: Survival Horror and its Remediations." *Games and Culture* 4:2 (April 2009): 115–126.

Kirkpatrick, Graeme. "Controller, Hand, Screen: Aesthetic Form in the Computer Game." *Games and Culture* 4:2 (April 2009): 127–143.

Klingmann, Anna. *Brandscapes: Architecture in the Experience Economy*. Cambridge: MIT Press, 2007.

Kolnai, Aurel. *On Disgust*. Edited by Barry Smith and Carolyn Korsmeyer. Chicago: Open Court, 2004.

Korsmeyer, Carolyn. *Savoring Disgust: The Foul and the Air in Aesthetics*. Oxford: Oxford University Press, 2011.

Krentz, Jayne Ann, ed. *Dangerous Men and Adventurous Women*. Philadelphia: University of Pennsylvania Press, 1992.

Kristeva, Julia. *Desire in Language: A Semiotic Approach to Literature and Art*. New York: Columbia University Press, 1980.

Krzywinska, Tanya. "Hands-On Horror." *ScreenPlay: Cinema/Videogames/Interfaces*. Edited by Geoff King and Tanya Krzywinska, 206–223. London: Wallflower Press, 2002.

Kushner, David. "The Wizardry of Id." *Spectrum Online* (September 22, 2004), http://web.archive.org/web/20050325063428/http://www.spectrum.ieee.org/WEBONLY/publicfeature/aug02/id.html.

Kuznets, Lois Rostow. *When Toys Come Alive: Narratives of Animation, Metamorphosis, and Development*. New Haven: Yale University Press, 1994.

Kwiatek, Brandon. "An Age-Old Terror: The Spirit of the Dark Ride Has Been Around for Centuries." *Skew* 11 (October 1995), http://skew.ot.com/eleven/dark.html.

Laine, Tarja. "Cinema as Second Skin." *New Review of Film and Television Studies* 4:2 (2006): 93–106.

Laurel, Brenda. *Computers as Theatre*. Reading: Addison-Wesley, 1991.

Law, John. *Scare Tactic: The Life & Films of William Castle*. Bloomington: iUniverse, 2000.

Le Cain, Maximilian. "Tarantino and the Vengeful Ghosts of Cinema." *Senses of Cinema* 32 (April–June 2004), http://www.sensesofcinema.com/2004/32/tarantino/.

Lee, Linda J. "Guilty Pleasures: Reading Romance Novels as Reworked Fairy Tales." *Marvels & Tales* 22, no.1 (2008): 52–66.

Leibniz, Gottfried Wilhelm. *Discourse on Metaphysics and the Monadology*. New York: Dover, 2005.

Lévi-Strauss, Claude. *The Raw and the Cooked*. New York: Harper & Row, 1970.

———. *Structural Anthropology*. New York: Basic, 1963.

Levisohn, Aaron M. "The Body as a Medium: Reassessing the Role of Kinesthetic Awareness in Interactive Applications." Multimedia '07 Proceedings of the 15th International Conference on Multimedia. New York: ACM, 2007, http://dl.acm.org/citation.cfm?id=1291352.

Lim, Dennis. "Dante's Inferno: A Horror Movie Brings Out the Zombie Vote to Protest Bush's War." *Village Voice* (November 22, 2005), http://www.villagevoice.com/2005-11-22/film/dante-s-inferno/.

Lingis, Alphonso F. "Sense and Non-Sense in the Sexed Body." *Philosophy Social Criticism* 4 (1977): 345–65.

Lohmann, Jennifer. "'Beauty and the Beast' Themes in Romance Novels." Master's paper for the M. S. in L. S. degree, University of North Carolina, April 2006, http://etd.ilsunc.edu:8080.

Lonsway, Brian. *Making Leisure Work: Architecture and the Experience Economy*. New York: Routledge, 2009.

Lowry, Brian. "Political Anger Finds 'Homecoming' on TV." *Daily Variety* 289:42 (November 30, 2005): 4.

Lutz, Deborah. *The Dangerous Lover: Gothic Villains, Byronism, and the Nineteenth-Century Seduction Narrative.* Columbus: Ohio State University Press, 2006.

Macpherson, Fiona. "Taxonomising the Senses." Philosophical Studies 153 (2011): 123–142.

MacRea, Rob. "The Boo Business." *Haunted Attraction Magazine* 39 (2005), http://www.hauntedattraction.com/39/current issue_boobbiz.shtm.

Maddrey, Joseph. *Nightmares in Red, White and Blue: The Evolution of the American Horror Film.* Jefferson, NC: McFarland, 2004.

Margolis, Ann. "In Defense of Romantic Fiction." Paper presented at the Dyson College of Arts and Sciences, 2009, http://digitalcommons.pace.edu/dyson_mspublishing/10.

Marks, Laura U. *Touch: Sensuous Theory and Multisensory Media.* Minneapolis: Minnesota University Press, 2002.

Marling, Karal Ann. *Designing Disney's Theme Parks: The Architecture of Reassurance.* New York: Flammarion, 1998.

McCarthy, Caroline. "Could the 'War of the Worlds' Scare Happen Today?" *CNET News* (October 31, 2007), http://news.cnet.com/Could-the-War-of-the-Worlds-scare-happen-today/2100-1025_3-6216098.html#ixzz12CLwo7nQ.

McCrea, Christian. "Gaming's Hauntology: Dead Media in *Dead Rising, Siren* and *Michigan: Report from Hell,* in *Horror Video Games: Essays on the Fusion of Fear and Play,* ed. B. Perron. Jefferson, NC: McFarland, 2009.

McDonagh, Maitland. *Broken Mirrors, Broken Minds: The Dark Dreams of Dario Argento.* London: Sun Tavern Fields, 1991.

McGonigal, Jane. "This Was Never a Game." *Avant Game* (June 27, 2008), http://blog.avantgame.com/2008/06/this-was-never-game.html.

McGrath, Roberta. "Natural Magic and Science Fiction: Instruction, Amusement and the Popular Show, 1795–1895." *Cinema: The Beginnings and the Future.* Edited by Christopher Williams, 24–32. London: Westminster University Press, 1996.

McKay, Jade, and Elizabeth Parsons. "Out of Wedlock: The Consummation and Consumption of Marriage in Contemporary Romance Fiction." *Genders* 50 (2009): n.p., http://www.genders.org/g50/g50_mckayparsons.html.

McLuhan, Marshall, and Quentin Fiore. *The Medium is the Massage: An Inventory of Effects.* New York: Gingo Press, 1967.

Merleau-Ponty, Maurice. *Phenomenology of Perception.* Translation by Colin Smith. London: Routledge and Kegan Paul, 1962.

Metz, Christian. *Film Language: A Semiotics of the Cinema.* Translated by Michael Taylor. New York: Oxford University Press, 1974.

Milbank, Alison. "Gothic Femininities." In *The Routledge Companion to Gothic,* edited by Catherine Spooner & Emma McEvoy, chapter 19. London: Routledge, 2007.

Miller, Kathleen. "A Little Extra Bite: Dis/Ability and Romance in Tanya Huff and Charlaine Harris's Vampire Fiction." *Journal of Popular Romance Studies* 1, no. 1 (2010), http://jprstudies.org/2010/08/a-little-extra-bite-disability-and-romance-in-tanya-huff-and-charlaine-harris-vampire-fiction-by-kathleen-miller/.

Miller, Kathleen Ann. "Haunted Heroines: The Gothic Imagination and the Female *Bildungsromane* of Jane Austen, Charlotte Brontë, and L. M. Montgomery." *The Lion and the Unicorn* 34 (2010): 125–147.

Miller, Susan. *Disgust: The Gatekeeper Emotion.* London: Routledge, 2004.

Mittell, Jason. "Serial Boxes." *Just TV* (January 20, 2010), http://justtv.wordpress.com/2010/01/20/serial-boxes/.

Modleski, Tania. *Loving With a Vengeance: Mass Produced Fantasies for Women.* London: Routledge, 2007; originally published, 1982.

Munsterberg, Hugo. *The Photoplay: A Psychological Study.* London: Routledge, 2001.

"NBC and Vivendi Universal Entertainment Unite to Create NBC Universal, CNBC." *CNBC Europe* (Tuesday, April 10, 2007), http://www.cnbc.com/id/18037310/NBC_and_Vivendi_Universal_Entertainment_Unite_to_Create_NBC_Universal.

Ndalianis, Angela. *Neo-Baroque Aesthetics and Contemporary Entertainment.* Cambridge: MIT Press, 2004.

Neale, Stephen. *Genre.* London: British Film Institute, 1980.

Neale, Steve. "*Halloween*: Suspense, Aggression and the Look." In *Planks of Reason: Essays on the Horror Film*. Edited by Barry Keith Grant and Christopher Sharrett, 356–62. Lanham: Scarecrow Press, 1984.

Newman, Kim. *Nightmare Movies: A Critical History of the Horror Film, 1968–88*. London: Bloomsbury, 1988.

Orenstein, Catherine. *Little Red Riding Hood Uncloaked: Sex, Morality, and the Evolution of a Fairy Tale*. New York: Basic, 2002.

Orr, Mary. *Intertextuality: Debates and Contexts*. Cambridge: Polity Press, 2008.

Parker, James. "Don't Fear the Reaper: Learning to Love the Slasher-film Renaissance." *The Atlantic* (April 2009), http://www.theatlantic.com/magazine/archive/2009/04/don-8217-t-fear-the-reaper/7318/.

Paul, William. *Laughing, Screaming: Modern Hollywood Horror and Comedy*. New York: Columbia University Press, 1994.

PC Gamer. "Violence is Golden." *PC Gamer* 1, no. 4 (March 1994): 42–45.

Pearce, Celia. "Story as Play Space: Narrative in Games." In *Game On: The History and Culture of Videogames*, edited by Lucien King. London: Laurence King, 2002.

Pearl, Cyril. "Zombie Politics." *Video Business* 26:25 (June 19, 2006): 16.

Perron, Bernard. "A Cognitive Psychological Approach to Gameplay Emotions." Paper presented at the 2009 conference, *Breaking New Ground: Innovation in Games, Play, Practice and Theory*, at Brunel University, London, United Kingdom, September 1–4, 2009, http://www.aestheticsofplay.org/papers/perron2.htm.

———. "Coming to Play at Frightening Yourself: Welcome to the World of Horror Video Games." Paper presented at the 2005 conference, *Aesthetics of Play*, in Vancouver, British Columbia, Canada, October 14–15, 2005, http://www.aestheticsofplay.org/perron.php.

———, ed. *Horror Video Games: Essays on the Fusion of Fear and Play*. Jefferson, NC: McFarland, 2009.

Peucker, Brigitte. *The Material Image: Art and the Real in Film*. Stanford: Stanford University Press, 2007.

Phoebe. "Elan Lee: The *Rolling Stone* Interview, Part 1." *WorkBook Project // Cultural Hacker* (July 7, 2010), http://workbookproject.com/culturehacker/2010/07/07/elan-lee-the-rolling-stone-interview-part-i/.

———. "Elan Lee: The *Rolling Stone* Interview, Part 2." *WorkBook Project // Cultural Hacker* (July 7, 2010), http://workbookproject.com/culturehacker/2010/07/07/elan-lee-the-rolling-stone-interview-part-ii/.

———. "Elan Lee: The *Rolling Stone* Interview, Part 3." *WorkBook Project // Cultural Hacker* (July 7, 2010), http://workbookproject.com/culturehacker/2010/07/07/elan-lee-the-rolling-stone-interview-part-iii/.

Potteiger, Matthew, and Jamie Purinton. *Landscape Narrative: Design Practices for Telling Stories*. New York: John Wiley & Sons, 1998.

Potter, Lee Ann. "'Jitterbugs' and 'Crackpots.' Letters to the FCC about the 'War of the Worlds' Broadcast." *Prologue Magazine* 35:3 (Fall 2003), http://www.archives.gov/publications/prologue/2003/fall/war-of-worlds.html.

Prince, Stephen. "True Lies: Perceptual Realism, Digital Images, and Film Theory." *Film Quarterly* 49:3 (Spring 1996): 27–37.

Propst, Lisa G. "Bloody Chambers and Labyrinths of Desire: Sexual Violence in Marina Warner's Fairy Tales and Myths." *Marvels & Tales* 22, no.1 (2008): 125–142.

Radway, Janice A. *Reading the Romance: Women, Patriarchy, and Popular Literature*. Chapel Hill: University of North Carolina Press, 1991; originally published 1984.

Rappaport, Hal B. "The Legend of Castle Dracula." *Haunted Attraction Magazine* 29 (accessed February 20, 2007): n.p., http://www.hauntedattraction.com/29/spotlight1.htm.

Regis, Pamela. *A Natural History of the Romance Novel*. Philadelphia: University of Pennsylvania Press, 2003.

Riley, Benjamin. "Vampire Misogyny: Violence in 'True Blood.'" *Pop Matters* (September 10, 2010), http://www.popmatters.com/pm/feature/130459-vampire-misogyny-violence-in-true-blood.

Robben, Antonius, C. G. M. "Death and Anthropology: An Introduction." *Death, Mourning, and Burial: A Cross-Cultural Reader*. Edited by Antonius Robben, C. G. M., 1–16. Malden: Wiley-Blackwell, 2004.

Rodaway, Paul. *Sensuous Geographies: Body Sense, and Place*. London: Routledge, 1994.

Rodowick, D.N. "The Enemy Within: The Economy of Violence in *The Hills Have Eyes.*" *The Planks of Reason: Essays on the Horror Film.* Edited by Barry K. Grant and Christopher Sharrett, 321–330. Lanham: Scarecrow Press, 1984.

Roscoe, Jane. "*The Blair Witch Project* Mock Documentary Goes Mainstream." *Jump Cut: A Review of Contemporary Media* 43 (July 2000): 3–8.

Rose, Frank. "Secret Websites, Coded Messages: The New World of Immersive Games." *Wired Magazine* 16:1 (December 20, 2007), http://www.wired.com/entertainment/music/magazine/16-01/ff_args#ixzz12BDwRMLB.

Sartre, Jean-Paul. *The Emotions: Outline of a Theory.* New York: Citadel, 2000.

Saville, Anthony. *Leibniz and the Monadology.* London: Routledge, 2000.

Sceats, Sarah. "Oral Sex: Vampiric Transgression and the Writing of Angela Carter." *Tulsa Studies in Women's Literature* 20, no. 1 (Spring 2001): 107–21.

Schaefer, Eric. "'You Gotta Tell 'Em to Sell 'Em': Distribution, Advertising and Exhibition of Exploitation Film." In *"Bold! Daring! Shocking! True!" A History of Exploitation Films, 1919–1959.* Durham: Duke University Press, 1999.

Schatz, Thomas. *Hollywood Genres: Formulas, Filmmaking, and the Studio System.* New York: McGraw-Hill, 1981.

Secord, J. A. "Portraits of Science: Quick and Magical Shaper of Science." *Science Magazine* 297:5587 (September 6, 2002): 1648–49.

Seidman, Robert. "True Blood Averages 12.4 Million Per Episode Across Platforms in Second Season." TV by Numbers (September 19, 2009), http://tvbythenumbers.zap2it.com/2009/09/19/true-blood-averages-12-4-million-per-episode-across-platforms-in-second-season/27753/.

———. "True Bloody Momentum for True Blood: 5.3 Million and Another Record!" TV by Numbers (August 25, 2009), http://tvbythenumbers.zap2it.com/2009/08/25/true-bloody-momentum-for-true-blood-5-3-million-and-another-record/25336/.

Selinger, Eric Murphy. "Rereading the Romance." *Contemporary Literature* 48, no. 2 (Summer 2007): 307–324.

Semeneko, Aleksei. "Quentin Tarantino's Milk Shake: On the Problem of Intertext and Genre." In *Intertextuality and Intersemiosis*, edited by Marina Grishakova and Markku Lehtimäki, 134–150. Tartu: Tartu University Press, 2004.

Sharrett, Christopher. "'Fairytales for the Apocalypse': Wes Craven on the Horror Film." *Literature/Film Quarterly* 13: 3 (1985): 139–147.

———. "The Idea of Apocalypse in *The Texas Chainsaw Massacre.*" In *The Planks of Reason: Essays on the Horror Film*, edited by Barry K. Grant and Christopher Sharrett, 255–76. Lanham, Scarecrow Press, 1984.

Silver, Anna. "Twilight is Not Good for Maidens: Gender, Sexuality, and the Family in Stephenie Meyer's Twilight Series." *Studies in the Novel* 42, no.'s 1 & 2 (Spring & Summer 2010): 121–138.

Simons, Ronald C. *Boo!: Culture, Experience, and the Startle Reflex.* Oxford: Oxford University Press, 1996.

Sobchack, Vivian. *Carnal Thoughts: Embodiment and Moving Image Culture.* Berkeley: California University Press, 2004.

Stafford, Barbara Maria. *Artful Science: Enlightenment Entertainment and the Eclipse of Visual Education.* Cambridge: MIT Press, 1994.

Stam, Robert. *Subversive Pleasures: Bakhtin, Cultural Criticism, and Film.* Baltimore: Johns Hopkins University Press, 1989.

Stanley, T. L. "HBO Markets Bloodsucker Beverage." *Brandweek* 50.29 (August 3, 2009): 21.

Sypher, Wylie. *Rococo to Cubism in Art and Literature.* New York: Vintage, 1960.

Szalosky, Melinda. "Sounding Images in Silent Film: Visual Acoustics in Murnau's Sunrise." *Cinema Journal* 41:2 (Winter 2002): 109–131.

Tamborini, Ron. "A Model of Empathy and Emotional Reactions to Horror." In *Horror Films Current Research on Audience Preferences and Reactions*, edited by James B. Weaver III and Ron Tamborini, 103–24. New Jersey: Lawrence Erlbaum, 1996.

Telotte, J. P. "Through a Pumpkin's Eye: The Reflexive Nature on Horror." In *American Horrors: Essays on the Modern American Horror Film*, edited by Gregory A. Waller,

114–28. Urbana: Illinois University Press, 1987.

Tuve, Rosemond. *Elizabethan and Metaphysical Imagery: Renaissance Poetic and Twentieth-Century Critics.* Chicago: University of Chicago Press, 1947.

Umstead, R. Thomas. "HBO Sinks Its Teeth Into 'True Blood' Campaign." *Multichannel News* 29.29 (July 28, 2009): 12–13.

Vender, David. *Three Mistakes About the Senses.* Ph.D. thesis, University of Tasmania, 2010, http://eprints.utas.edu.au/10779/.

Walker, Alissa "Did HBO's 'True Blood' Campaign Achieve Immortality or Just Plain Suck?" *FastCompany.Com* (Monday, June 15, 2009), http://www.fastcompany.com/blog/alissa-walker/designerati/did-seasons-true-blood-campaign-achieve-immortality-or-just-plain-suc.

Waller, Gregory A., ed. *American Horrors: Essays on the Modern American Horror Film.* Urbana: Illinois University Press, 1987.

Waltl, Markus, Christian Timmerer, Benjamin Rainer, and Hermann Hellwagner. "Sensory Effects for Ambient Experiences in the World Wide Web." Institute of Information Technology Alpen-Adria-University Klagenfurt. Technical Report No TR/ITEC/11/1.13 (July 2011).

Warner, Marina. *From the Beast to the Blonde: On Fairy Tales and Their Tellers.* London: Vintage, 1995.

_____. *Phantasmagoria: Spirit Visions, Metaphors, and Media into the Twenty-First Century.* Oxford: Oxford University Press, 2006.

Waterworth, John A. "Creativity and Sensation: The Case for Synaesthetic Media." *Leonardo* 30:4 (1997): 27–330.

Weitz, Scott. "Robert Rodriguez's *Planet Terror* Soundtrack." *Film Edge* (April 5, 2007), http://www.filmedge.net/Grind/PTC-Drev.htm.

Williams, Linda. "Film Bodies: Gender, Genre, and Excess." *Film Quarterly* 44, no. 4 (Summer 1991): 2–13.

_____. *Screening Sex.* Durham: Duke University Press, 2008.

Wood, Robin. "Return of the Repressed." *Film Comment* 14:4 (1978): 24–32.

Wright, Laura Bell. *The Appeal of Vampire Romance: Why Do Readers Like These Stories?* A Master's in Library Services, School of Information and Library Science, University of North Carolina at Chapel Hill, 2003, www.ils.unc.edu/MSpapers/2890.pdf.

Wright, Will. *Sixguns and Society: A Structural Study of the Western.* Berkeley: University of California Press, 1975.

Wyatt, Justin. *High Concept: Movies and Marketing in Hollywood.* Austin: Texas University Press, 1994.

Wyatt, Neal, Georgine Olson, et al. "Core Collections in Genre Studies." *Romance Fiction 101. Reference & User Services Quarterly* 47, no. 2 (2008): 120–125.

Zaldron. "Doom 3 Technology." *Doom World* (September 26, 2010), http://www.doomworld.com/lordflathead/zaldron.html.

Index

abject 19, 35, 108, 141
Abrams, J.J. 184; *see also Cloverfield*
Abu Ghraib 22, 21, 37
Adventures of Spiderman (ride, Universal) 8, 9, 64, 68, 70, 72, 199, 200
aesthetics 9, 13, 17, 20, 43, 48, 58, 59, 60, 61, 102, 126, 130, 140, 144, 147, 154, 157, 166, 169, 170, 172, 175, 192; disgust 6, 99, 103, 104, 105, 120, 181; horror 5, 15, 19, 23, 29, 33, 37, 144, 161, 175
affective 4, 20, 24, 32, 34, 39, 46, 47, 48, 57, 58, 63, 70, 71, 72, 96, 102, 126, 158, 163, 202
A.I. *see* artificial intelligence
A.I. Artificial Intelligence 165, 167, 168
Aja, Alexandre 23, 25, 26; *see also The Hills Have Eyes* films
Alien films 143, 151
Alien Wars 156, 157
amusement park 7, 57, 58, 59, 63, 68, 109, 199; *see also* theme park
Animal Crossing 54
animatronics 64, 68
Anita Blake Vampire Hunter 1, 8, 73, 74, 75, 78, 79, 80, 83, 84, 90, 93, 94, 97–9, 104, 105; *see also* Hamilton, Laurel K.
apocalypse 19, 21, 22, 23, 27, 33, 34, 35, 90
Arens, William 35
ARG (alternative reality game) 167, 168, 169, 170, 172, 175, 176, 184, 186, 189, 190, 191, 192, 193; *see also* The Beast; transmedia; viral marketing
Argento, Dario 19, 33, 113
Aristotle 50
Arkham Asylum *see Batman: Arkham Asylum*
art cinema 110, 130
art-horror 29, 57; *see also* Carroll, Noel
artificial intelligence 40, 41, 45, 46, 54
artificial life *see* artificial intelligence
Artisan Entertainment 171

Asimov, Isaac 45
Austen, Jane 81, 82, 83; *see also Pride and Prejudice; Zombies*
automaton 51, 52, 53, 54, 68
avatar 6, 7, 37, 40, 41, 42, 44, 45, 46, 47, 48, 49, 50, 51, 54, 55, 69, 146

Bakhtin, Mikhail 11, 109, 110, 11, 112, 116, 117, 118, 121, 122, 123, 127, 136, 142
Bardot, Brigitte 133, 134, 135
Barker, Jennifer 4, 19, 72, 87, 106
Barnum, P.T. 113, 169
baroque and neo-baroque 55, 190, 191, 192; *see also* Gesamtkunstwerk/Total Artwork
Barthes, Roland 10, 122
Bataille, Georges 93, 94, 98, 99
Batman 48, 49, 146, 186, 187, 188; *see also The Dark Knight*
Batman: Arkham Asylum 1, 48, 49, 146, 158, 191
Bava, Lamberto 19, 31, 113
Bava, Mario 112
The Beast 167, 168; *see also A.I. Artificial Intelligence;* ARG
Benjamin, Walter 17, 29
Benson-Allott, Caitlin 126
Bioshock 158
Bishop, Kyle 21, 22
Blade Runner 149
The Blair Witch Project 12, 163, 165, 170–2, 177, 191, 205; *Curse of the Blair Witch* 171; *see also* transmedia
Blake, Rachel 175, 176; *see also Lost*
Bolter, Jay David 63, 147, 162; *see also* remediation
Boyle, Danny 37
Bredekamp, Horst 53
Brontë sisters 81, 82, 83, 84
Brooks, Peter 44
Bruno, Giuliana 4, 5, 6, 7, 19, 20, 31, 39, 44, 48, 72, 189

Buck-Morss, Susan 17
Buffy the Vampire Slayer 74, 76, 90, 200

Cabin Fever 15
Campert, Remco 49, 50
Campfire 177, 178; see also True Blood
Cannibal Holocaust 33
cannibalism 16, 21, 26, 28, 33, 35, 36, 127, 141, 151, 196
Careri, Giovanni 191–2
Carmack, John 143, 144, 154, 159, 160, 161; see also *Doom* video games; Romero, John
carnivalesque 11, 33, 58, 107, 109, 110, 111, 112, 113, 118, 119, 121, 122, 123, 126, 127, 141; and Cervantes 109, 110, 111, 112, 122; and Rabelais 109, 110, 111, 112, 122; and Shakespeare 109, 11, 112; see also Bakhtin, Mikhail; dialogic
Carolyn, Axelle 20, 21
Carpenter, John 16, 19, 121, 126, 131, 154
Carroll, Noel 29, 57, 71
Castle, William 166–7; Emergo 166; and *Homicidal* 166; *House on Haunted Hill* 166; and Percepto 166; and the senses 167; *The Tingler* 166
Child's Play 46, 119
cineliterate *see* media literate
cinephilia 106, 122, 123, 128, 130, 137; and horror-philia 12, 120, 123; see also fans; media literate
cinesthesia 5, 6, 9, 31, 33
cinesthetic subject *see* cinesthesia
Citizen Kane 149
Clover, Carol J. 70, 128, 131, 132, 138, 139, 140, 141
Cloverfield 12, 165, 173, 183, 184, 186
Cochin, Charles-Nicolas 52, 53
cognition 1, 3, 4, 5, 7, 11, 12, 16, 17, 20, 29, 30, 34, 39, 48, 49, 50, 51, 58, 70, 86, 102, 114, 145, 146, 154, 165, 169, 173, 176, 181, 183, 186, 189, 192; see also intelligence
Colicchio, Tom 181, 183; see also True Blood
Collins, Jim 110, 149, 162
Collodi, Carlo 45, 51
Commander Keen 159
Coney Island 57, 64, 65, 198, 199
conglomeration 7, 9, 10, 59, 60, 63, 146, 165, 185, 190, 192
contagion 34, 35, 96
convergence 10, 185
Convoy 129
corporeal 1, 3, 4, 5, 7, 12, 17, 28, 48, 49, 51, 58, 64, 69, 70, 97, 102, 114, 192
Craven, Wes 15, 19, 23, 25, 26, 121, 131, 137, 196
The Crazies 165, 173, 183, 184, 186
Creatures video games 54
crossmedia 7, 9, 10, 11, 13, 57, 59, 60, 61, 62, 76, 146, 147, 151, 165, 170, 172, 176, 185, 192, 198, 199; see also transmedia
Cthulhu Mythos 151, 204
cyborg 40; see also robot

Dance Central 50
The Dark Knight 1, 12–3, 165, 186–9, 191; see also Batman; Joker; transmedia; viral marketing
dark ride 7, 8, 56, 59, 62, 64, 65, 68, 69, 70, 71, 72, 199; see also horror rides
Davies, Jody 9, 76, 92
Dawn of the Dead 11, 21, 31, 33, 108, 119, 124, 127, 129
Day of the Dead 21, 31, 36, 124, 127
death 22, 28, 35, 36, 56, 68, 69, 91, 93, 94, 95, 96, 97, 98, 99, 117, 132, 133, 160, 200
Death Proof 1, 11, 12, 107, 109, 110, 113, 114, 116, 120, 121, 122, 123, 125, 126, 128–41; see also Tarantino, Quentin
Death Race 129
de Certeau, Michel 47, 51
Deleuze, Gilles 55
Deodata, Ruggero 19
Descartes, René 53
desire 8, 9, 16, 35, 75, 77, 78, 84, 85, 86, 87, 88, 89, 90, 91, 92, 94, 95, 96, 97, 98, 99, 100, 103, 104, 105, 106, 176; and horror 69, 70, 78, 99, 103, 120, 121
dialogue 11, 20, 109, 110, 111, 113, 117, 122, 125, 127, 128, 130, 131, 133, 136, 137, 140, 142; see also Bakhtin; horror and self-reflexivity; intertextuality
Digital Kitchen 178, 206; see also True Blood
Dika, Vera 119, 120, 131
Dillard, R.H.W. 70
Dinehart, Stephen 172, 173, 174, 176, 184, 186, 190
Dirty Mary, Crazy Larry 129
disgust 6, 11, 29, 34, 35, 36, 78, 96, 97, 98, 99, 103, 104, 105, 108, 109, 117, 120, 181, 202
Disney, Walt 64, 65, 67, 68, 199
Disney Imagineers 67, 68, 199
Disneyland 8, 58, 65, 67, 68, 199
Doom buggy *see* Omnimover
Doom video games 1, 12, 142, 143, 144, 146, 147, 150, 151, 152–55, 157–62
Dracula 15, 58, 62, 83, 84, 90, 199; see also vampire
Drag Me to Hell 121
dramatic play 184, 185, 186, 190; and performativity 166, 170, 172, 173, 181, 183, 185, 187, 191, 192, 193; see also Dinehart, Stephen
Draper, Tim 164; see also transmedia; viral marketing
DreamWorks 147, 161
Dundy, Skip 64, 199

Eisenstein, Sergei 29
Electronic Arts 41, 43, 54, 147, 160
emotions 1, 3, 4, 5, 16, 20, 23, 28, 29, 35, 36, 38, 48, 57, 69, 70, 72, 77, 78, 79, 84, 85, 86, 89, 101, 102, 103, 104, 141, 166, 176, 202; and video games 145, 146, 150, 151, 157, 162
entertainment 1, 3, 4, 5, 8, 9, 11, 12, 52, 57,

Index

59, 60, 61, 62, 67, 70, 110, 144, 146, 147, 149, 150, 152, 157, 162, 164, 167, 168, 169, 172, 185
equilibrioception 8, 50, 51, 70; *see also* senses; sensorium
eroticism 8, 75, 76, 77, 85, 88, 89, 92, 93, 94, 96, 98, 99, 102, 104, 105, 106; and horror 8, 76, 85, 95, 96, 97, 99, 100, 104, 105, 106, 181
Evil Dead 11, 33, 108, 131; and *Army of Darkness* 33, 162; and *Evil Dead II* 11, 33, 108, 131, 143, 151
The Exorcist 163
The Experience Economy 165, 166, 192
exploitation cinema 12, 112, 113, 116, 111, 122, 126, 127, 128, 129, 130, 131, 135, 136, 137, 140, 196, 202; and car-chase films 112, 114, 128, 129, 131, 135, 137; and girl-action films 128; and girl-gang films 12, 128, 129, 135, 137; and Roger Corman 112; and Tura Satana 129
Eye Pet 41

Fair Game 137, 138, 139
fairy tales 8, 9, 87–89, 91, 97, 106; animal-groom 88, 89; and Charles Perrault 89; feminist writings 88, 89; and the French Conteuses 89
fans 10, 11, 13, 23, 80, 83, 90, 100, 103, 115, 120, 130, 164, 165, 169, 175, 183, 184, 185, 186, 189, 205; *see also* cinephilia
Fantasmagorie 67
Faster Pussycat! Kill! Kill! 112, 129, 137
Feehan, Christine 8, 75, 76, 85, 87, 89, 95; Dark Carpathians series 79, 85, 87, 95
final girl 12, 128, 131, 133, 134, 136, 137, 138–141
first person games 41, 51, 105, 142, 143, 152, 153, 159, 160
42 Entertainment 168, 189; *see also* Lee, Elan; Weisman, Jordan
found footage 21, 171
franchise 9, 12, 13, 60, 61- 62, 147, 164, 172, 173, 174, 184, 185, 191, 192
Frankenstein 40, 46, 58, 62, 83
Frantz, Sarah 84
French New Wave 130
Fresnadillo, Juan Carlos 6, 21
Freud, Sigmund 118
Friday the 13th 119, 127, 139
From Dusk Till Dawn 129
Fulci, Lucio 19, 31, 32, 33, 112

game controller 7, 44, 46, 48, 49, 50, 51, 158
Game Cube 41, 49
gameplay 4, 12, 41, 43, 45, 46, 48, 49, 50, 51, 54, 55, 70, 145, 147, 148, 150, 153, 154, 160, 163, 165, 168
los ganados 42, 43, 47, 54, 55, 164; *see also* living dead; *Resident Evil*; zombies
genre 3, 4, 7, 8, 9, 10, 11, 12, 15, 16, 19, 21, 31, 32, 36, 40, 57, 59, 60, 61, 63, 72, 73, 75, 76, 77, 78, 80, 81, 83, 85, 87, 90, 91, 103, 106, 109, 110, 111, 119, 120, 112, 113, 117, 121, 122, 122, 123, 124, 126, 127, 128, 130, 131, 145, 163, 164, 167, 175; and Tarantino 128–42; and video games 41, 143, 144, 145, 146, 147, 151, 159, 160
Gesamtkunstwerk/Total Artwork 190; *see also* baroque; neo-baroque
ghost train 57, 59, 65, 68
Gilmore, James 166
Godard, Jean Luc 128, 130, 150
gore 6, 15, 24, 30, 31, 33, 102, 112, 120, 196; *see also* splatter
Gothic horror *see* horror genre
Grand Theft Auto 154
Grindhouse see Planet Terror; Death Proof
grindhouse 107, 112, 113, 116, 118, 120, 121, 122, 124, 125, 127, 128, 129, 130, 131, 136, 140
gross-out horror *see* horror
The Grudge 129
Grusin, Richard 63, 147, 162; *see also* remediation
Gulf War 39
Gunning, Tom 57, 150, 157
Gurfinkel, Jenka 192
Gwenllian-Jones, Sara 175

Half-Life 154
Halloween (1978) 19, 70, 131, 154, 155, 202
Halloween (2007) 6, 16, 18, 119, 121
Halo video games 154, 161, 165, 168
Hamilton, Laurell K. 8, 73, 74, 75, 79, 97, 102; *see also* Anita Blake Vampire Hunter
Hansen, Miriam 57, 102
Hanso Foundation 173, 174, 175, 176; *see also Lost*
Hantke, Steffan 71
haptic 5, 19, 20, 23, 34, 39, 40, 44, 50, 63, 65, 72, 158, 189; *see also* touch
Harris, Charlaine 79, 101, 201; *see also* Sookie Stackhouse
Harrison, Kim 79; Hollows series 79
Harvey Dent 186, 187, 188, 189, 191; *see also The Dark Knight*
Haunted Mansion (ride, Disneyland) 1, 58, 62, 65, 67, 68, 199
hearing 6, 8, 17, 20, 22, 28, 31, 32, 34, 69, 95, 100, 125; 156; *see also* senses; sensorium; sound
Heavy Rain 158
Heller-Nicholas, Alexandra 138, 141
heteroglossia 122, 127; *see also* dialogic; intertextuality
The Hills Have Eyes films 1, 6, 15, 16, 23–30, 36, 37, 129, 196
Hitchcock, Alfred 15, 131, 133
Hollywood 31, 61, 62, 102, 109, 110, 202
Homecoming 22
Hooper, Tobe 19, 21, 23, 27, 112, 121, 131

INDEX

horizontal integration 60, 62
horror genre 1, 2, 3, 7, 8, 9, 15, 16, 17, 19, 24, 28, 29, 33, 36, 38, 39, 57, 59, 63, 69, 70, 71, 72, 75, 76, 90, 91, 105, 110, 121, 163; apocalyptic 19, 20, 21, 22, 23, 27, 33, 34, 35, 90; body-horror/body destruction 28, 30, 33, 34, 38, 120, 127; and comedy/laughter 108, 109, 111, 112, 118, 119, 120, 121, 125, 181, 202; comics 60, 61, 63, 72, 74, 146, 156, 186, 191; and cult 10, 11, 13, 110, 122, 135, 137, 151, 164, 175, 176, 185, 190; and family 20, 23, 25, 26, 27, 28, 196; films 6, 22, 23, 25, 26, 27, 29, 30, 31, 34, 35, 43–4, 56, 61, 62, 63, 69, 70, 71, 104, 106, 121, 123, 151; Gothic 31, 63, 85, 106; gross-out 11, 15, 107, 108, 109, 112, 118, 120, 122; hybrids 79, 82, 83, 106, 129; Italian 19, 24, 32–34, 38, 113, 196; Japanese 163; New Horror 6, 15, 16, 17, 19, 20, 21, 23, 26, 29, 30, 33, 34, 37, 72, 196; and performance 12, 13, 28, 41, 50, 54, 111, 121, 127, 135; and pre-cinema 66, 67, 68; rides 7, 8, 56, 57–9, 63, 64, 68, 70, 71, 72, 199; and romance 77; and self-reflexivity 11, 114, 119, 125, 126, 129, 131, 133–42; and September 11/9–11 20, 21, 37–9; slasher films 11, 128, 131; and society 6, 15, 16, 17, 19, 37–9, 120, 121; survival horror 40, 41, 42–5, 146; television 62, 63, 68, 72, 75, 76, 77, 90, 99–104, 106, 112, 146, 163, 164, 165, 167, 171, 173, 176; torture porn/gorn 120, 129; video games 12, 43, 51, 54, 63, 143, 144, 146, 150, 151, 152, 154, 161; *see also* apocalypse; sensorium, and horror
horror-paranormal romance *see* paranormal romance
Hostel films 15, 16, 21, 33, 37, 121
Huff, Tanya 76; Blood Books 76; Blood Ties 76
Human Centipede 37

I Know What You Did Last Summer 131
I Love Bees 168, 169; *see also* ARG; transmedia; viral marketing
I Spit on Your Grave 137
I Walked with a Zombie 35
id software 12, 143, 144, 151, 152, 153, 154, 155, 158, 159, 160, 161, 162
ideology 15, 16, 20, 39, 87, 88, 89, 112, 120, 121, 196
Indiana Jones Adventure: Temple of the Forbidden Eye (ride, Disneyland) 8, 68, 72
intelligence 1, 2, 3, 7, 9, 10, 11, 12, 16, 17, 20, 25, 29, 30, 40, 41, 45, 48, 50, 54, 58, 72, 81, 83, 108, 113, 114, 123, 131, 142, 144, 145, 166, 169, 181, 185, 186, 202
intertextuality 8, 10, 11, 12, 16, 17, 63, 110, 114, 122, 123, 125, 126, 129, 130, 135, 136, 142, 143, 145, 149, 150, 151, 169; *see also* Bakhtin; dialogue; horror genre, and self-reflexivity
Italian horror 19, 24, 31, 33, 38, 112, 113, 126, 146, 196

It's a Small World (ride, Disneyland) 68
It's a Wonderful Life 149

Jacquet-Droz, Pierre 53
Jean-Claude, the Vampire 73, 75, 90, 93, 94, 97, 98; *see also* Anita Blake Vampire Hunter
Jenkins, Henry 47, 167, 168, 185
The Joker 186, 187, 188, 189; *see also* The Dark Knight; transmedia; viral marketing
Jurassic Park (ride, Universal) 8, 68, 71

Kawin, Bruce R. 69
Kepler, Johannes 53
Kill Bill films 129, 136, 140
kinesthetics 5, 8, 20, 39, 70, 72
King Kong 15, 88, 129
Kolnai, Aurel 34, 35, 96, 103
Korsmeyer, Carolyn 96, 99, 103, 104, 181
Kracauer, Siegfried 30
Kristeva, Julia 35, 94, 123, 124, 127
Krzywinska, Tanya 43, 44
Kuznets, Lois Rostow 45

Laine, Tarja 86, 87
Last House on the Left 23, 137
Le Cain, Maximilian 130
Lee, Elan 167, 168, 170; *see also* 42 Entertainment
Leibniz, Gottfried 55
Leon S. Kennedy (character) 41, 42, 43, 45, 46, 47, 48, 51, 55; *see also Resident Evil* games
Lévi-Strauss, Claude 29, 119
Levisohn, Aaron M. 51
Levy, Pierre 169
Lingis, Alphonso 86, 87, 104, 105
living dead 6, 7, 21, 23, 31, 34–7, 40, 41, 45, 71, 96, 117, 119, 120, 121, 122, 123, 124, 127, 146; *see also* zombies
Lonsway, Brian 166, 192
Lost 1, 12, 165, 173–6, 184, 186, 191, 205, 206
The Lost Experience see *Lost*
Lotman, Yuri 140, 141
Luna Park 57, 64, 65
Lutz, Deborah 81, 83, 84

Macpherson, Fiona 50, 200
mad science 41, 46, 54, 151
magic lantern 63, 67, 68
Marks, Laura 4, 19, 23, 44, 87, 106
Marvel Entertainment 9, 10, 74
The Matrix 146
Max Payne video games 146, 147, 148, 149, 150
McCrea, Christian 144, 145
McLuhan, Marshall 158
Medal of Honor video games 147, 160
media history 63, 144, 146, 150, 151, 158, 162
media hybrids 63, 59, 146, 147
media literate 10, 130, 137, 145, 169
meta-genre 11, 110, 120, 123, 169, 175, 176, 183

meta-horror 113, 114, 181
meta-text *see* meta-genre
Meyer, Stephenie 76, 91; *see also Twilight* series
Michael Myers (character) 15, 16, 17, 18, 154, 155
Microsoft 165, 167
Miller, Susan 36
Mittell, Jason 169
modernity 57, 102, 141
Modleski, Tania 80, 85, 87
monster 5, 8, 12, 15, 16, 23, 25, 26, 27, 29, 38, 40, 70, 71, 73, 79, 80, 82, 84, 85, 89, 91, 94, 95, 96, 97, 106, 118, 124, 129, 138, 139, 178, 184
Morricone, Ennio 113
The Mummy films 1, 7, 8, 56, 57, 59, 60, 61, 62, 63; *see also* The Revenge of the Mummy (ride)
My Name Is Nobody 136
My Name Is Trinity 136
myth 7, 27, 29, 40, 41, 43, 46, 51, 54, 80, 82, 86, 106, 110, 119, 140, 141, 151, 175, 176, 191, 192, 204

Nakata, Hideo 163
necromancer 46, 73, 80, 97
New Horror *see* horror genre
New York World's Fair 1964 68, 199
Night of the Living Dead 21, 23, 31, 119, 121, 122
A Nightmare on Elm Street 119, 131
Nilson, Fred 161
Nintendogs 41
nociception 8, 70; *see also* senses; sensorium
normality 16, 17, 19, 23, 25, 26, 28, 91, 94, 177
Nosferatu 15, 90

Omnimover 65, 67, 68

Pan-American Exposition, 1901 64, 199
Pan's Labyrinth 129
paranormal romance 1, 8, 9, 72, 73–92, 94, 96, 97, 104, 105, 106, 164, 193; and zombies 59, 79, 81, 82, 90, 95, 96–7, 106; *see also* romance
Paul, William 11, 58, 108, 109, 112, 116, 118, 119, 120
Pearson, Roberta 175
Pentium chip 159, 160
Pepper's Ghost 66, 67, 68; and Pepper, John 66, 67
perception 1, 3, 4, 5, 6, 11, 12, 17, 19, 20, 29, 30, 31, 33, 39, 48, 50, 51, 58, 70, 87, 104, 113, 114, 136, 145, 154, 155, 157, 162, 163, 166, 170
Perron, Bernard 145, 146, 150, 162
Peter Pan (ride, Disneyland) 68
Peucker, Brigitte 6, 19, 31, 32, 33, 34, 36
phenomenology 4, 49
Pine, Joseph 166

Pinocchio 45
Pirates of the Caribbean (ride, Disneyland) 68
Pixar 10
Planet Terror 1, 11, 101, 108, 109, 110, 113, 114, 115, 117, 121–8, 129, 131, 141; *see also* Rodriguez, Robert
Playstation 41, 49, 60; iMove 7
Polidori, John 83, 90
postmodernism 60, 88, 89, 130
Prince, Stephen 157
Prometheus 40, 41, 43, 46, 51, 53, 54, 83
proprioception 8, 50, 70; *see also* senses; sensorium
Psycho 15, 17, 19, 23, 131, 133, 171
psychogeography 4, 20, 28, 39, 46
Pulp Fiction 129

Quake video games 151, 158, 160, 161

Radcliffe, Ann 83
Raimi, Sam 11, 108, 110, 112, 121, 143, 162
rape-revenge films 12, 128, 131, 135, 137, 138, 139
reboot 21, 23, 31, 36, 37, 83, 151
Red vs Blue 160–1
Regency romance horror reboots 81, 82, 83; *Emma and the Vampires* 82; *Emma and the Werewolves* 82; and Grahame-Smith, Seth 81; *Jane Bites Back* 82, 83; *Jane Slayre* 82; *Little Vampire Women* 82; *Mansfield Park and Mummies: Monster Mayhem, Matrimony, Ancient Curses, True Love, and Other Dire Delights* 82; *Mr. Darcy, Vampyre* 82; *Pride and Prejudice and Zombies* 81, 82; *Pride and Prejudice and Zombies: Dreadfully Ever After* 82; *Sense and Sensibility and Sea Monsters* 82; *Vampire Darcy's Desire: A Pride and Prejudice Adaptation* 82; *Wuthering Bites* 82
remediation 7, 63, 64, 65, 67, 68, 146, 147, 148, 162, 171; *see also* Bolter, Jay David; Grusin, Richard
Reservoir Dogs 129, 135
Resident Evil films and video games 1, 7, 40–7, 49, 51, 54, 55, 146, 164, 197
Revenge of the Mummy (ride, Universal) 1, 7, 8, 56, 57, 59, 60, 63, 64, 68, 69, 71
Rice, Anne 76, 201
Ringu/The Ring 163
Robert, Etienne Gaspard 67
robot 40, 45, 54, 64, 129, 168
Rodaway, Paul 11, 30, 48, 114, 154
Rodriguez, Robert 11, 107, 108, 110, 113, 114, 120, 121, 122, 124–8, 129, 141
roller coaster 8, 58, 59, 63, 64, 68, 69, 71, 72
romance genre 8, 9, 73, 74, 75, 76, 77, 78, 79, 80–90, 92, 106, 200; young adult romance 78; *see also* paranormal romance
Romero, George A. 11, 19, 20, 21, 23, 31, 35, 36, 41, 71, 108, 112, 121, 122, 124, 146, 183

222 INDEX

Romero, John 143, 159, 160, 161; *see also* Carmack, John; *Doom* video games
Roscoe, Jane 172
Roth, Eli 15, 16, 33, 34, 129, 132

Sally Corporation 58, 198
Savini, Tom 127
Saw films 15, 37, 120, 121, 129
The Scary Adventures of Snow White (ride, Disneyland) 1
Schivelbusch, Wolfgang 57
Schwartz, Vanessa R. 57
science fiction 40, 54, 78, 80, 143, 149, 151, 164, 167, 175, 183, 199; and horror 40, 54, 143, 151
Scream films 15, 131
The Searchers 140
Selinger, Eric 81, 83
Semenko, Aleksei 136
senses 1, 3, 4, 5, 6, 7, 8, 9, 12, 16, 17, 19, 20, 29, 30, 31, 32, 33, 34, 39, 44, 48, 49, 50, 51, 57, 58, 62, 65, 67, 70, 71, 72, 76, 86, 87, 93, 96, 101, 102, 103, 104, 105, 106, 114, 117, 121, 131, 142, 144, 154, 155, 156, 157, 162, 164, 165, 166, 169, 176, 181, 183, 186, 189, 192; immediate impact on 5, 8, 11, 17, 34, 64, 69, 76, 114, 158, 162, 186, 189; and mediation 19, 30, 48, 71, 72, 86, 114; *see also* sensorium
sensorium 1, 5, 6, 9, 11, 13, 16, 17, 19, 20, 25, 29, 30, 39, 49, 51, 57, 61, 72, 75, 91, 94, 102, 106, 114, 144, 151, 158, 163, 165, 166, 175, 181, 185, 186, 189, 192; and horror 3, 4, 5, 7, 19, 94, 95, 96, 99, 102–3, 104, 106, 154–5, 163–4, 169, 181, 185, 186, 192, 193; *see also* senses
sensory intelligence 17, 181; *see also* intelligence
sequel 10, 15, 28, 31, 56, 82, 119, 131, 143
serial 10, 63, 80, 168, 175, 186, 191
sex 74, 75, 76, 77, 78, 86, 91, 92, 93, 94, 96, 98, 100, 101, 102, 106, 113, 114, 131, 133, 138, 139, 164, 181; and violence 9, 75, 88, 89, 99, 103, 104, 105, 116, 117, 132, 137, 138
sexuality 8, 25, 75, 77, 78, 88, 91, 92, 96, 98, 99, 104, 105, 129, 138, 141, 181
Sharrett, Christopher 27
She Devils on Wheels 137
Shelley, Mary 83, 84
sight 3, 4, 5, 6, 7, 8, 17, 19, 20, 31, 33, 35, 39, 44, 69, 70, 71, 72, 76, 101, 102, 103, 104, 105, 108, 116, 126, 130, 137, 138, 148; *see also* senses; sensorium
Simons, Ronald 69
The Sims 54
site-seeing 5, 7, 20, 44, 189; *see also* Bruno, Giulia
Sizemore, Susan 76, 79; Prime Series 79
smell 8, 9, 17, 33, 34, 69, 71, 93, 95, 96, 101, 102, 103, 104, 117, 165, 189; *see also* senses; sensorium

Sobchack, Vivian 4, 5, 6, 9, 19, 29, 30, 31, 33, 87, 102, 106
social networks 12, 164, 173, 192
Sookie Stackhouse (character) 1, 8, 73, 75, 79, 83, 84, 99, 100–2, 105; *Cub Dead* 101; *see also* Harris, Charlaine; *True Blood*
sound 6, 9, 20, 23, 28, 33, 46, 47, 49, 59, 61, 64, 65, 67, 95, 96, 101, 102, 104, 106, 113, 117, 125, 129, 130, 144, 147, 148, 154, 156, 160, 161, 164, 189; *see also* hearing
Southern Vampire Series *see* Sookie Stackhouse
Space Invaders 54
special effects 24, 28, 40, 58, 123, 126, 127, 128
spectatorship 1, 4, 6, 7, 12, 16, 19, 20, 21, 23, 29, 31, 32, 33, 34, 39, 44, 46, 48, 53, 57, 65, 69, 70, 71, 72, 77, 78, 87, 102, 104, 106, 108, 114, 117, 119, 123, 127, 141, 162, 163, 165, 169, 181, 186, 190; and ocular-centrism 4, 5
Spielberg, Steven 147, 165
splatter 31, 33, 37, 73, 126, 156, 181, 196; *see also* gore
Spore 41, 54
Stafford, Barbara Maria 52
Stoker, Bram 83, 199
supernatural 8, 17, 40, 53, 76, 79, 81, 84, 164, 173, 175
synaesthesia 6, 8, 9, 11, 20, 31, 33, 34, 50, 53, 65, 69, 72, 102, 104, 114, 117, 189

taboo 16, 90, 91, 96, 99, 141
Tarantino, Quentin 11, 107, 110, 113, 114, 120, 121, 122, 125, 128, 129, 130, 131, 133, 135, 136, 137, 138, 140, 141
technological mediation 7, 40, 44, 154, 155, 158, 162
techno-textuality 143, 145; *see also* intertextuality
Telotte, J.P. 69, 70
Terminator 2: 3D (ride, Universal) 58
Texas Chainsaw Massacre films 16, 21, 23, 24, 27, 36, 37, 129, 131, 171, 196
theatricality 12, 13, 41, 63, 64, 121, 123, 162, 173, 186, 190, 192, 193; *see also* horror genre and performativity; virtuosity
theme park 1, 3, 4, 5, 7, 8, 10, 39, 50, 57, 58, 59, 60, 61, 63, 64, 68, 70, 72, 165, 166; *see also* amusement park
third person games 41, 146
30 Days of Night 16
Thompson, Frederick 64, 199
Tilyou, George 64
Tomb Raider 154
Toolbox Murders 129
touch 5, 8, 9, 17, 20, 23, 30, 32, 33, 38, 39, 44, 49, 69, 71, 72, 85, 86, 87, 93, 95, 96, 101, 102, 103, 104, 106, 117, 158, 165, 189; *see also* senses; sensorium
Transformers 184

transmedia 1, 2, 10, 12, 13, 59, 60, 61, 62, 123, 163–9, 172–186, 189–93, 205; and extended storytelling 12, 164, 173; and horror 12, 59, 60, 164, 165, 169, 171–2, 173, 175, 176, 181, 183, 184, 186; *see also* ARG; crossmedia; viral marketing
A Trip to the Moon (ride) 59, 64, 199
Truck Stop Women 137
True Blood 1, 9, 12, 75, 76, 90, 99, 101–6, 165, 173, 176–183, 186, 191; *see also* ARG; Campfire; Digital Kitchen; transmedia; viral marketing
28 Days Later 21, 37, 41; *see also* Boyle, Danny
28 Weeks Later 1, 6, 21, 37, 38, 39, 41, 121, 129; *see also* Fresnadillo, Juan Carlos
Twilight series 76, 90, 91, 92, 181

uncanny 45, 46
undead *see* living dead
Under a Killing Moon 148, 149, 150
Undying 43
Universal Studios 7, 8, 56, 58, 59, 60, 61, 62, 64, 68, 70, 199
urban fantasy *see* paranormal romance

vampire 8, 9, 73, 74, 75, 76, 77, 79, 80, 82, 83, 84, 86, 89, 90, 91, 92, 93, 94, 95, 96, 97, 98, 99, 100, 101, 103, 105, 106, 176, 177, 178, 179, 180, 181, 182, 183, 186
Vanishing Point 129, 135, 137
Vaucanson, Jacques de 53
vertical integration 61, 62, 202
video card 160, 161; and ATI 161; and NVIDIA 161
Vietnam War 21, 120
violence 5, 6, 15, 16, 19, 24, 25, 26, 36, 37, 39, 74, 80, 99, 100, 103, 131, 137, 138; *see also* sex, and violence
virtuosity 12, 51, 52, 53, 127, 150, 151, 152, 157, 158, 161, 162, 172, 191
visceral 8, 19, 36, 70, 72, 83, 96, 106, 113, 120, 123, 166

vision *see* sight
viral marketing 1, 12, 13, 22, 163, 164, 165, 166, 168, 172, 173, 176, 177, 178, 180, 183, 184, 186, 187, 188, 189, 190, 191, 192; and horror 170–2; *see also* ARG; transmedia
virus 37, 38, 39, 41, 97, 164, 183
Vivendi Universal *see* Universal Studios
VUP (viewer/user/player) 173, 176, 185, 186, 189, 190, 191, 192

The Walt Disney Company 9, 10, 58, 205; *see also* Disney, Walt; Disneyland
The War of the Worlds 170, 172
Warner, Marina 8, 35, 36, 88, 89, 97
Weisman, Jordan 167, 168; *see also* Elan, Lee; 42 Entertainment
Welles, Orson 149, 170
Wells, H.G. 170, 199
White Zombie 35
Wii, Nintendo 7, 40, 41, 42, 43, 46, 47, 48, 49, 50, 51, 55
Williams, Linda 9, 70, 76, 77, 78, 86, 102; and body genres 77, 78
Wolf Creek 15, 16, 129
Wolfenstein video games 159, 160
WolfQuest 54
Wood, Robin 25, 26

Xbox 7, 50, 167, 168; Kinect 7, 50
The X-files 76

YouTube 12, 164, 177, 184, 191

Zombi 2 1, 32, 33, 164; *see also* Fulci, Lucio
Zombie, Rob 6, 16, 17
zombies 6, 7, 20, 21, 22, 31, 32, 33, 35, 37, 41, 42, 45, 46, 58, 90, 95–7, 107, 108, 114, 115, 117, 123, 124, 125, 126, 127, 129, 146, 151, 155, 156, 158, 163; and virus 37, 38, 39, 41, 183; *see also* living dead; paranormal romance zombies